Excel® PivotTables and PivotCharts

Your visual blueprint™ for creating dynamic spreadsheets, 2nd Edition

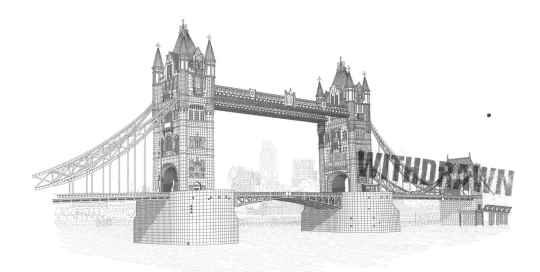

by Paul McFedries

WILEY

Wiley Publishing, Inc.

Excel® PivotTables and PivotCharts: Your visual blueprint™ for creating dynamic spreadsheets, 2nd Edition

Published by
Wiley Publishing, Inc.
10475 Crosspoint Boulevard
Indianapolis, IN 46256

www.wiley.com

Published simultaneously in Canada

Library of Congress Control Number: 2010926851

ISBN: 978-0-470-59161-1

Manufactured in the United States of America

10 9 8 7 6 5 4 3 2 1

Trademark Acknowledgments

Contact Us

For general information on our other products and services please contact our Customer Care Department within the U.S. at 877-762-2974, outside the U.S. at 317-572-3993 or fax 317-572-4002.

For technical support please visit www.wiley.com/techsupport.

The Tower Bridge

Truly a 19th century architectural wonder, London's Tower Bridge took 432 construction workers eight years to build. Architect Horace Jones designed the massive bascule bridge—a type of counterweighted drawbridge—and at its completion in 1894, it was the largest and most sophisticated of its kind ever built.

Discover more about London's historic architecture in *Frommer's England 2010* (ISBN 978-0-470-47070-1), available wherever books are sold or at www.Frommers.com.

Disclaimer

In order to get this information to you in a timely manner, this book was based on a pre-release version of Microsoft Office 2010. There may be some minor changes between the screenshots in this book and what you see on your desktop. As always, Microsoft has the final word on how programs look and function; if you have any questions or see any discrepancies, consult the online help for further information about the software.

Sales

Contact Wiley
at (877) 762-2974
or (317) 572-4002.

Credits

Executive Editor
Jody Lefevere

Project Editor
Kristin DeMint

Technical Editor
Namir Shammas

Copy Editor
Kim Heusel

Editorial Director
Robyn Siesky

Editorial Manager
Cricket Krengel

Business Manager
Amy Knies

Senior Marketing Manager
Sandy Smith

Vice President and Executive Group Publisher
Richard Swadley

Vice President and Executive Publisher
Barry Pruett

Project Coordinator
Lynsey Stanford

Graphics and Production Specialists
Carrie Cesavice
Joyce Haughey
Andrea Hornberger
Jennifer Mayberry

Quality Control Technician
Lauren Mandelbaum

Proofreading and Indexing
Penny Stuart
Potomac Indexing, LLC

Media Development Project Manager
Laura Moss

Media Development Assistant Project Manager
Jenny Swisher

Media Development Associate Producer
Marilyn Hummel

Screen Artist
Jill A. Proll

Illustrator
Cheryl Grubbs

Special Help
Rebekah Worthman

About the Author

Paul McFedries is a full-time technical writer. Paul has been authoring computer books since 1991 and he has more than 70 books to his credit. Paul's books have sold more than three million copies worldwide. These books include the Wiley titles *Teach Yourself VISUALLY Excel 2010; Excel 2010 Visual Quick Tips; Teach Yourself VISUALLY Windows 7;* and *Teach Yourself VISUALLY Office 2008 for Mac*. Paul is also the proprietor of Word Spy (www.wordspy.com and twitter.com/wordspy), a Web site that tracks new words and phrases as they enter the language. Paul invites you to drop by his personal Web site at www.mcfedries.com or to follow him on Twitter at twitter.com/paulmcf.

Author's Acknowledgments

It goes without saying that writers focus on text, and I certainly enjoyed focusing on the text that you'll read in this book. However, this book is more than just the usual collection of words and phrases. A quick thumb-through of the pages will show you that this book is also chock full of images, from sharp screen shots to fun and informative illustrations. Those images sure make for a beautiful book, and that beauty comes from a lot of hard work by Wiley's immensely talented group of designers and layout artists. They are all listed in the Credits section on the previous page, and I thank them for creating another gem. Of course, what you read in this book must also be accurate, logically presented, and free of errors. Ensuring all of this was an excellent group of editors that included project editor Kristin DeMint, copy editor Kim Heusel, and technical editor Namir Shammas. Thanks to all of you for your exceptional competence and hard work. Thanks, as well, to acquisitions editor Jody Lefevere for asking me to write this book.

How to Use This Visual Blueprint Book

Who This Book Is For

This book is for advanced computer users who want to take their knowledge of this particular technology or software application to the next level.

The Conventions in This Book

❶ Steps

This book uses a step-by-step format to guide you easily through each task. Numbered steps are actions you must do; bulleted steps clarify a point, step, or optional feature; and indented steps give you the result.

❷ Notes

Notes give additional information — special conditions that may occur during an operation, a situation that you want to avoid, or a cross reference to a related area of the book.

❸ Icons and Buttons

Icons and buttons show you exactly what you need to click to perform a step.

❹ Extra or Apply It

An Extra section provides additional information about the preceding task — insider information and tips for ease and efficiency. An Apply It section takes the code from the preceding task one step further and allows you to take full advantage of it.

❺ Bold

Bold type shows text or numbers you must type.

❻ Italics

Italic type introduces and defines a new term.

❼ Courier Font

`Courier font` indicates the use of scripting language code such as statements, operators, or functions, and code such as objects, methods, or properties.

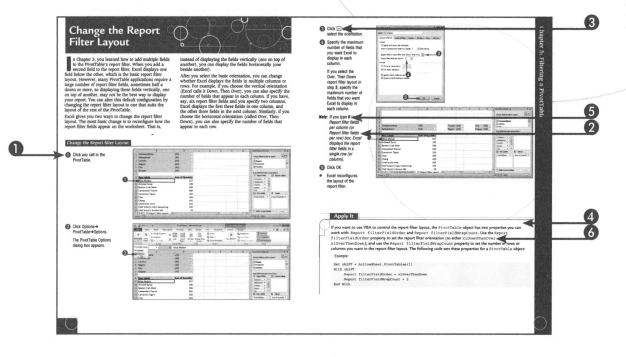

TABLE OF CONTENTS

TABLE OF CONTENTS

TABLE OF CONTENTS

Understanding Data Analysis

The PivotTables and PivotCharts that you learn about in this book are part of the larger category of *data analysis*. You can get the most out of these tools if you have a broader understanding of what data analysis is, what its benefits are, and what other tools are available to you.

Data analysis is the application of tools and techniques to organize, study, reach conclusions and sometimes also make predictions about a specific collection of information. A sales manager might use data analysis to study the sales history of a product, determine the overall trend, and produce a forecast of future sales. A scientist might use data analysis to study experimental findings and determine the statistical significance of the results. A family might use data analysis to find the maximum

mortgage it can afford or how much it must put aside each month to finance retirement or the kids' education.

The point of data analysis is to understand information on some deeper, more meaningful level. By definition, *raw data* is a mere collection of facts that by themselves tell you little or nothing of any importance. To gain some understanding of the data, you must manipulate it in some meaningful way. This can be something as simple as finding the sum or average of a column of numbers or as complex as employing a full-scale regression analysis to determine the underlying trend of a range of values. Both are examples of data analysis, and Excel offers a number of tools — from the straightforward to the sophisticated — to meet even the most demanding needs.

Data

The "data" part of data analysis is a collection of numbers, dates, and text that represents the raw information you have to work with. In Excel, this data resides inside a worksheet and you get it there in one of two ways: You enter it by hand or you import it from an external source. You can then either leave the data as a regular range, or you can convert it into a table for easier data manipulation.

Data Entry

In many data analysis situations, the required data must be entered into the worksheet manually. For example, if you want to determine a potential monthly mortgage payment, you must first enter values such as the current interest rate, the principal, and the term. Manual data entry is suitable for small projects only, because entering hundreds or even thousands of values is time consuming and can lead to errors.

Imported Data

Most data analysis projects involve large amounts of data, and the fastest and most accurate way to get that data onto a worksheet is to import it from a non-Excel data source. In the simplest scenario, you can copy the data — from a text file, a Word table, or an Access datasheet — and then paste it into

a worksheet. However, most business and scientific data is stored in large databases, and Excel offers tools to import the data you need into your worksheet. See Appendixes B and C for more about these tools.

Table

After you have your data in the worksheet, you can leave it as a regular range and still apply many data analysis techniques to the data. However, if you convert the range into a *table*, Excel treats the data as a simple flat-file database and enables you to apply a number of database-specific analysis techniques to the table. To learn how to do this, see Chapter 2.

Data Models

In many cases, you perform data analysis on worksheet values by organizing those values into a *data model*, a collection of cells designed as a worksheet version of some real-world concept or scenario. The model includes not only the raw data, but also one or more cells that represent some analysis of the data. For example, a mortgage amortization model would have the mortgage data — interest rate, principal, and term — and cells that calculate the payment, principal, and interest over the term. For such calculations, you use formulas and Excel's built-in functions, as described in Appendix A.

Formulas

A *formula* is a set of symbols and values that perform some kind of calculation and produce a result. All Excel formulas have the same general structure: an equals sign (=) followed by one or more *operands* — which can be a value, a cell reference, a range, a range name, or a function name — separated by one or more *operators*, which are the symbols that combine the operands in some way, such as the plus sign (+) and the multiplication sign (*). For example, the formula =A1+A2 adds the values in cells A1 and A2.

Functions

A *function* is a predefined formula that is built in to Excel. Each function takes one or more inputs — called *arguments,* such as numbers or cell references — and then returns a result. Excel offers hundreds of functions and you can use them to compute averages, determine the future value of an investment, compare values, and much more.

What-If Analysis

One of the most common data analysis techniques is *what-if analysis*, where you set up worksheet models to analyze hypothetical situations. The what-if part comes from the fact that these situations usually come in the form of a question: "What happens to the monthly payment if the interest rate goes up by 2 percent?" "What will the sales be if you increase the advertising budget by 10 percent?" Excel offers four what-if analysis tools: data tables, Goal Seek, Solver, and scenarios.

Data Tables

A *data table* is a range of cells where one column consists of a series of values, called *input cells*. You can then apply each of those inputs to a single formula, and Excel displays the results for each case. For example, you can use a data table to apply a series of interest rate values to a formula that calculates the monthly payment for a loan or mortgage.

Goal Seek

You use Excel's Goal Seek tool when you want to manipulate one formula component — called the *changing cell* — in such a way that the formula produces a specific result. For example, in a *break-even analysis*, you determine the number of units of a product that you must sell for the profit to be 0. Given a formula that calculates profit, you can use Goal Seek to determine the break-even point.

Solver

You use Excel's Solver tool when you want to manipulate multiple formula components — called the *changing cells* — in such a way that the formula produces the optimal result. For example, you can use Solver to tackle the so-called *transportation problem*, where the goal is to minimize the cost of shipping goods from several product plants to various warehouses around the country.

Scenarios

A *scenario* is a collection of input values that you plug into formulas within a model to produce a result. The idea is that you make up scenarios for various situations — for example, best-case, worst-case, and so on — and Excel's Scenario Manager saves each one. Later you can apply any of the saved scenarios, and Excel automatically applies all the input values to the model.

Introducing the PivotTable

Tables and external databases can contain hundreds or even thousands of records. Analyzing that much data can be a nightmare without the right kinds of tools. To help you, Excel offers a powerful data analysis tool called a *PivotTable*. This tool enables you to summarize hundreds of records in a concise tabular format. You can then manipulate the layout of — or *pivot* — the table to see different views of your data.

This book teaches you everything you need to know (and, indeed, just about everything there *is* to know) about PivotTables. You learn how to create them, edit them, pivot them, format them, calculate with them, and much more. You can get more out of the rest of the book if you take a few minutes now to get acquainted with some PivotTable background and basics.

Database Analysis

To understand PivotTables, you need to see how they fit in with Excel's other database-analysis features. Database analysis has three levels of complexity: lookup and retrieval, criteria and table functions, and multiple variables. As you move from one level to another, the need for PivotTables becomes apparent.

Lookup and Retrieval

The simplest level of database analysis involves the basic lookup and retrieval of information. For example, if you have a database that lists the company sales reps and their territory sales, you can use a data form (or even Excel's Find feature) to search for a specific rep and to look up the sales in that rep's territory.

Criteria and Table Functions

The next level of database analysis complexity involves more sophisticated lookup and retrieval systems in which you apply criteria to work with a subset of the data. You can then use this subset to apply subtotals and Excel's table functions (such as the DSUM() function, which sums those table cells that meet some specified criteria). For example, suppose that each sales territory is part of a larger region and you want to know the total sales in the eastern region. You can either subtotal by region or set up your criteria to match all territories in the eastern region and use DSUM() to get the total. To get more specific information, such as the total eastern region sales in the second quarter, you just add the appropriate conditions to your criteria.

Multiple Variables

The next level of database analysis applies a single question to multiple variables. For example, if the company in the preceding example has four regions, you might want to see separate totals for each region broken down by quarter. One solution would be to set up four different criteria and four different DSUM() functions. But what if there were a dozen regions? Or a hundred? Ideally, you need some way of summarizing the database information into a sales table that has a row for each region and a column for each quarter. This is exactly what PivotTables do and, as you see with Excel's PivotTable Wizard in Chapter 2, you can create your own PivotTables with just a few mouse clicks.

PivotTables help you analyze large amounts of data by performing three operations: grouping the data into categories, summarizing the data using calculations, and filtering the data to show just the records you want to work with.

Grouping

A PivotTable is a powerful data-analysis tool in part because it automatically groups large amounts of data into smaller, more manageable categories. For example, suppose you have a data source with a Region field where each cell contains one of four values: East, West, North, and South. The original data may contain thousands of records, but if you build your PivotTable using the Region field, the resulting table has just four rows — one each for the four unique Region values in your data.

You can also create your own grouping after you build your PivotTable. For example, if your data has a Country field, you can build the PivotTable to group together all the records that have the same Country value. When you have done that, you can further group the unique Country values into continents: North America, South America, Europe, and so on. See Chapter 4 to learn how to group PivotTable values.

Summarizing

In conjunction with grouping data according to the unique values in one or more fields, Excel also displays summary calculations for each group. The default calculation is Sum, which means for each group, Excel totals all the values in some specified field. For example, if your data has a Region field and a Sales field, a PivotTable can group the unique Region values and display the total of the Sales values for each one. Excel has other summary calculations, including Count, Average, Maximum, Minimum, and Standard Deviation.

Even more powerful, a PivotTable can display summaries for one grouping broken down by another. For example, suppose your sales data also has a Product field. You can set up a PivotTable to show the total Sales for each Product, broken down by Region.

Filtering

A PivotTable also enables you to view just a subset of the data. For example, by default the PivotTable's groupings show all the unique values in the field. However, you can manipulate each grouping to hide those that you do not want to view; see Chapter 4 for more. Each PivotTable also comes with a report filter — see the section "Explore PivotTable Features" later in this chapter — that enables you to apply a filter to the entire PivotTable. For example, suppose your sales data also includes a Customer field. By placing this field in the PivotTable's report filter, you can filter the PivotTable report to show just the results for a single Customer.

PivotTable Limitations

PivotTables come with certain limitations and restrictions that you need to be familiar with. See the section "Explore PivotTable Features" later in this chapter for explanations of the PivotTable terminology used here:

- The maximum number of row fields is 1,048,576. (If you are using a version of Excel prior to 2007, the maximum number is 65,536.)

- The maximum number of column fields is 16,384. (If you are using a version of Excel prior to 2007, the maximum number is 256.)

- The maximum number of page fields is 256.
- The maximum number of data fields is 256.
- The maximum number of unique items that can appear in a row, column, or page field is 1,048,576. (If you are using Excel 2003, the maximum number is 32,500; if you are using a version of Excel prior to 2003, the maximum number is 8,000.)
- The size and number of PivotTables are limited by how much available memory your system has.

Learn PivotTable Benefits

f Excel comes with so many powerful data analysis tools and features, why do you need to learn how to build and work with PivotTables? The short answer is that PivotTables are a useful weapon to add to your data-analysis arsenal. The long answer is that PivotTables are worth learning because they come with not just one or two, but a long list of benefits.

PivotTables are easy to build and maintain; they perform large and complex calculations amazingly fast; you can quickly and easily update them to account for new data; PivotTables are dynamic, so components can be easily moved, filtered, and added to; they are fully customizable so you can build each report the way you want; and, finally, PivotTables can use most of the formatting options that you can apply to regular Excel ranges and cells.

PivotTables Save Time

These days, most people have far too much to do and far too little time in which to do it. Computers are supposed to help us with this problem by reducing the amount of time spent on routine tasks, such as adding up rows of numbers. Some computer features have the opposite effect — e-mail, for example, takes up increasing amounts of time — but

PivotTables is not one of these features. The chore PivotTables are designed to replace — cross-tabulating massive amounts of data — is inherently time consuming. But PivotTables, by virtue of being easy to use, lightning fast, and readily updated, reduce that time to a mere fraction of what it was, resulting in true time savings.

Easy

Perhaps the most important benefit of PivotTables is that they do not come with a daunting learning curve. After you understand the basic features, you can use Excel's Summarize with PivotTable command to build a simple PivotTable report with as little as five or six mouse clicks; see the section "Explore PivotTable Features" later in this chapter. Even the most complex PivotTables are not much harder to build because the PivotTable Tools tab offers everything you need to configure and format a PivotTable.

Fast

The average PivotTable must do quite a bit of work when it generates its report: It must analyze hundreds or even thousands of records, each of which may have a dozen or more fields; extract the unique values from one or more fields; calculate the data summary for each unique item; and then lay

everything out on the worksheet. Amazingly, for all but the largest data sources, this entire process usually only takes a second or two.

Updateable

PivotTables are often used in situations where the original data changes. When that happens, the PivotTable can become out of date. However, each PivotTable "remembers" the original data upon which the report was based. This means that when a PivotTable is out of date, you do not need to re-create the report from scratch. Instead, you can run the Refresh Data command, which instantly updates the PivotTable with the latest data. You can even set up your PivotTable to refresh its data automatically. For the details on refreshing PivotTables, see Chapter 3.

PivotTables Are Flexible

One of the traits that makes a PivotTable a powerful data analysis tool is its flexibility. For example, when you create a PivotTable, the resulting report is not set in stone. Instead, you can move components from one part of the PivotTable to another, filter the results, add and remove data, and more. Another aspect of the flexibility of PivotTables is their versatility, which means that you can create them from more than just Excel ranges and tables.

Dynamic

Every PivotTable is a dynamic creation that you can reconfigure to produce the kind of report you need. Specifically, most of the fields that you add to the PivotTable you can also move from one part of the report to another. This is called *pivoting* the data and it causes Excel to reconfigure the PivotTable and recalculate the results. Excel produces the updated PivotTable immediately, so you can use this feature as needed, making PivotTables even more powerful and useful. See Chapter 4 to learn how to pivot data.

Manipulable

You can easily and quickly manipulate your PivotTable layout to get the results you are looking for. For example, you can always add new fields to any part of the PivotTable, usually with just a few mouse clicks, and you can easily remove any fields that you no longer need. Also, as you learned in the previous section, you can group and filter the PivotTable results to work with just the data you need.

Versatile

If you could create PivotTables only from an Excel range or table, they would still be enormously useful. However, Excel has made PivotTables versatile enough to handle many other types of data. You can create them from Access tables, Word tables, text files, Web pages, XML data, and from tables in powerful database systems such as SQL Server and Online Analytical Processing (OLAP) servers. See Chapter 10 to build advanced PivotTables; see Chapter 11 to build a PivotTable from an OLAP Cube.

PivotTables Suit Your Needs

Although many of the PivotTables that you create will be for your own use, you are also likely to set up PivotTables for other people to view, either on-screen, on paper, or even on the Web (see Chapter 3). In these more public situations, you will usually want to set up your PivotTable so that it looks its best. To that end, Excel has given PivotTables a number of features that enable you to customize and format them as needed.

Customizing

Each PivotTable comes with a number of options that you can use to customize both the report as a whole and individual PivotTable components. For example, you can hide items, sort the data, and customize the report printout. You can also customize the calculations used in the report, either by changing to one of Excel's built-in calculations or by defining custom calculations. For more about custom calculations, see Chapter 8.

Formatting

After you have the PivotTable result you want, you can spend time dressing up the report to make the data easier on the eyes. Fortunately, most of the cells in a PivotTable act as regular Excel cells. This means you can format them in the same way by changing the font, applying colors and borders, using numeric and date formats, and much more. See Chapter 5 to learn about customizing your PivotTable fields.

Learn When to Use PivotTables

One of the keys to using Excel's data-analysis tools is knowing which tool to use under which circumstance. If you want to glean one or two facts about your data, then a formula or two is often all you need. For more elaborate needs, especially ones where you need to build a worksheet version of some real-world concept, a data model is required. If you want to "interrogate" your data by plugging various values into a formula and comparing the results, a data table is best.

If you are looking for a particular or optimal result, use Goal Seek for simple models or Solver for more complex models.

PivotTables, too, are best used only in certain scenarios. Those where a PivotTable is your best data-analysis tool — or at least a worthwhile one to consider — depend on one of three factors: the structure of the underlying data, the analysis you require, and your (or your manager's) reporting needs.

Data Structure

More than any other factor, the structure of your data determines whether a PivotTable is a good data analysis choice. Certain types of data simply cannot be analyzed in a PivotTable, while other data sets would produce largely useless results. In general, the best data structure for

PivotTables is one where the data exists in a tabular format with consistent and repeated data, such as those found in databases of transactions. For more detailed information on setting up your data for a PivotTable report, see Chapter 2.

Tabular Data

Your data is a good candidate for a PivotTable analysis if it exists in tabular format. This means that the data is arranged in a row-and-column structure, with the same number of columns used in each row. If your data is scattered around the worksheet and cannot be rearranged into tabular format, you cannot build a PivotTable from it.

Consistent and Repeated Data

You should consider a PivotTable analysis if your tabular data also has consistent and repeated values. *Consistent values* means that each column contains the same type of data in the same format. For example, one column contains only customer names, another contains only order dates, and yet another contains only invoice amounts. *Repeated values* means that at least one column contains only a limited number of values that

repeat throughout the records. For example, a Region column may contain just four values — East, West, North, and South, for example — that are repeated over hundreds or thousands of records.

Transactional Data

The perfect type of data to benefit from a PivotTable analysis is *transactional* data that records frequent, consistent exchanges of information. Common examples of transactional data include customer orders, accounts receivable data, experiment results, inventory totals, product sales, survey answers, and production schedules. This transactional data creates the same data structure for each record, has consistent data, and has repeated values in at least one field, all which makes this kind of data ideal for a PivotTable approach.

Analysis Required

When deciding whether to build a PivotTable from your data, think about the type of analysis you require. What is your goal? What do you need to know? What secret do you suspect is hidden within all that data? Generally, building a PivotTable is a good idea if you are seeking one or more of the following as part of your analysis of the data: a list of unique values in a field, a summary of a large amount of data, the relationships between two or more fields, and the trend of the data over time.

Unique Values

When faced with a huge amount of data, you may find that one of the first things you want from that data is a list of the unique values in some field. For example, in a database of thousands of orders, you may simply want to know which customers placed orders. The PivotTable is your best choice here because extracting a list of the unique values that occur in a field is one of the things that PivotTables do best.

Summary

Analyzing data often means summarizing it in some way: totaling it, counting it, finding the average or maximum value, and so on. Excel has worksheet functions, subtotals, and other tools for this kind of analysis, but none is suitable for summarizing large amounts of data, particularly if you want to view the results in a compact report. To do that, you must build a PivotTable.

Relationships

One of the biggest problems you face when confronted with a large data set is determining the relationships that exist between one field and another. Which customers are buying which products? How do product defects vary by manufacturing plant? PivotTables are ideal for this kind of analysis because they can break down the values in one field with respect to another. For example, you can display the total sales generated by each of your salespeople, and then break that down by customer, country, product, category, and so on.

Trends

If your data includes a field with date or time values, you may be interested to see how a particular field varies over time. This *trend analysis* can be extremely useful, and Excel has several powerful tools to help you see the trend. However, a PivotTable is an excellent choice if you want to summarize one field and break it down according to the date or time values. How do sales vary throughout the year? How do manufacturing defects vary throughout the day or week?

Reporting Needs

The final aspect to consider when deciding whether to analyze your data with a PivotTable is your reporting needs. In other words, what do you want to end up with? Choose the PivotTable route if you want to end up with a report that is flexible and can easily handle frequent changes.

Flexibility

Build a PivotTable to analyze your data if you want the flexibility to change the report quickly and easily. If you need to switch the layout — for example, to switch from a vertical layout to a horizontal one — you can pivot any field with a click and drag of the mouse. If you need to view subsets of the results, you can filter the report based on the values in a particular field.

Frequent Changes

Choose a PivotTable if you think your underlying data will change frequently. You can easily update the PivotTable to use the latest data, so your report is always accurate and up to date. It is also easy to change the structure of the PivotTable by adding a new field that has been inserted into the data, so you can always incorporate new data.

Explore PivotTable Features

You can get up to speed with PivotTables very quickly after you learn a few key concepts. You need to understand the features that make up a typical PivotTable, particularly the four areas — row, column, data, and page — to which you add fields from your data.

You also need to understand some important PivotTable terminology that you will encounter throughout this book, including terms such as *source data*, *pivot cache*, and *summary calculation*.

Ⓐ Report Filter

Displays a drop-down list that contains the unique values from a field. When you select a value from the list, Excel filters the PivotTable results to include only the records that match the selected value.

Ⓒ Row Area

Displays vertically the unique values from a field in your data.

Ⓓ Data Area

Displays the results of the calculation that Excel applied to a numeric field in your data.

Ⓔ Row Field Header

Identifies the field contained in the row area. You also use the row field header to filter the field values that appear in the row area.

Ⓕ Column Field Header

Identifies the field contained in the column area. You also use the column field header to filter the field values that appear in the column area.

Ⓑ Column Area

Displays horizontally the unique values from a field in your data.

	A	B	C	D	E	F
1	Country	(All)				
2						
3	Sum of ExtendedPrice	OrderDate				
4	Salesperson	1st Quarter	2nd Quarter	3rd Quarter	4th Quarter	Grand Total
5	Andrew Fuller	$7,488.78	$24,374.17	$17,309.15	$21,272.04	$70,444.14
6	Anne Dodsworth	$2,471.98	$4,187.10	$10,245.95	$9,405.36	$26,310.39
7	Janet Leverling	$28,793.05	$33,901.93	$10,469.46	$34,861.69	$108,026.13
8	Laura Callahan	$18,684.31	$7,465.81	$10,800.40	$19,082.08	$56,032.60
9	Margaret Peacock	$41,088.53	$24,474.10	$29,947.73	$33,299.42	$128,809.78
10	Michael Suyama	$3,899.44	$13,806.01	$5,481.65	$19,939.27	$43,126.37
11	Nancy Davolio	$14,402.07	$14,824.31	$32,077.16	$31,844.50	$93,148.04
12	Robert King	$18,940.34	$12,605.92	$25,520.43	$3,404.50	$60,471.19
13	Steven Buchanan	$2,520.40	$7,537.67	$12,085.80	$8,572.57	$30,716.44
14	Grand Total	$138,288.90	$143,177.02	$153,937.73	$181,681.43	$617,085.08
15						
16						

PT-Employee Sales By Quarter / PT-Customer Order T...

Ⓖ Data Field Header

Specifies both the calculation (such as Sum) and the field (such as Invoice Total) used in the data area.

Ⓗ Field Items

The unique values for the field added to the particular area.

PivotTable Glossary

PivotTables come with their own terminology, much of which may be unfamiliar to you, even if you have extensive experience with Excel. To learn PivotTables faster, you should understand not only the terms on the previous page, but also the words and phrases that appear in this glossary.

Data

The calculated values that appear within the data area.

Drop Area

A region of the PivotTable onto which you can drop a field from the source data or from another area of the PivotTable. Excel displays each drop area with a blue border.

External Data

Source data that comes from a non-Excel file or database. You can use Microsoft Query to import external data into your Excel worksheet (see Appendix B). Or you can use Excel's other data import tools (see Appendix C).

Labels

The nondata area elements of the PivotTable. The labels include the field buttons, field items, and report filter drop-down list.

Outer Field and Inner Field

When you have multiple fields in the row or column area — see Chapter 3 — Excel places the fields either beside each other in the row area, or one on top of the other in the column area. In either case, the field that is closest to the data area is called the *inner field*, and the field that is farthest from the data area is called the *outer field*.

Pivot

To move a field from one drop area of the PivotTable to another.

Pivot Cache

This is the source data that Excel keeps in memory to improve PivotTable performance.

Source Data

The original data from which you built your PivotTable. The source data can be an Excel range or table, an Access table or query, a Word table, a text file, a Web page, an XML file, SQL Server data, or OLAP server data, among others.

Summary Calculation

The mathematical operation that Excel applies to the values in a numeric field to yield the summary that appears in the data area. Excel offers 11 built-in summary calculations: Sum, Count, Average, Maximum, Minimum, Product, Count Numbers, Standard Deviation (sample), Standard Deviation (population), Variance (sample), and Variance (population). For more, see Chapter 8. You can also create custom calculations (see Chapter 9).

Introducing the PivotChart

When you begin the process of building a PivotTable, Excel actually gives you a choice between building a PivotTable or a PivotChart. In basic terms, a PivotChart is to a PivotTable what a regular chart is to a range. That is, the former is a graphical representation of the latter. So the PivotChart enables you to visualize the PivotTable results by displaying the data area values in chart form.

However, it is also possible to say that a PivotChart is to a regular chart what a PivotTable is to a regular range. In other words, the PivotChart goes far beyond the capabilities of a simple chart because the PivotChart comes with most of the same features that make PivotTables so powerful: You can filter the results to see just the data you need, and you can pivot fields from one area of the PivotChart to another to get the layout you want. See Chapter 9 to learn how to create and work with PivotCharts.

PivotChart Concepts

As you might expect, PivotCharts have a number of elements in common with PivotTables, but there are also some key differences. The following items explain these differences and introduce you to some important PivotChart concepts.

Chart Categories (X-Axis)

Like a PivotTable, a PivotChart automatically groups large amounts of data into smaller, more manageable groups. For example, if you have data with a Category field containing values such as Beverages, Condiments, Confections, and so on, if you build your PivotChart using the Category field, the resulting chart will display one chart category (X-axis value) for each unique Category field value. This is the equivalent of a row field in a PivotTable.

Chart Data Series

Also, as with a PivotTable, you can break down your data in terms of a second field. For example, your data may have an Order Date field. If you add that field to the PivotChart, Excel creates one data series for each unique value in that field. This is the equivalent of a Column field in a PivotTable.

Chart Values (Y-Axis)

You can't have a PivotTable without a data field, and the same is true with a PivotChart. When you add a numeric field for the summary calculation, Excel displays the results as chart values (Y-axis). This is the equivalent of a data field in a PivotTable.

Dynamic PivotCharts

Perhaps the biggest difference between a PivotChart and a regular chart is that each PivotChart is a dynamic object that you can reconfigure as needed, just like a PivotTable. You can pivot fields from one area of the chart to another, you can add fields to different chart areas, and you can place multiple fields in any chart area.

Filtering

Like a PivotTable, you can use the unique values in another field to filter the results that appear in the PivotChart. For example, if your source data has a Country field, you could add it to the PivotChart and use it to filter the chart results to show just those from a specific country. This is the equivalent of a page field in a PivotTable.

Pros and Cons

PivotCharts have advantages and disadvantages, and understanding their strengths and weaknesses will help you decide when and if you should use them. On the positive side, a PivotChart is a powerful data analysis tool because it combines the strengths of Excel's charting capabilities — including most of the options available with regular charts — with the features of a PivotTable. Also, creating a basic PivotChart is just as easy as creating a PivotTable. In fact, if you already have a PivotTable, you can create the equivalent PivotChart with just a couple mouse clicks.

On the negative side, PivotCharts share the same caveats that come with regular charts, particularly the fact that if you do not choose the proper chart type or layout, your data will not be easily understood. Moreover, a PivotChart can quickly become extremely confusing when you have multiple category fields or data series fields. Finally, PivotCharts have inherent limitations that restrict the options and formatting you can apply. For more on PivotChart limitations, see Chapter 9.

PivotChart Features

PivotCharts carry over some of the same terminology that you saw earlier for PivotTables, including the concepts of the *report filter*, *data area*, and *field button*.

However, PivotCharts also use a number of unique terms such as *category axis* and *series axis* that you need to understand to get the most out of PivotCharts.

Ⓐ **Field Buttons**

Displays a drop-down list with unique values from a category field, data series field, or report filter field that you use to filter the PivotChart data.

Ⓑ **Category Items**

The unique values from a field that define the chart's categories.

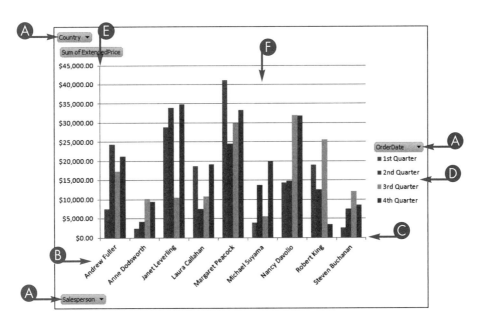

Ⓒ **Category Axis**

The chart axis (X-axis) that displays the category items.

Ⓓ **Data Series Items**

The unique values from a field that define the chart's data series. The item names appear in the chart legend.

Ⓔ **Series Axis**

The chart axis (Y-axis) that displays the values of the data series items.

Ⓕ **Data Area**

Displays the charted results of the calculation that Excel applied to a numeric field in your data.

Prepare Your Worksheet Data

The most common method for building a PivotTable is to use data that exists in an Excel worksheet. You can make this task much easier by taking a few minutes to prepare your worksheet data for use in the PivotTable. Ensuring your data is properly prepared will also ensure that your PivotTable contains accurate and complete summaries of the data.

Preparing your worksheet data for use in a PivotTable is not difficult or time consuming. At a minimum, you must ensure that the data is organized in a row-and-column format, with unique headings at the top of each column

and accurate and consistent data — all numbers or all text — within each column. You also need to remove blank rows, turn off automatic subtotals, and format the data. In some cases, you may also need to add range names to the data, filter the data, and restructure the data so that worksheet labels appear within a column in the data. You may not need to perform all or even any of these tasks, but you should always ensure that your data is set up according to the guidelines you learn about in this section.

Organize Your Data

In the simplest case, Excel builds a PivotTable from worksheet data by finding the unique values in a specific column of data and *summarizing* — summing or counting — that data based

on those unique values. For this to work properly, you need to ensure that your data is organized in such a way that Excel can find those unique values and compute accurate summaries.

Row-and-Column Format

You can perform some Excel tasks on data that is scattered here and there throughout a worksheet, but building a PivotTable is not one of them. To create a PivotTable, your data must be organized in a basic row-and-column format, where each column represents a particular aspect of the data, and each row represents an example of the data. For example, in a parts table, you might have columns for the part name, part number, and cost, and each row would display the name, number, and cost for an individual part.

Unique Column Headings

The first row in your data must contain the headings that identify each column. Excel uses these headings to generate the PivotTable field names, so the headings must be unique and they must reside in a single cell.

Incorporate Labels as Columns

Many worksheets use *labels* — cells that contain descriptive text — as headings to differentiate one section of the worksheet from another. For example, a parts table might have separate sections for each warehouse, and labels such as "East Warehouse" and "West Warehouse" off the side of or

above the appropriate section. Unfortunately, this setup prevents you from using the warehouse data as part of the PivotTable — in the page field, for example. To fix this, create a new column with a unique heading, such as "Warehouse," and copy the label value to each row in the section.

East Warehouse

Description	Number	Quantity	Cost	Total Cost	Retail	Gross Margin
Gangley Pliers	D-178	5,700	$10.47	$59,679.00	$ 17.95	71.4%
HCAB Washer	A-201	20,123	$ 0.12	$ 2,414.76	$ 0.25	108.3%
Finley Sprocket	C-098	10,237	$ 1.57	$16,072.09	$ 2.95	87.9%
6" Sonotube	B-111	860	$15.24	$13,106.40	$ 19.95	30.9%

West Warehouse

Description	Number	Quantity	Cost	Total Cost	Retail	Gross Margin
Langstrom 7" Wrench	D-017	755	$18.69	$14,110.95	$ 27.95	49.5%
Thompson Socket	C-321	5,893	$ 3.11	$18,327.23	$ 5.95	91.3%
S-Joint	A-182	3,023	$ 6.85	$20,707.55	$ 9.95	45.3%
LAMF Valve	B-047	6,734	$ 4.01	$27,003.34	$ 6.95	73.3%

Warehouse	Description	Number	Quantity	Cost	Total Cost	Retail	Gross Margin
East	Gangley Pliers	D-178	5,700	$10.47	$59,679.00	$ 17.95	71.4%
East	HCAB Washer	A-201	20,123	$ 0.12	$ 2,414.76	$ 0.25	108.3%
East	Finley Sprocket	C-098	10,237	$ 1.57	$16,072.09	$ 2.95	87.9%
East	6" Sonotube	B-111	860	$15.24	$13,106.40	$ 19.95	30.9%
West	Langstrom 7" Wrench	D-017	755	$18.69	$14,110.95	$ 27.95	49.5%
West	Thompson Socket	C-321	5,893	$ 3.11	$18,327.23	$ 5.95	91.3%
West	S-Joint	A-182	3,023	$ 6.85	$20,707.55	$ 9.95	45.3%
West	LAMF Valve	B-047	6,734	$ 4.01	$27,003.34	$ 6.95	73.3%

To get your data ready for PivotTable analysis, you may also need to run through a few more preparatory chores, including deleting blank rows, ensuring the data is consistent and accurate, and turning off subtotals and the AutoFilter feature.

Ensure Accurate Data

One of the most important concepts in data analysis is that your results are only as accurate as your data. This is sometimes referred to, whimsically, as GIGO: Garbage In, Garbage Out. PivotTables are no exception: You can be sure that the summaries displayed in the report are accurate only if you are sure that the values used in the data field column are accurate. This applies to the other PivotTable fields, as well. For example, if you have a column that is supposed to contain just a certain set of values — for example, North, South, East, and West — you need to check the column to make sure there are no typos or extraneous data items.

Turn Off Automatic Subtotals

Excel PivotTables are designed to provide you with numeric summaries of your data: sums, counts, averages, and so on. Therefore, you do not need to use Excel's Automatic Subtotals feature within your data. In fact, Excel will not create a PivotTable from worksheet data that has subtotals displayed. Therefore, you should remove all subtotals from your data. Click inside the data, click Data→Subtotal, and then click Remove All.

Delete Blank Rows

It is common to include one or more blank rows within a worksheet to space out the data and to separate different sections of the data. This may make the data easier to read, but it can cause problems when you build your PivotTable because Excel includes the blank rows in the PivotTable report. To avoid this, run through your data and delete any blank rows.

Ensure Consistent Data

It is important that each column contains consistent data. First, ensure that each column contains the same kind of data. For example, if the column is supposed to hold part numbers, make sure it does not contain part names, costs, or anything other than part numbers. Second, ensure that each column uses a consistent data type. For example, in a column of part names, be sure each value is text; in a column of costs, make sure each value is numeric.

Turn Off AutoFilter

If you want to use only a subset of the worksheet data in your PivotTable, do not use Excel's AutoFilter feature. If you do, Excel will still use some or all the hidden rows in the PivotTable report, so your results will not be accurate. Instead, you need to use Excel's Advanced Filter feature and have the results copied to a different worksheet location. You can then use the copied data as the source for your PivotTable report.

Use Repeated Data

The power of the PivotTable lies in its ability to summarize huge amounts of data. That summarization occurs when Excel detects the unique values in a field, groups the records together based on those unique values, and then calculates the total (or whatever) of the values in a particular field. For this to work, at least one field must contain repeated data, preferably a relatively small number of repeated items.

Create a Table for a PivotTable Report

You can make your PivotTable easier to maintain by converting the underlying worksheet data from a regular range to a table. In Excel, a table is a collection of related information with an organizational structure that makes it easy to add, edit, and sort data. In short, a table is a type of database where the data is organized into rows and columns: Each column represents a database field, which is a single type of information, such as a name, address, or phone number; each row represents a database record, which is a collection of associated field values, such as the information for a specific contact. A table differs from a regular Excel range in that Excel offers a set of tools that makes it easier for you to add new records, delete existing records, sort and filter data, and more.

How does a table help you maintain your PivotTables? Using a regular range as the PivotTable source data works well when you insert or delete rows within the range. After the insertions or deletions, you can refresh the PivotTable and Excel automatically updates the report to reflect the changes. However, this does not work if you add new data to the bottom of the range, which is the most common scenario. In this case, you need to rebuild the PivotTable and specify the newly expanded range. You can avoid this extra step by converting your source data range into an Excel table. In this case, Excel keeps track of any new data added to the bottom of the table, so you can refresh your PivotTable at any time.

Create a Table for a PivotTable Report

Note: This chapter uses the Orders02.xlsx spreadsheet, available at www.wiley.com/go/pivottablesvb2e, or you can create your own sample database.

1 Click a cell within the range that you want to convert to a table.

2 Click the Insert tab.

3 Click Table.

You can also choose the Table command by pressing Ctrl+T.

The Create Table dialog box appears.

- Excel selects the range that it will convert to a table.

- If you want to change the range, click here and then click and drag the mouse over the new range.

④ Click OK.

Excel converts the range to a table.

- Excel applies a table format to the range.

- The Table Tools contextual tab appears.

- AutoFilter drop-down lists appear in each field heading.

⑤ Click the Design tab to see Excel's table design tools.

Extra

To add a record to the end of the table, click inside the table, press Ctrl+End to move to the last field in the last record, and then press Tab. To add a record within the table, right-click the record above which you want to insert the new record, and then click Insert→Table Rows Above. Type your data for the first field and then press Tab to move to the second field. For the rest of the fields, type your data and press Tab to move to the next field.

After you create a table, Excel's Design tab offers a number of tools that enable you to format the table. For example, use the Table Styles gallery to change the overall format applied to the table. You can also use the check boxes in the Table Style Options group to turn formatting such as Banded Rows on and off.

Build a PivotTable from an Excel Table

If the data you want to cross-tabulate exists as an Excel table, you can use the Summarize with PivotTable command to easily build a PivotTable report based on your data. You need only specify the location of your source data and then choose the location of the resulting PivotTable.

Excel creates an empty PivotTable in a new worksheet or in the location you specified. Excel also displays PivotTable Field List, which contains four areas with the following labels: Report Filter, Column Labels, Row Labels, and Values. To complete the PivotTable, you must populate some or all of these areas with one or more fields from your data.

When you add a field to the Row Labels, Column Labels, or Report Filter area, Excel extracts the unique values from the field and displays them in the PivotTable in the row,

column, or page field, respectively. For example, if you add the Salesperson field to the Row Labels area, Excel updates the PivotTable's row area to display the unique salesperson names as headings that run down the leftmost column of the report. Similarly, if you add the Country field to the Report Filter area, Excel updates the PivotTable's page field to display the unique country names.

When you add a field to the Values area, Excel performs calculations based on the numeric data in the field. The default calculation is sum, so if you add, for example, the Sale Amount field to the Values area, Excel sums the Sale Amount values. How Excel calculates these sums depends on the fields you have added to the other areas. For example, if you add just the Salesperson field to the row area, Excel displays the sum of the Sale Amount values for each salesperson. You can also use other calculations such as Average and Count (see Chapter 8).

Build a PivotTable from an Excel Table

① Click a cell within the table that you want to use as the source data.

② Click Design→Summarize with PivotTable.

The Create PivotTable dialog box appears.

③ Select the New Worksheet option.

● If you want to place the PivotTable in an existing location, select the Existing Worksheet option, and then use the Location range box to select the worksheet and cell where you want the PivotTable to appear.

④ Click OK.

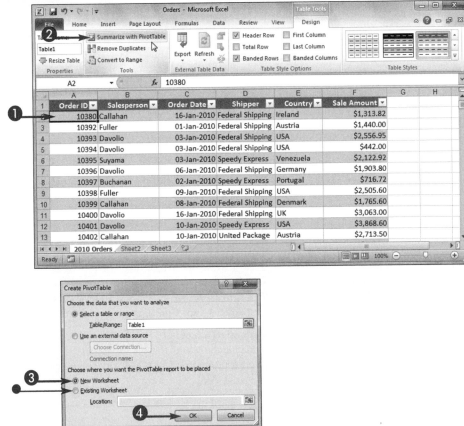

- Excel creates a blank PivotTable.

- Excel displays the PivotTable Field List.

5 Click and drag a field and drop it inside the Row Labels area.

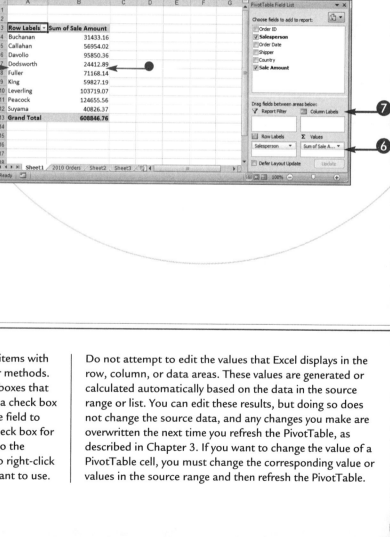

- Excel adds the field's unique values to the PivotTable's row area.

6 Click and drag a numeric field and drop it inside the Values area.

- Excel sums the numeric values based on the row values.

7 If desired, click and drag fields and drop them in the Column Labels area and the Report Filter area.

Each time you drop a field in an area, Excel updates the PivotTable to include the new data.

Extra

If you are not comfortable dragging items with the mouse, Excel gives you two other methods. The first method is to use the check boxes that appear beside each field. If you click a check box for a text or date field, Excel adds the field to the Row Labels area; if you click a check box for a numeric field, Excel adds the field to the Values area. The second method is to right-click a field, and then click the area you want to use.

Do not attempt to edit the values that Excel displays in the row, column, or data areas. These values are generated or calculated automatically based on the data in the source range or list. You can edit these results, but doing so does not change the source data, and any changes you make are overwritten the next time you refresh the PivotTable, as described in Chapter 3. If you want to change the value of a PivotTable cell, you must change the corresponding value or values in the source range and then refresh the PivotTable.

Build a PivotTable from an Excel Range

I n the previous section, you learned how to build a
PivotTable report from an Excel table. This is the
easiest way to build a PivotTable because, by
definition, an Excel table has the required structure to
successfully create a PivotTable. However, if your data is
not in the form of a table — that is, your data resides in a
regular Excel range — you can still build a PivotTable
report from that data. In this case, you need to make sure
that your data is in the correct format to build a PivotTable
report. See the earlier section "Prepare Your Worksheet" for
a list of characteristics to look for and techniques you can
use to put your data into the proper arrangement.

When you run Excel's Insert PivotTable command, Excel
prompts you to specify the location of the source data and
it asks whether you want to store the PivotTable report on
a new worksheet or in an existing worksheet location.
When that is done, Excel creates an empty PivotTable in
the location you specified and displays the PivotTable Field
List. As you saw in the previous section, the PivotTable
Field List contains four areas: Report Filter, Column Labels,
Row Labels, and Values. To complete the PivotTable, you
must populate some or all of these areas with one or more
fields from your data. In most cases, you do this by
clicking and dragging a field and dropping it inside the
area you want to work with. Each time you do that, Excel
updates the PivotTable report with the new data.

Build a PivotTable from an Excel Range

① Click a cell within the range that you
want to use as the source data.

② Click Insert→PivotTable.

The Create PivotTable dialog box
appears.

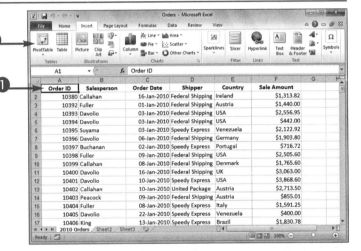

③ Ensure that the displayed range
address is correct.

● If the range address is incorrect,
click here and then click and drag
with your mouse to select the range.

④ Select the New Worksheet option.

● If you want to place the PivotTable
in an existing location, select the
Existing Worksheet option, and then
use the Location range box to select
the location.

⑤ Click OK.

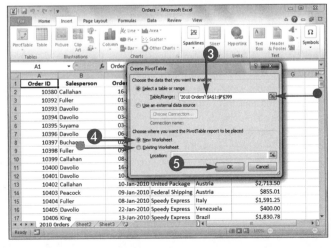

- Excel creates a blank PivotTable.

- Excel displays the PivotTable Field List.

6 Follow steps **6** to **8** in the previous section to add fields to the Row Labels, Values, Column Labels, and Report Filter areas.

- Excel creates the PivotTable.

Extra

Once you add a field to the Report Filter, Column Labels, Rows Labels, or Values area, you do not have to keep the field in that area. For example, you may have accidentally dropped a field in the Report Filter area instead of the Row Labels area. To fix this, click and drag the field from the existing area and then drop it inside the new area. Similarly, if you no longer want a field to appear in the PivotTable, click and drag the field from its existing area and then drop it outside the PivotTable Field List.

When you drop a field inside an area, Excel automatically updates the PivotTable report with the new data, and this process usually does not take more than a second or two. However, if your data source is extremely large, it might take Excel a noticeably long time to update the PivotTable report when you drop a field inside an area. If you find that you have to wait too long for each update, you can tell Excel not to perform the update each time you add a field. Click the Defer Layout Update check box. When you are ready to see the updated PivotTable, click the Update button.

Recreate an Existing PivotTable

he source data that underlies a PivotTable rarely remains static. You, or someone else, may add or delete records, edit the existing data, or add or delete fields. Therefore, you will need to update your PivotTable from time to time to reflect these changes. In most cases, particularly when you use an Excel table as the source data, you need only refresh the PivotTable to incorporate any changes to the original data. See Chapter 3 to learn how to refresh an existing PivotTable.

However, you may find that in certain cases, refreshing the PivotTable does not incorporate all the changes that have been made to the source data. Similarly, you may have an important meeting or presentation coming up and you want to make sure that your PivotTable is using the most up-to-date information. In both situations, you can ensure that your PivotTable uses the latest source data by re-creating the PivotTable. You do this by reselecting the updated table or range.

Recreate an Existing PivotTable

① Click a cell within the existing PivotTable.

② Click Options→Change Data Source.

The Change PivotTable Data Source dialog box appears.

Note: If you based your PivotTable on a table, Excel automatically selects the table. In this case, you can skip to step **5**.

③ Adjust the range address to include the updated data.

● You can also click here and then click and drag with your mouse to select the updated range.

④ Click OK.

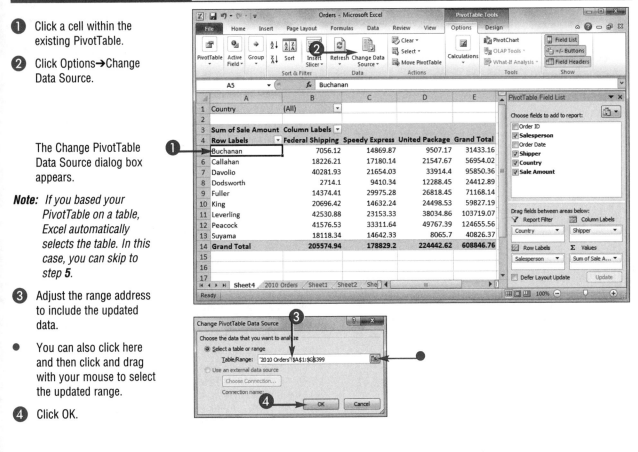

Excel re-creates the PivotTable.

If any fields were removed from the source data, Excel removes those fields from the PivotTable and from the PivotTable Field List.

● If any fields were added to the source data, Excel adds those fields to the PivotTable Field List, such as the Customer field shown here.

⑤ Use the PivotTable Field List to add any new fields to the PivotTable.

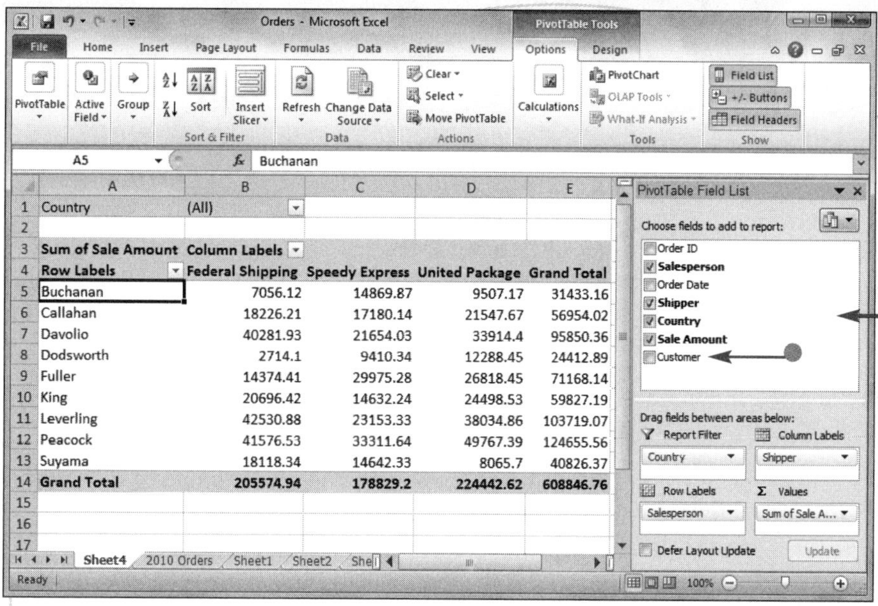

Apply It

You can also use the Change PivotTable Data Source dialog box to select a completely different table or range for your PivotTable. Note, too, that it is not uncommon to have the source data for a PivotTable in one workbook and the PivotTable itself in a different workbook. In this case, in step **6**, you may prefer to type the range address in the Range text box. If so, then you need to specify not only the source data's range address, but also the workbook file name and the name of the worksheet that contains the range. Here is the following general format to use:

```
'[WorkbookName.xls]SheetName'!RangeAddress
```

For example, suppose the source data resides in a workbook named Orders.xlsx, on a worksheet named Orders 2010, and in the range $A$1: $F$399. Here is the address you would type in the Range dialog box in step **6**:

```
'[Orders.xlsx]Orders 2010'!$A$1:$F$399
```

Turn the PivotTable Field List On and Off

Y ou can give yourself more room to display your PivotTable report by turning off the PivotTable Field List when you do not need it. You can then turn the PivotTable Field List back on when you need to add, move, or delete fields.

By default, when you click inside the PivotTable, Excel displays the PivotTable Field List, and then hides the PivotTable Field List again when you click outside of the PivotTable report. However, if you want to work with the PivotTable Tools, then you need to leave at least one cell in the PivotTable report selected. Fortunately, Excel also enables you to turn the PivotTable Field List off and on by hand.

You can also use the programming language VBA to toggle the PivotTable Field List, as shown in the following macro (see Chapter 16 for the basics on using VBA with PivotTables):

```
Example:
Sub ToggleFieldList()
    '
    ' Work with the active workbook
    '
    With ActiveWorkbook
        '
        ' Toggle the current value of the
        ' workbook's ShowPivotTableFieldList
        ' property between True and False
        '
        .ShowPivotTableFieldList = Not
  .ShowPivotTableFieldList
    End With
End Sub
```

Turn the PivotTable Field List On and Off

Turn Off the PivotTable Field List

Note: This chapter uses the Orders03.xlsm and PivotTables03.xlsm spreadsheets, available at www.wiley.com/go/pivottablesvb2e, or you can create your own sample files.

1 Click inside the PivotTable.

2 Click Options→Field List.

● You can also click the Close button.

Excel turns off the PivotTable Field List.

Turn On the PivotTable Field List

1 Click inside the PivotTable.

2 Click Options→Field List.

Excel turns on the PivotTable Field List.

Customize the PivotTable Field List

By default, the PivotTable Field List pane is divided into two sections: the Fields Section lists the available fields and appears at the top of the pane, and the Areas Section lists the PivotTable areas and appears at the bottom of the pane. You can customize this layout to suit the way you work.

For example, you can choose the Field Section and Areas Section Side-By-Side option, which puts the Fields Section on the left and the Areas Section on the right. This is useful if your source data comes with a large number of fields.

Another option is Fields Section Only, which hides the Areas Section. This is useful if you add fields to the PivotTable by right-clicking the field name and

then clicking the area to which you want the field added. In this case, hiding the Areas Section gives you more room to display fields.

A third option is Areas Section Only (2 by 2), which hides the Fields Section. This option is useful if you have finished adding fields to the PivotTable and you want to concentrate on moving fields between the areas and filtering the fields (see Chapter 4). This option arranges the areas in two rows and two columns.

The final option is Areas Section Only (1 by 4). This is the same as the Areas Section Only (2 by 2) options, except that Excel displays the areas in a single column. This gives each area a wider display, which is useful if some of your fields have very long names.

Customize the PivotTable Field List

1 Click any cell inside the PivotTable.

2 Click here.

● Excel displays the list of PivotTable Field List options.

3 Click the option you want to use.

● Excel customizes the PivotTable Field List based on your selection.

Select PivotTable Items

In many of the sections in this book, you apply formatting or settings to some or all of the PivotTable's cells, or you perform some action on some or all of the PivotTable's cells. Before you can do any of this, however, you must first select the cell or cells you want to work with. You can speed up your PivotTable work considerably by becoming familiar with the various methods that Excel offers for selecting elements in a PivotTable report.

If you are familiar with Excel, then you probably already know the basic techniques for selecting cells. For example, you select a single cell by clicking it, and you

select a range by dragging your mouse from the top-left corner of the range to the bottom-right corner. You can also select random cells by holding down Ctrl and clicking the cells you want. You can use all the standard techniques to select cells within a PivotTable report. However, Excel also offers several methods that are unique to PivotTables. For example, you can select one or more row or column fields, just the PivotTable labels, just the PivotTable data, or the entire table. Excel also offers handy Ribbon buttons for most of these techniques, so you can customize the Quick Access Toolbar for one-click access to PivotTable selection techniques.

Select PivotTable Items

Select a Row or Column Field

① For a column, move the mouse pointer just above the column label.

The mouse pointer changes to a black, downward-pointing arrow (↓).

● For a row, move the mouse pointer just to the left of the row label.

The mouse pointer changes to a right-pointing arrow (→).

② Click the mouse.

● Excel selects the column.

Select the Entire PivotTable

① Click any cell within the PivotTable.

② Click Options→Select→Entire PivotTable.

You can also move the mouse pointer to the top or left edge of the upper-left PivotTable cell (the pointer changes to ↓ or →) and then click.

Excel selects the entire table.

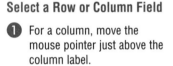

Select Data Only

1. Select the entire PivotTable, as described in the previous task.

2. Click Options→ Select→Values.

● Excel selects just the PivotTable's data area.

If you select a field instead of the entire table, click Options→ Select→Values to select just that field's data.

Select Labels Only

1. Select the entire PivotTable, as described in the task "Select the Entire PivotTable," or the PivotTable data, as described in the previous task.

2. Click Options→ Select→Labels.

● Excel selects just the PivotTable's labels.

If you select a field instead of the entire table, click Options→ Select→Labels to select just that field's labels.

Extra

You can make your PivotTable selection chores even easier by incorporating one or more extra buttons on the Quick Access Toolbar. Excel offers extra buttons for the Values, Labels, and Labels and Values commands that appear when you click Options→Select in the PivotTable Tools context tab.

Right-click the Quick Access Toolbar and then click Customize Quick Access Toolbar to display the Customize tab of the Excel Options dialog box. Use the Choose Commands From list to click PivotTable Tools→Options Tab and then scroll down the list until you see the following buttons:

BUTTON	NAME	DESCRIPTION
	Select Labels	Selects the PivotTable labels
	Select Labels and Values	Selects the PivotTable's labels and values
	Select PivotTable Values	Selects the PivotTable values

Click the button you want and then click Add. When you finish, click OK to close the Excel Options dialog box.

Remove a PivotTable Field

After you complete your PivotTable, the resulting report is not set in stone. You see in Chapter 4 and in other parts of this book that you can change the PivotTable view, format the PivotTable cells, add custom calculations, and much more. You can also remove fields from the PivotTable report, as you learn in this section.

Removing a PivotTable field comes in handy when you want to work with a less detailed report. For example, suppose your PivotTable report shows the sum of sales data from four items in the Region field — East, Midwest, South, and West — that appear in the row area. This data is broken down by fiscal quarter, where each item in the Quarter field appears in the column area. If you decide you want to simplify the report to show just the total for

each region, then you need to remove the Quarter field from the PivotTable.

Remove a field from a PivotTable only if you are sure you will not need the field again in the future. You can always add fields back into the PivotTable report, but deleting a field and then adding it back again is inefficient. If you only want to take a field out of the PivotTable report temporarily, consider hiding the field (see Chapter 4 for more on hiding rows and fields).

Similarly, you do not need to go through the process of removing a field if you know that the field has been removed from the original data source. Instead, refresh the PivotTable and Excel removes the deleted field for you automatically. See the section "Refresh PivotTable Data" for more.

Remove a PivotTable Field

Remove a Field from the PivotTable Report

1 Click any cell inside the PivotTable.

2 In the PivotTable field list, click the check box of the field you want to remove.

● Excel removes the field from the PivotTable report.

Remove All Fields from the PivotTable Report

1 Click any cell inside the PivotTable.

2 Click Options→ Clear→Clear All.

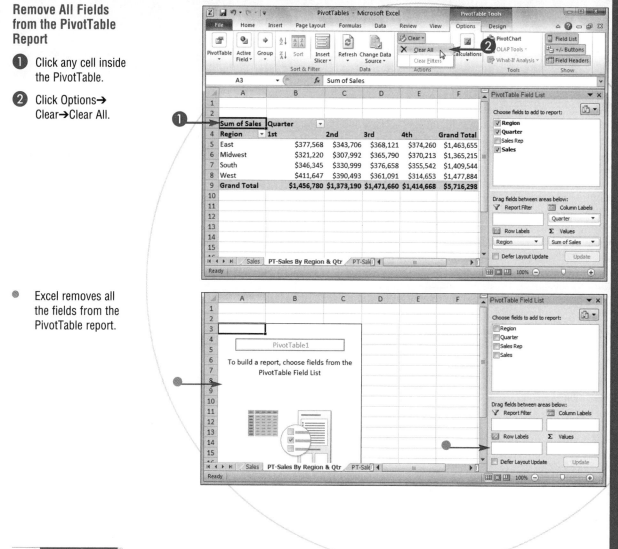

● Excel removes all the fields from the PivotTable report.

Apply It

Removing fields is particularly handy when you work with multiple fields in a single area, as described in the sections "Add Multiple Fields to the Row or Column Area," "Add Multiple Fields to the Data Area," and "Add Multiple Fields to the Report Filter." If you find that a PivotTable with multiple fields in one area is too confusing or too cumbersome to manipulate, removing one or more of those fields can simplify the layout and help you get more out of your PivotTable.

It is worth noting here that you cannot delete part of a field. For example, if you have a Region field, you cannot delete the Midwest item, for example. If you select a cell, row, or column within the PivotTable and press Delete, Excel displays an error message telling you that you cannot delete part of the PivotTable report. Again, it is possible to hide individual rows and columns within a PivotTable (see Chapter 4 for more).

Refresh PivotTable Data

Whether your PivotTable is based on financial results, survey responses, or a database of collectibles such as books or DVDs, the underlying data is probably not static. That is, the data changes over time as new results come in, new surveys are undertaken, and new items are added to the collection. You can ensure that the data analysis represented by the PivotTable remains up to date by refreshing the PivotTable, as shown in this section.

Refreshing the PivotTable means rebuilding the report using the most current version of the source data. However, this is not the same as rebuilding the PivotTable, as described in the section "Re-create an Existing PivotTable" in Chapter 2. Instead, when you refresh a PivotTable, Excel keeps the report layout as is

and simply updates the data area calculations with the latest source data. Also, depending on the type of source data you are using, Excel removes from the report any fields that have been deleted from the source data, and it displays in the PivotTable Field List any new fields that have been added to the source data.

Excel offers two methods for refreshing a PivotTable: manual and automatic. A manual refresh is one that you perform yourself, usually when you know that the source data has changed, or if you simply want to be sure that the latest data is reflected in your PivotTable report. An automatic refresh is one that Excel handles for you. For PivotTables based on Excel ranges or tables, you can tell Excel to refresh a PivotTable every time you open the workbook that contains the report.

Refresh PivotTable Data

Refresh Data Manually

1. Click any cell inside the PivotTable.

2. Click Options→Refresh.

   You can also press Alt+F5.

- To update every PivotTable in the current workbook, either click the Options→Refresh menu and then click Refresh All, or press Ctrl+Alt+F5.

   Excel updates the PivotTable data.

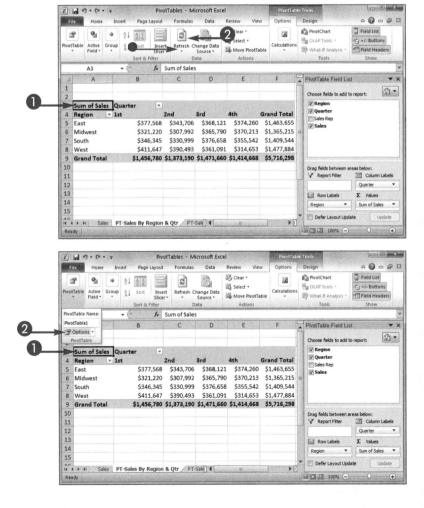

Refresh Data Automatically

1. Click any cell inside the PivotTable.

2. Click Options→ PivotTable→Options.

The PivotTable Options dialog box appears.

③ Click the Data tab.

④ Click Refresh data when opening the file.

⑤ Click OK.

Excel applies the refresh options.

Apply It

For certain types of source data, you can set up a schedule that automatically refreshes the PivotTable at a specified interval. This is useful when you know the source data changes frequently and you do not want to be bothered with constant manual refreshes.

Click any cell inside the PivotTable, click Options→Refresh, and then click Connection Properties. Note that if this command is not enabled, it means your source data does not support automatic refreshing at preset intervals. For example, this command is not enabled when you use an Excel range or table as the data source. However, for data that comes from other types of data source types, particularly external data, this command is enabled. See Chapter 10 to learn how to build a PivotTable from data sources other than Excel ranges and tables. If you want to refresh the PivotTable automatically at a specified interval, click Refresh every, and then use the spin box to specify the refresh interval in minutes.

Note, however, that you might prefer not to have the source data updated too frequently. Depending on where the data resides and how much data you are working with, the refresh could take some time, which would slow down the rest of your work.

Display the Details Behind PivotTable Data

The main advantage to using PivotTables is that they give you an easy method for summarizing large quantities of data into a succinct report for data analysis. PivotTables show you the forest instead of the trees. However, there may be times when you need to see some of the trees that comprise the forest. For example, if you are studying the results of a marketing campaign, your PivotTable may show you the total number of mouse pads sold as a result of a direct marketing piece. However, what if you want to see the details underlying that number? If your source data contains hundreds or thousands of records, you would need to filter the data in some way to see just the records you want.

Fortunately, Excel gives you an easier way to do this by enabling you to directly view the details that underlie a specific data value. This is called *drilling down* to the

details. When you drill down into a specific data value in a PivotTable, Excel returns to the source data, extracts the records that comprise the data value, and then displays the records in a new worksheet. For a PivotTable based on a range or list, this extraction takes but a second or two, depending on how many records there are in the source data.

This section shows you how easy it is to drill down into your PivotTable data. In fact, it is so easy and so useful that many people find themselves frequently drilling down to peek behind the data. Unfortunately, because Excel creates a new worksheet each time, this often results in a workbook that is cluttered with many extra worksheets. Therefore, this section also shows you how to delete the detail worksheets.

Display the Details Behind PivotTable Data

Display the Details

1 Right-click the data value for which you want to view the underlying details.

The data value's shortcut menu appears.

2 Click Show Details.

You can also double-click the data value.

- Excel displays the underlying data in a new worksheet.

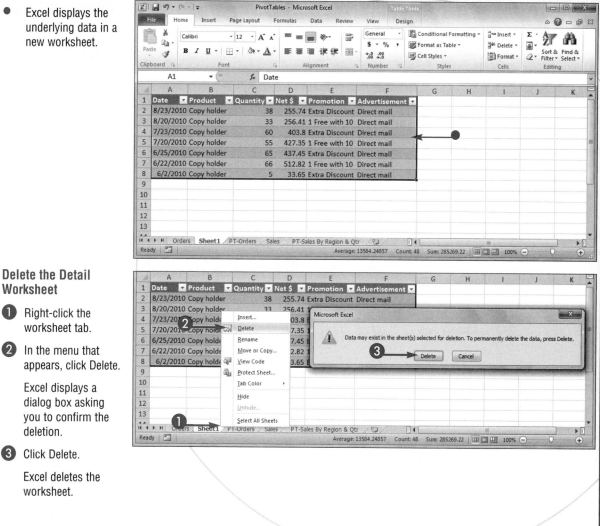

Delete the Detail Worksheet

① Right-click the worksheet tab.

② In the menu that appears, click Delete.

Excel displays a dialog box asking you to confirm the deletion.

③ Click Delete.

Excel deletes the worksheet.

Extra

When you attempt to drill down to a data value's underlying details, Excel may display the error message "Cannot change this part of a PivotTable report." This error means that the feature that normally enables you to drill down has been turned off. To turn this feature back on, click any cell inside the PivotTable and then click Options→PivotTable→Options to display the PivotTable Options dialog box. Click the Data tab, click Enable Show Details, and then click OK.

The opposite situation occurs when you distribute the workbook containing the PivotTable and you do not want the other users drilling down and cluttering the workbook with detail worksheets. In this case, click Options→PivotTable→Options, click the Data tab, click Enable Show Details, and then click OK.

There may be times when you want to see all of a PivotTable's underlying source data. If the source data is a range or table in another worksheet, then you can see the underlying data by displaying that worksheet. If the source data is not so readily available, however, then Excel gives you an easy way to view all the underlying data. Right-click the PivotTable's Grand Total cell and then click Show Details. Excel displays all of the PivotTable's underlying data in a new worksheet.

Create a Chart from PivotTable Data

Excel charts are a great way to analyze data because they enable you to visualize the numbers and see the relationships between different aspects of the data. This is particularly useful in a PivotTable because it is often necessary to visualize the relationship between different columns or different rows. In Chapter 10, you learn how to create a PivotChart. However, if you just need a simple chart, or if you want to avoid the limitations that are inherent with a PivotChart, you can create a regular chart using the PivotTable data, as you learn in this section.

If you try to create a chart directly from a PivotTable, Excel creates a PivotChart. To create a regular chart from

a PivotTable, you must first copy the PivotTable data that you want to graph, and then paste the values into another part of the worksheet. You can then build your chart using this copied data. In this case, you run through the various steps provided by the Chart Wizard to specify the chart type, chart options, and chart location.

Note, though, that this method produces a static chart. This means that if your PivotTable data changes, your chart does not change automatically. Instead, you need to re-create your chart from scratch. However, it is possible to create a dynamic chart that changes whenever your PivotTable does. See the tip at the end of this section for details.

Create a Chart from PivotTable Data

① Select the PivotTable data you want to use for your chart.

② Click Home→Copy.

You can also press Ctrl+C.

Excel copies the PivotTable data.

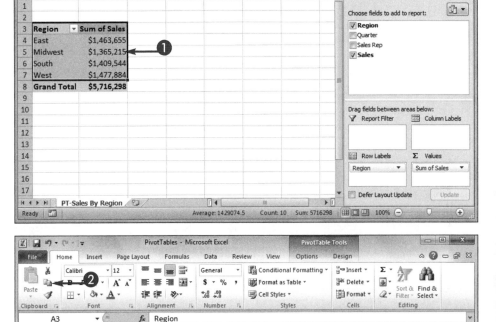

③ Click the cell where you want the copied data to appear.

④ Click Home→ Paste→Paste Values.

Excel pastes just the labels and data from the copied PivotTable.

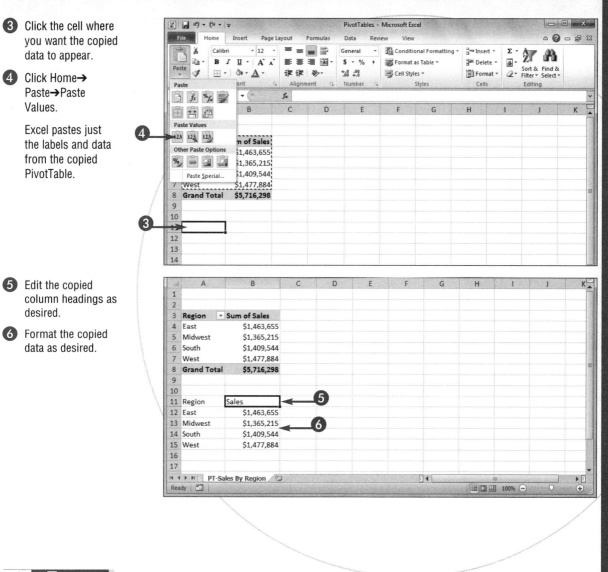

⑤ Edit the copied column headings as desired.

⑥ Format the copied data as desired.

continued ➡

Extra

PivotTables often result in large workbooks because Excel must keep track of a great deal of extra information to keep the PivotTable performance acceptable. In Chapter 4, you learn how to *pivot* the data, which means move a field to a different area of the PivotTable. To ensure that the recalculation involved in pivoting happens quickly and efficiently, Excel maintains a copy of the source data in a special memory area called the *pivot cache*.

When you copy a PivotTable and then paste it, Excel also pastes the pivot cache. This is wasteful because the pasted data does not and cannot make use of the pivot cache. This is why you must be sure to choose the Paste Values command instead of the regular Paste command.

As you learn in Chapter 10, a PivotChart, although very similar to a regular Excel chart, comes with a number of limitations on chart types, layout, and formatting. A PivotChart also comes with its own pivot cache, a concept you learned about in the tip for the section "Create a Chart from PivotTable Data." This means that PivotCharts can use up a great deal of memory and can greatly increase the size of a workbook.

If you simply want to visualize your data, you can avoid the limitations and resource requirements of a PivotChart by creating a regular chart instead. You do this by using the Insert tab's Charts group to select the chart type and subtype you want to create. With a regular chart, you have access to all the available charting features, so you can use all the options presented by the Chart Tools contextual tab to lay out and design your graph.

Create a Chart from PivotTable Data *(continued)*

⑦ Select the copied data.

⑧ Click Insert.

⑨ Click the chart type you want to insert.

⑩ Click a chart subtype.

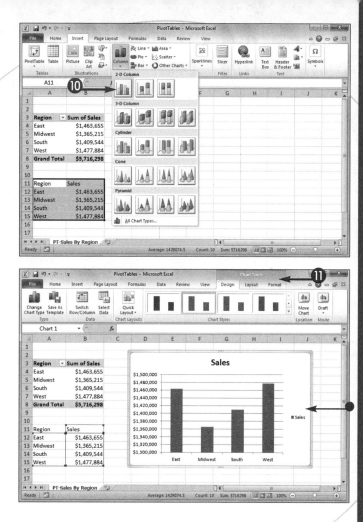

● Excel inserts the chart.

⑪ Use the Chart Tools tabs to modify the chart design, layout, and formatting as desired.

Apply It

The chart you learn how to create in this section is static, so whenever your PivotTable gets new values, you must re-create the chart from scratch. This is useful for PivotTables that do not change fields, items, or data. However, if you have a PivotTable that changes frequently, you might prefer to create a dynamic chart that updates automatically when changes occur in your PivotTable data.

To create a dynamic chart, use formulas instead of copy and paste to create a replica of the PivotTable data. That is, for each cell in the PivotTable that you want to use in your chart, create a formula in another cell that references the PivotTable cell. For example, in cell A11, type the formula **=B3** to reference the Region label; similarly, in cell B11, type the formula **=B3** to reference the Sum of Sales label. Do the same for the data values. Note that for large PivotTable reports, Excel gives you an easier method: copy the PivotTable data, and then click Home→Paste→Paste Link. When you finish, you should have the same labels and values in a replica of the PivotTable. You can then base your chart on this replicated data. Because you are using formulas to reference the original data, any changes to the PivotTable are automatically reflected in your chart.

Enable the Classic PivotTable Layout

When you create a new PivotTable report in Excel 2010, the program sets up the PivotTable so that you must add and remove a field using the PivotTable Field List: you either click and drag a field and drop it on or outside of one of the areas in the Fields Section, or you click the field's check box to add it to or remove it from a default area.

Using the PivotTable Field List is straightforward, but Excel offers an alternative method for manipulating fields in a report. This method uses the *classic* PivotTable layout, which gets its name because it was the layout used in previous versions of Excel. In the classic layout, Excel adds *in-grid drop zones* to the PivotTable. These zones correspond to the row, column, data, and report

filters, and they are called drop zones because you can use them to click and drag fields from the PivotTable Field List and drop them directly on the PivotTable. You can also use these zones to click and drag existing PivotTable fields, which enables you to move fields from one part of the report to another, or to remove fields from the PivotTable.

As you learn in this section, you can configure a PivotTable created in Excel 2010 to use the classic layout. Note, too, that in some cases Excel may display the classic layout automatically. This occurs when you open a workbook created in a previous version of Excel and that workbook contains one or more PivotTables.

Enable the Classic PivotTable Layout

① Click a cell within the PivotTable.

Note: *A new, unpopulated PivotTable appears here so that later on you can more easily see the drop zones. However, you can use this technique on any existing PivotTable.*

② Click Options→ PivotTable→Options.

The PivotTable Options dialog box appears.

③ Click the Display tab.

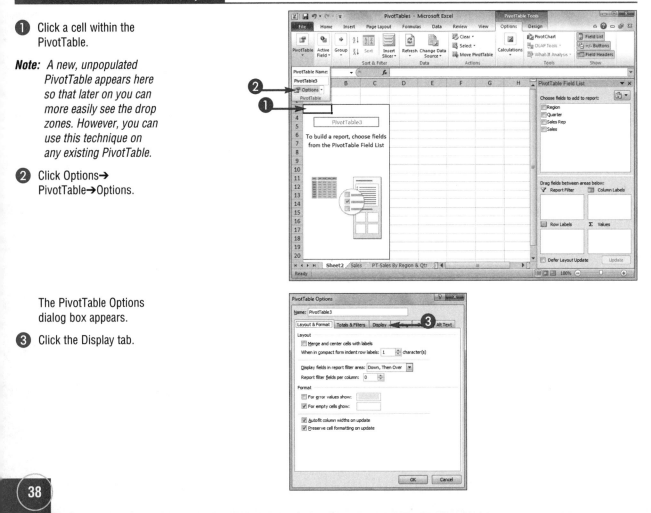

④ Select the Classic PivotTable layout check box.

⑤ Click OK.

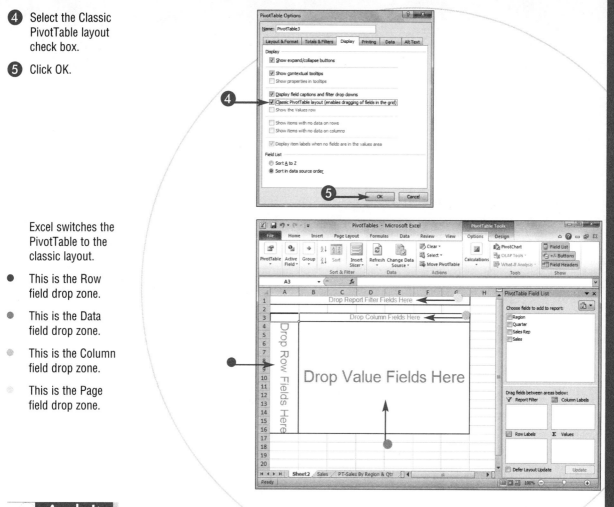

Excel switches the PivotTable to the classic layout.

● This is the Row field drop zone.

● This is the Data field drop zone.

● This is the Column field drop zone.

● This is the Page field drop zone.

Apply It

To return to the Excel 2010 PivotTable layout, follow steps **1** to **3**, deselect the Classic PivotTable layout check box, and then click OK. Note that you can also use VBA to toggle the classic layout on and off. This enables you to set up a shortcut key for the macro or add the macro to the Quick Access Toolbar. In your VBA code, you set the `PivotTable` object's `InGridDropZones` property to either `True` (to display the classic layout) or `False` (to use the default layout). Here's an example macro that toggles the classic layout on and off:

```
Sub ToggleClassicPivotTableLayout()
    '
    ' Work with the current PivotTable
    ' (click any cell in the PivotTable)
    '
    With Selection.PivotTable
        '
        ' Toggle the current value of the
        ' PivotTable's InGridDropZones
        ' property between True and False
        '
        .InGridDropZones = Not .InGridDropZones
    End With
End Sub
```

Add Multiple Fields to the Row or Column Area

The PivotTables you have seen so far have been restricted to a single field in any of the four areas: row, column, data, and page. However, you are free to add multiple fields to any one of these areas. This is a very powerful technique because it allows you to perform further analysis of your data by viewing the data differently.

In this section, you learn how to add multiple fields to a PivotTable's row and column areas. Also see the sections "Add Multiple Fields to the Data Area" and "Add Multiple Fields to the Report Filter." Adding multiple fields to the row and column areas enables you to break down your data for further analysis. For example, suppose you are analyzing the results of a sales campaign that ran

different promotions in several types of advertisements. A basic PivotTable might show you the sales for each Product (the row field) according to the Advertisement in which the customer reported seeing the campaign (the column field). You might also be interested in seeing, for each product, the breakdown in sales for each promotion. You can do that by adding the Promotion field to the row area, as you see in the example used in this section.

Even more powerfully, after you add a second field to the row or column area, you can change the field positions to change the view, as described in Chapter 4. Note that the field in the row or column area that is closest to the data area is called the *inner field* and the field farthest from the data area is called the *outer field*.

Add Multiple Fields to the Row or Column Area

Add a Field to the Row Area

1 Click a cell within the PivotTable.

Add a Field to the Row Area

2 Select the check box of the text or date field you want to add.

● Excel adds the field to the PivotTable's row area.

Add a Field to the Row or Column Area

1 Click a cell within the PivotTable.

2 In the PivotTable Field List, click and drag the field you want to add and drop the field in either the Row Labels section or the Column Labels section.

● Excel adds the field to the PivotTable.

First PivotTable:

Sum of Quantity	Column Labels			
Row Labels	Direct mail	Magazine	Newspaper	Grand Total
Copy holder	322	555	562	1439
Glare filter	402	719	587	1708
Mouse pad	752	1596	1012	3360
Printer stand	338	546	460	1344
Grand Total	1814	3416	2621	7851

PT-Multiple Row-Col Fields

Second PivotTable:

Sum of Quantity	Column Labels				
	Direct mail		Direct mail Total	Magazine	Maga
Row Labels	1 Free with 10	Extra Discount		1 Free with 10	Extra Discount
Copy holder	154	168	322	341	214
Glare filter	220	182	402	352	367
Mouse pad	385	367	752	836	760
Printer stand	176	162	338	264	282
Grand Total	935	879	1814	1793	1623

PT-Multiple Row-Col Fields

Extra

You can also add a field to the row or column area of a PivotTable by dragging. To do this, you must first activate the PivotTable's classic layout, as described in the section "Enable the Classic PivotTable Layout." In the PivotTable Field List, click the field you want to add and then drag it to the PivotTable. When the mouse pointer is over the area to which you want to add the field, drop the field. Note that when you hover the mouse pointer over a PivotTable area, Excel displays a border around the area to help you identify it.

Also note that *where* you drop the field within the row or column area is significant. In the row area, for example, you can either drop the new field to the right or to the left of the existing field. If you drop it to the right, Excel displays each item in the original field, broken down by the items in the new field. In the last screenshot in the previous section, you see each item in the Product field broken down by the two items in the Promotion field. Conversely, if you drop the new field to the left of the existing field, Excel displays each item in the new field broken down by the items in the original field.

Add Multiple Fields to the Data Area

In this section you learn how to add multiple fields to the PivotTable's data area. Also see the sections "Add Multiple Fields to the Row or Column Area" and "Add Multiple Fields to the Report Filter." Adding multiple fields to the data area enables you to see multiple summaries for enhancing your analysis. For example, suppose you are analyzing the results of a sales campaign that ran different promotions in several types of advertisements. A basic PivotTable might show you the sum of the Quantity sold (the data field) for each Product (the row field) according to the Advertisement in which the customer reported seeing the campaign (the column field). You might also be interested in seeing, for each product and advertisement, the net dollar amount sold. You can do that by adding the Net $ field to the data area, as you see in the example used in this section.

Even more powerfully, you are not restricted to using just sums in each data field. Excel enables you to specify a number of different summary functions in the data area, so you can apply a different function to each field. For example, you can view the sum of the Quantity field and the average of the Net $ field. You learn how to change the summary function in Chapter 8.

Add Multiple Fields to the Data Area

Add a Field to the Data Area with a Check Box

1 Click a cell within the PivotTable.

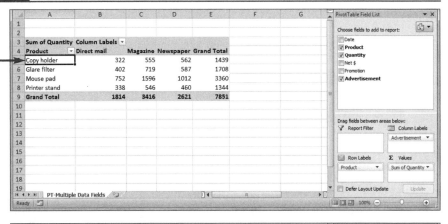

2 Click the check box of the numeric field you want to add.

● Excel adds the field to the PivotTable's data area.

Add a Field to the Data Area by Dragging

1. Click a cell within the PivotTable.

2. In the PivotTable Field List, click and drag the field you want to add and drop the field in the Values section.

- Excel adds the field to the PivotTable.

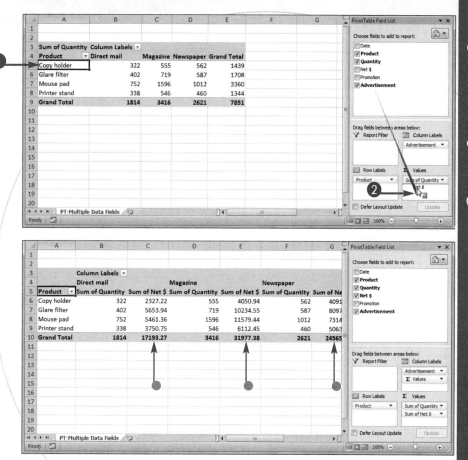

Extra

You can also add a field to the PivotTable's data area by dragging. To do this, you must first activate the PivotTable's classic layout, as described in the section "Enable the Classic PivotTable Layout." In the PivotTable Field List, click and drag the field you want to add and then drag it to the PivotTable. When the mouse pointer is over the data area, drop the field. Note that when you hover the mouse pointer over the data area, Excel displays a border around the area to help you identify it.

When you add a second field to the data area, Excel moves the labels — for example, Sum of Quantity and Sum of Net $ — into the column area for easier reference. This is also reflected in the addition of a Values button in the Column Labels section of the PivotTable Field List. This enables you to pivot the values within the report. You learn how to pivot fields from one part of a PivotTable report to another in Chapter 4.

Add Multiple Fields to the Report Filter

In this section, you learn how to add multiple fields to the PivotTable's report filter area. Also see the sections "Add Multiple Fields to the Row or Column Area" and "Add Multiple Fields to the Data Area." Adding multiple fields to the report filter enables you to apply multiple filters to the PivotTable to enhance your analysis. For example, suppose you are analyzing the results of a sales campaign that ran different promotions in several types of advertisements. A basic PivotTable might show you the sum of the Quantity sold (the data field) for each Product (the column field) by Date (the row field), with a filter for the type of Advertisement (the page field). You might also be interested in filtering the data even further to show specific Promotion items. You can do that by adding the Promotion field to the report filter, as you see in the example used in this section.

To get the most out of this technique, you need to know how to use a report filter field to filter the data shown in a PivotTable. For example, you can use the Advertisement field to display the PivotTable results for just the Magazine item. With the Promotion field also added to the report filter, you can filter the PivotTable even further to display just the results for the 1 Free with 10 item. In Chapter 5, you learn how to apply a report filter and how to reconfigure the report filter layout, respectively.

Add Multiple Fields to the Report Filter

Add a Field to the Report Filter by Right-clicking

1. Click a cell within the PivotTable.

2. Right-click the text or date field you want to add.

3. Click Add to Report Filter.

• Excel adds the field to the PivotTable's report filter.

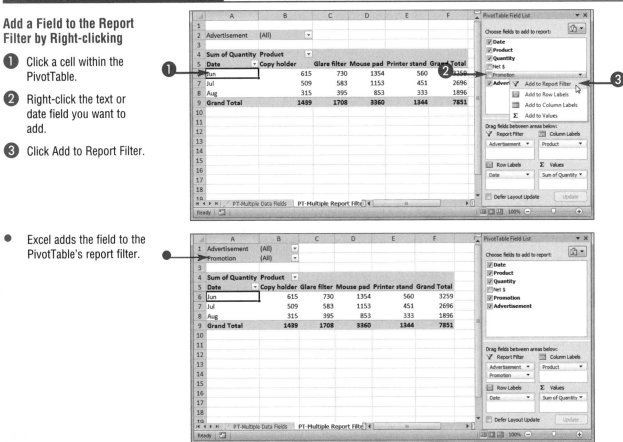

Add a Field to the Report Filter by Dragging

1. Click a cell within the PivotTable.

2. In the PivotTable Field List, click and drag the field you want to add and drop the field in the Report Filter section.

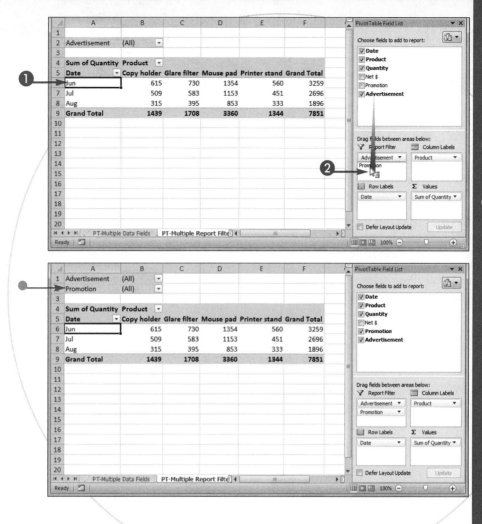

- Excel adds the field to the PivotTable's report filter.

Extra

You can also add a field to the PivotTable's report filter by dragging. To do this, you must first activate the PivotTable's classic layout, as described in the section "Enable the Classic PivotTable Layout." In the PivotTable Field List, click and drag the field you want to add and then drag it to the PivotTable. When the mouse pointer is over the report filter, drop the field. Note that when you hover the mouse pointer over the report filter, Excel displays a border around the area to help you identify it.

Earlier, you learned that the order of the fields with the PivotTable's row and column areas is important because it changes how Excel breaks down the data; see the section "Add Multiple Fields to the Row or Column Area." The order of the fields in the report filter is not important because the resulting filter is the same. For example, suppose you have a collection of shirts, and you want to see only those that are white and short-sleeved. You can do this by first pulling out all the white shirts and then going through those to find all the short-sleeved ones. However, you get the same result if you first take out all the short-sleeved shirts and then find all of those that are white.

Publish a PivotTable to a Web Page

When you analyze data, it is often important to involve other people in the process. For example, you might want to have other people help with some or all of the analytical tasks. Similarly, you might want to share your results with other interested parties. If the other people have Excel, you can share the workload or the results simply by sending each person a copy of the workbook that contains the PivotTable. However, although Excel is extremely popular, not everyone uses it.

Whether you are sharing the work or the results, a related problem involves updates to the PivotTable data. You know you can always refresh the PivotTable to see the latest data; see the section "Refresh PivotTable Data."

However, it is inconvenient to have to send out a new copy of the workbook each time you update the PivotTable.

You can solve both problems by placing your PivotTable on a Web page, either on the Internet or on your corporate intranet site. After the PivotTable is in Web page format, anyone — even people who do not use Excel — can view the PivotTable. It is also possible to set up the Web page version of the PivotTable to be updated automatically whenever you save the original workbook, so other people always see the latest data. Finally, you can also create interactive PivotTables, which means that other people can work with the PivotTable within the Web browser. This section shows you the steps involved in publishing a PivotTable to a Web page.

Publish a PivotTable to a Web Page

1 Select the entire PivotTable that you want to publish.

Note: See the section "Select PivotTable Items" to learn how to select an entire PivotTable.

2 Click File→Save As.

The Save As dialog box appears.

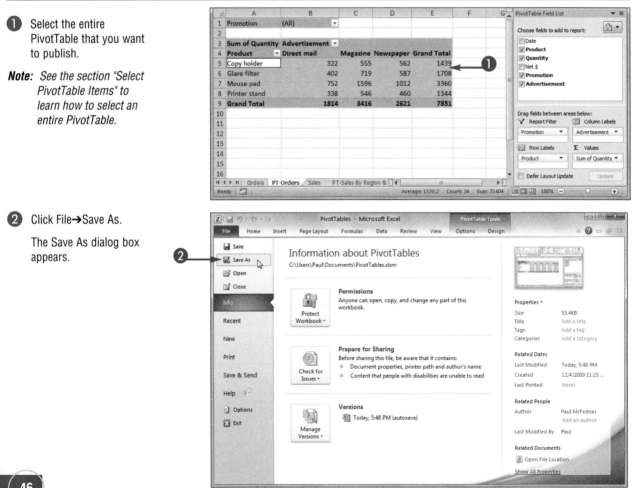

3 In the Save as type list, click Web Page.

4 Click Selection: PivotTable.

5 Click Publish.

The Publish as Web Page dialog box appears.

Apply It

You can tell Excel to add a title to the published PivotTable. This title appears in the Web page as text just above the PivotTable. To specify a title, click Change Title in the Save As dialog box to display the Set Title dialog box. Type the title that you want to appear over the PivotTable and then click OK to return to the Save As dialog box. You can also specify a title from the Publish as Web Page dialog box by clicking Change.

To ensure that the Web page version of your PivotTable is always up to date, you can tell Excel to update it for you automatically. In the Publish as Web Page dialog box, select AutoRepublish every time this workbook is saved. Unfortunately, activating this option means that every time you save the workbook, Excel displays a dialog box asking if you want to disable or enable the AutoRepublish feature. To bypass this dialog box, the next time the dialog box appears, select Enable the AutoRepublish Feature, select Do Not Show This Message Again, and then click OK.

continued ➡

When publishing a PivotTable, it is important to choose the proper location for the published Web page and its associated files. If you are putting the PivotTable Web page on an Internet site, save the Web page to whatever folder you use for your other Web site files, which will likely be a subfolder of Documents (or My Documents in XP). If you are putting the PivotTable Web page on your corporate intranet site, save the Web page to an appropriate

network folder. Ask your system administrator for the correct folder and whether you need a username and password.

After you publish an Internet-based PivotTable Web page to your computer, you must then use an FTP utility or similar program to upload the Web page and its associated files to your directory on the Web server.

Publish a PivotTable to a Web Page *(continued)*

6 Click the PivotTable you want to publish.

7 Click Browse.

● If you already know where you want the Web page saved, type the location and file name in this text box.

The Publish As dialog box appears.

8 Click the location where you want the Web page published.

9 Type a name for the Web page.

Note: *When typing a name for the Web page, do not use spaces and make sure the name ends with either .htm or .html.*

10 Click OK.

Note: *If Excel displays a dialog box listing one or more features that cannot be saved, click Yes to continue.*

Excel returns you to the Publish as Web Page dialog box.

⑪ Click the Open published web page In browser check box.

⑫ Click Publish.

Excel publishes the PivotTable to the Web page.

● Internet Explorer displays the PivotTable on the Web page.

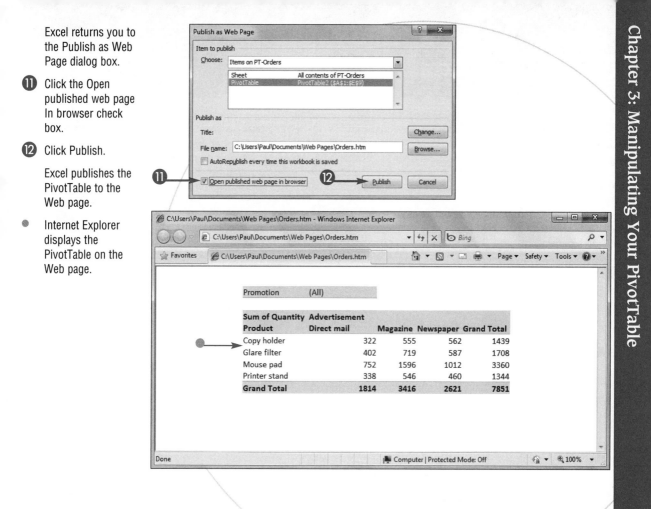

Apply It

Rather than publishing the PivotTable to a local folder and then using a separate FTP program to upload the file to your Web site, you can publish directly to the site using Excel. Follow steps **1** to **6** in this section to display the Publish as Web Page dialog box and select the PivotTable. In the File name text box, specify your FTP host name, directory, and file name using the following general syntax:

```
ftp://HostName/Directory/FileName
```

Here is an example:

```
ftp://www.mysite.com/reports/orders.htm
```

When you publish the Web page, your Web browser asks you to type your FTP username and password.

Convert a PivotTable to Regular Data

One of the major drawbacks of PivotTables is that they often require an inordinate amount of system resources. For example, it is not unusual to have source data that contains a large number of records or to have a PivotTable that is itself quite large and uses multiple fields in one or more areas. In such cases, the workbook containing the PivotTable can become huge and the memory used by Excel to store PivotTable data for faster performance can become excessive.

In situations where you need to manipulate the PivotTable frequently and where the source data changes, you have no choice but to put up with the burden that the PivotTable puts on your system. On the other hand, you may just be interested in the current PivotTable results and have no need to manipulate or refresh the data; similarly, you may not even need to keep the source data after you have built your PivotTable. In these scenarios, you can drastically reduce the resources used by the workbook by converting your PivotTable into regular data. When you do that, you can delete the PivotTable — see the section "Delete a PivotTable" — and the source data, assuming the source data is an Excel range or list that you no longer need.

Convert a PivotTable to Regular Data

① Select the entire PivotTable that you want to publish.

Note: See the section "Select PivotTable Items" to learn how to select an entire PivotTable.

② Click Home➔Copy.

You can also press Ctrl+C.

Excel copies the PivotTable data.

③ Click the cell where you want the regular data to appear.

④ Click Home→
Paste→Values &
Source Formatting.

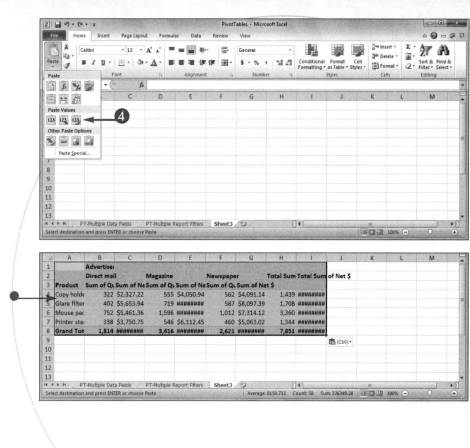

● Excel pastes the
PivotTable as
regular data.

Apply It

The Values & Source Formatting command is very useful in this scenario because it not only preserves whatever formatting you have applied to your PivotTable — see Chapter 5 to learn how to customize PivotTable fields — but it also preserves the data field's numeric formatting. However, there may be situations where you do not want to preserve any of the PivotTable's formatting. In that case, you need to click Home→Paste→Values instead. If you want to preserve only the data field's numeric formatting, click Home→Paste→Values & Number Formatting.

If you want to create a "snapshot" of the PivotTable that you can then use in other documents, you can take a picture of the PivotTable. Select the PivotTable and then click Home→Copy. Select the cell where you want the picture to appear and then click Home→Paste→Picture.

Delete a PivotTable

PivotTables are useful data-analysis tools, and now that you are becoming comfortable with them, you may find that you use them quite often. This will give you tremendous insight into your data, but that insight comes at a cost: PivotTables are very resource intensive, so creating many PivotTable reports can lead to large workbook file sizes and result in less memory available for other programs. You can reduce the impact that a large number of open PivotTables have on your system by deleting those reports that you no longer need.

Even if you create just a few PivotTables, you may find that you need them only temporarily. For example, you may just want to build a quick-and-dirty report to check a few numbers. Similarly, your source data may be preliminary, so you might want to create a temporary PivotTable for now, holding off on a more permanent version until your source data is complete. Finally, you might build PivotTable reports to send them to other people. When that is done, you may no longer need the reports yourself. For all these scenarios, you need to know how to delete a PivotTable report, and this section shows you how it is done.

Delete a PivotTable

① Click any cell within the PivotTable you want to delete.

② Click Options→ Select→Entire PivotTable.

Excel selects the PivotTable.

❸ Click Home➔Clear➔Clear All.

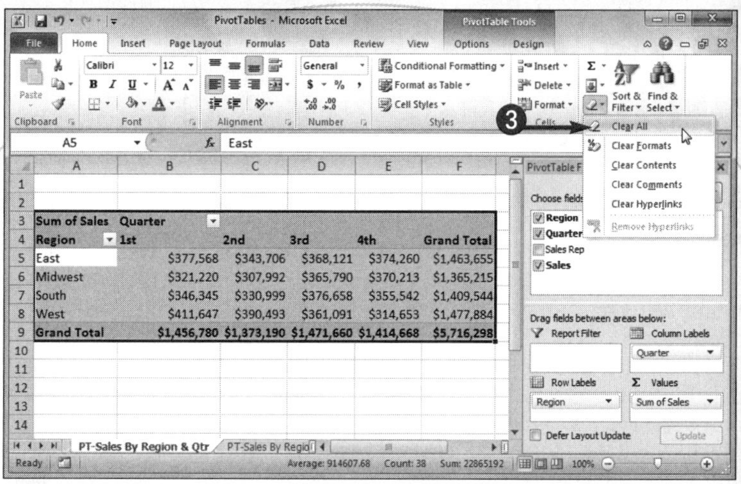

● Excel deletes the PivotTable.

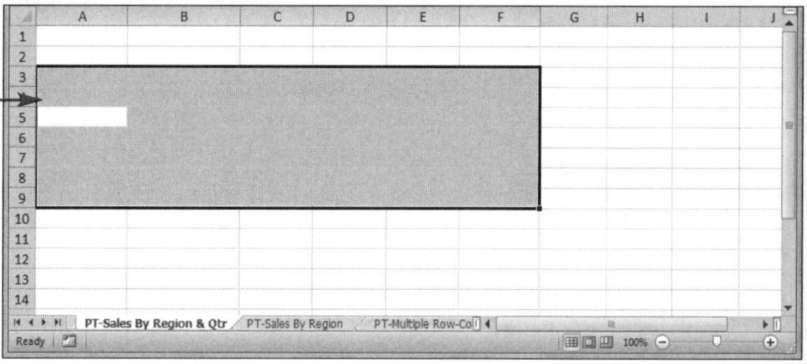

Apply It

If you create many temporary PivotTables, you should delete them to save system resources. However, this can become time consuming if you do it often. To save time, use the following VBA macro to automatically delete the first PivotTable on the active worksheet:

```
Sub DeletePivotTable()
    Dim objPT As PivotTable, nResult As Integer
    '
    ' Work with the first PivotTable
    ' on the active worksheet
    Set objPT = ActiveSheet.PivotTables(1)
    '
    ' Confirm
    nResult = MsgBox("Are you sure you want to delete the " & _
              "PivotTable named " & objPT.Name & "?", vbYesNo)
    If nResult = vbYes Then
        '
        ' Select the PivotTable
        objPT.PivotSelect ""
        '
        ' Delete it
        Selection.Clear
    End If
End Sub
```

Move a Field to a Different Area

A PivotTable is a powerful data-analysis tool because it can take hundreds or even thousands of records and summarize them into a compact, comprehensible report. However, unlike most of Excel's other data-analysis features, a PivotTable is not a static collection of worksheet cells. Instead, you can move a PivotTable's fields from one area of the PivotTable to another. This enables you to view your data from different perspectives, which can greatly enhance the analysis of the data. Moving a field within a PivotTable is called *pivoting* the data.

The most common way to pivot the data is to move fields between the row and column areas. If your PivotTable contains just a single nondata field, moving the field

between the row and column areas changes the orientation of the PivotTable between horizontal (column area) and vertical (row area). If your PivotTable contains fields in both the row and column areas, pivoting one of those fields to the other area creates multiple fields in that area. For example, pivoting a field from the column area to the row area creates two fields in the row area. This changes how the data breaks down, as described in Chapter 3.

You can also pivot data by moving a row or column field to the report filter and a page field to the row or column area. This is a useful technique when you want to turn one of your existing row or columns fields into a filter.

Move a Field to a Different Area

Move a Field between the Row and Column Areas

Note: This chapter uses the PivotTables04.xlsm spreadsheet, available at www.wiley.com/go/ pivottablesvb2e, or you can create your own sample file.

1. Click a cell within the PivotTable.

2. Click and drag a column field button and drop it within the Row Labels area.

● Excel displays the field's values within the row area.

You can also drag a field button from the Row Labels area and drop it within the Column Labels area.

Move a Row or Column Field to the Report Filter

① Click a cell within the PivotTable.

② Click and drag a row field button and drop it within the PivotTable's Report Filter area.

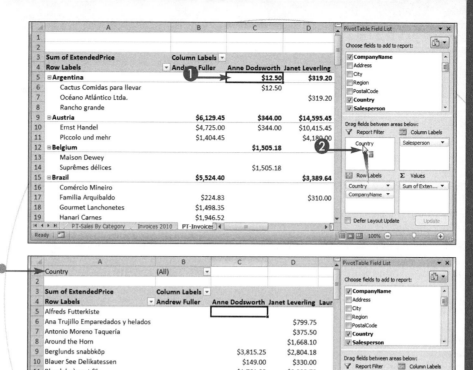

● Excel moves the field button to the report filter.

You can also drag a field button from the Column Labels area and drop it within the Report Filter area.

Apply It

You can also move any row, column, or report filter field to the PivotTable's data area. This may seem strange because row, column, and page fields are almost always text values, and the default data area calculation is Sum. How can you sum text values? You cannot, of course. Instead, Excel's default PivotTable summary calculation for text values is Count. So, for example, if you drag the Category field and drop it inside the data area, Excel creates a second data field named Count of Category. To learn more about working with multiple data area fields, see Chapter 3.

You can also pivot a field to a different area by dragging within the PivotTable itself. To do this, you must first activate the PivotTable's classic layout, as described in Chapter 3. In the PivotTable, click the button of the field you want to move and then drag it toward the other area. When the mouse pointer is over the area to which you want to move the field, drop the field. Note that when you hover the mouse pointer over a PivotTable area, Excel displays a border around the area to help you identify it.

Change the Order of Fields within an Area

You learned in Chapter 3 that you can add two or more fields to any area in the PivotTable. This enables you to break down the data in different ways (multiple row or column area fields), apply extra filters (multiple report filter fields), or display extra summaries (multiple data area fields). After you have multiple fields in an area, Excel enables you to change the order of those fields to reconfigure your data the way you prefer. This is another example of pivoting the data.

How you pivot within a field depends on the field. For row, column, and page fields, you pivot by dragging and dropping field buttons within the same area. For example,

if the row area of the PivotTable has the Product field on the outside (left) and the Promotion field on the inside (right), the PivotTable shows the sales of each product broken down by the promotion. If, instead, you prefer to see the sales of each promotion broken down by product, then you need to switch the order of the Product and Promotion fields.

If you have multiple data fields, you change the order of the data area fields by dragging and dropping any data field label. Note, however, that this does not change the data summaries themselves, just the order in which they appear in the PivotTable.

Change the Order of Fields within an Area

Change the Field Order Using the Excel 2010/2007 Layout

① Click any cell within the PivotTable.

② Click and drag the button of the field you want to move and then drop the field above or below an existing field.

● Excel reconfigures the PivotTable.

Change the Field Order Using the Classic Layout

Note: See Chapter 3 to learn how to display the classic layout.

1 Click and drag the button of the field you want to move.

● Excel displays a gray bar to show you where it will position the dropped field.

2 Within the row or column area, drop the field to the left or right of an existing field; within the report filter, drop the field above or below an existing field.

● Excel reconfigures the PivotTable.

Apply It

The most common situation for changing field order is to move a row field to the outer position. Here is a VBA macro that automates this process (see Chapter 16 for VBA basics):

Example:
```
Sub SwitchRowFields()
    Dim objPT As PivotTable
    Dim objPTField As PivotField
    ' Work with the first PivotTable on the active worksheet
    Set objPT = ActiveSheet.PivotTables(1)
    With objPT
        ' If there is just one row field, exit
        If .RowFields.Count = 1 Then Exit Sub
        ' Run through all the row fields
        For Each objPTField In .RowFields
            ' Is the current field the innermost field?
            If objPTField.Position = .RowFields.Count Then
                ' If so, make it the outer field
                objPTField.Position = 1
                ' We are done, so exit
                Exit Sub
            End If
        Next 'objPTField
    End With
End Sub
```

Change the Report Layout

Y ou saw in the previous section that if you display more than one field in an area of the PivotTable, you can change the order of those fields depending on how you want to view your report. When you have multiple fields in the row area, Excel displays each field in its own column, the field and subfield items all begin on the same row, and gridlines appear around every cell. This is called the *tabular report layout* and it is Excel's default report layout. Excel also comes with two other report layouts that you can use.

The third report layout is the *outline layout* that also displays each field in its own column. However, the

subfield items for each field item begin one row below the field item, and no gridlines appear around the cells (except for a single gridline under each item in the outer field). This is similar to the outlining used by Excel and Word.

The third report layout is the *compact layout*, which displays each field in a single column. The subfield items for each field item begin one row below the field item and are indented from the left. No gridlines appear around the cells (except for a single gridline under each item in the outer field).

Change the Report Layout

Change to the Outline Layout

1 Click any cell in the PivotTable.

2 Click Design→Report Layout→Show in Outline Form.

● Excel changes to the outline report layout.

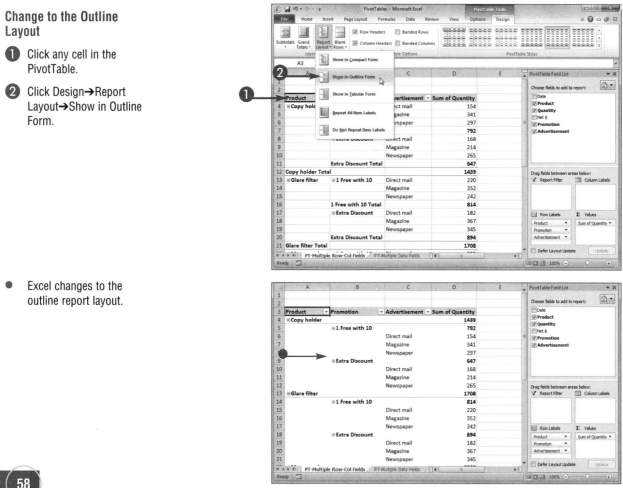

Change to the Compact Layout

1. Click any cell in the PivotTable.

2. Click Design→ Report Layout→ Show in Compact Form.

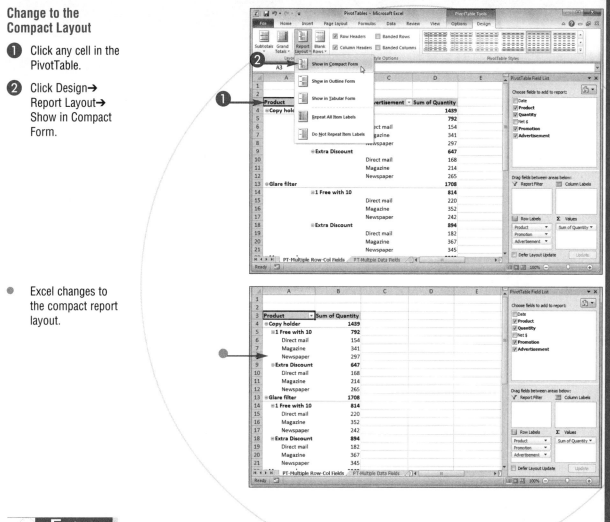

- Excel changes to the compact report layout.

Extra

Whichever layout you use, you can make the report a bit easier to read by displaying an extra blank line at the end of each item in the outer field. Click any item in the outer field and then click Options→Field Settings. Click the Layout & Print tab and then select the Insert blank line after each item label check box. Click OK to put the new settings into effect.

Apply It

You can control the amount by which each subfield item is indented in the compact report layout. Click any cell in the PivotTable and then click Developer→Visual Basic (or press Alt+F11) to open the Visual Basic Editor. Click View→Immediate Window (or press Ctrl+G) to display the Immediate window. Click inside the Immediate window, type the following statement, and then press Enter:

```
Selection.PivotTable.CompactRowIndent = 5
```

The higher the value, the greater the indent.

Sort PivotTable Data with AutoSort

When you create a PivotTable, Excel sorts the data in ascending order based on the items in the row and column fields. For example, if the row area contains the Product field, the vertical sort order of the PivotTable is ascending according to the items in the Product field. You can change this default sort order to one that suits your needs. Excel gives you two choices: You can switch between ascending and descending, or you can sort based on a data field instead of a row or column field.

Changing the sort order often comes in handy when you are working with dates or times. The default ascending sort shows the oldest items at the top of the field; if, instead, you are more interested in the most recent items, switch to a descending sort to show those items at the top of the field.

Sorting the PivotTable based on the values in a data field is useful when you want to rank the results. For example, if your PivotTable shows the sum of sales for each product, an ascending or descending sort of the product name enables you to easily find a particular product. However, if you are more interested in finding which products sold the most (or the least), then you need to sort the PivotTable on the data field.

Excel gives you two methods for sorting PivotTable items: You can have Excel sort the items automatically using the AutoSort feature, as you learn in this section; alternatively, you can create a custom sort order by manually adjusting the items; see the next section, "Move Row and Column Items."

Sort PivotTable Data with AutoSort

Sort a Row or Column Field

① Click ▼ beside the name of the row or column field you want to use for sorting.

② Click the sort order you want to use, such as Sort Z to A.

● Excel sorts the PivotTable.

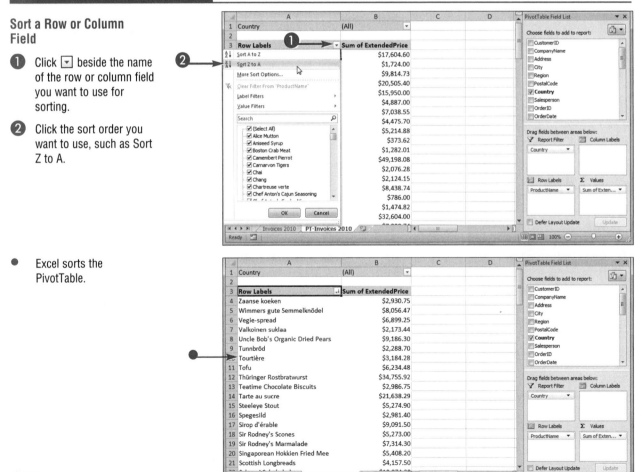

Sort a Data Field

① Right-click any cell in the data field.

② Click Sort.

③ Select the sort order you want to use, such as Sort Largest to Smallest.

● Excel sorts the PivotTable.

Extra

You can also sort a PivotTable using the buttons in the Options tab's Sort group. Click any cell in the field you want to sort, and then click either 🔼 for an ascending sort or 🔽 for a descending sort. For more sorting options, click the Options tab, and then click Sort to open the Sort dialog box. For example, if you do not want Excel to automatically sort the PivotTable each time you update the report, click More Options and then click Sort Automatically Every Time the Report is Updated.

In Excel, an ascending sort means that items are arranged in the following order: numbers, text, logical values, error values (such as #REF! and #N/A), and blank cells. A descending sort reverses this order, except for blank cells: error values (such as #REF! and #N/A), logical values, text, numbers, and blank cells.

Move Row and Column Items

As you saw in the previous section, Excel's AutoSort feature enables you to apply an ascending or a descending sort on a row or column field, or on a data item. However, there may be situations where these basic sort options do not fit your requirements. In these cases, you can solve the problem by coming up with a custom sort order, and Excel offers a couple of methods for doing just that.

For example, suppose you have a PivotTable that shows the sales generated by each employee, broken down by country. Showing the Country field items alphabetically makes sense in most situations, but suppose you are

preparing the report for managers who oversee the sales on each continent (North America, South America, Europe, and so on). In this case, it would be more convenient for those managers if you organized the PivotTable countries by continent. However, because there is no "continent" field to sort on, you need to sort the countries by hand.

To sort a PivotTable by hand, you need to move the row or column items individually. As you learn in this section, you can move individual row or column items either by using commands or by using your mouse to click and drag the items.

Move Row and Column Items

Use a Command to Move a Row and Column Item

1 Right-click the row or column item you want to move.

2 Click Move.

3 Click the command that represents the move you want to make, such as Move Up.

Excel moves the item.

4 Repeat steps **2** and **3** until the item is in the position you want.

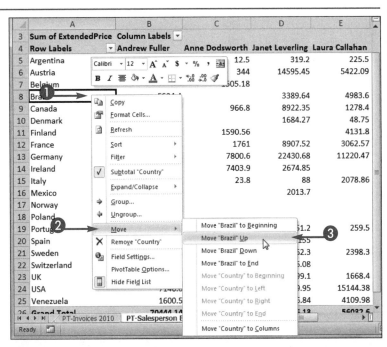

● Excel displays the item in the position you selected.

Click and Drag to Move Row and Column Items

1 Click the field item you want to move.

2 Move the mouse pointer to the top or bottom edge of the cell.

3 Click and drag the item and drop it in the position you want.

● Excel displays a gray bar to show you where it will position the dropped item.

● Excel displays the item in the position you selected.

	A	B	C	D	E
3	Sum of ExtendedPrice	Column Labels			
4	Row Labels	Andrew Fuller	Anne Dodsworth	Janet Leverling	Laura Callahan
5	Argentina		12.5	319.2	225.5
6	Austria	6129.45	344	14595.45	5422.09
7	Belgium		1505.18		
8	Brazil	5524.4		3389.64	4983.6
9	Canada	57.5	966.8	8922.35	1278.4
10	Denmark	1405.2		1684.27	48.75
11	Finland	5292.03	1590.56		4131.8
12	France	5279.51	1761	8907.52	3062.57
13	Germany	25984.1	7800.6	22430.68	11220.47
14	Ireland	2381.05	7403.9	2674.85	
15	Italy	3265.55	23.8	88	2078.86
16	Mexico	1351.15		2013.7	
17	Norway				
18	Poland				
19	Portugal			851.2	259.5
20	Spain			155	
21	Sweden	2844.5	3815.25	7462.3	2398.3
22	Switzerland			3276.08	
23	UK	2182.6	139.8	4199.1	1668.4
24	USA	7146.6	569	21189.95	15144.38
25	Venezuela	1600.5	378	5866.84	4109.98
26	Grand Total	70444.14	26310.39	108026.13	56022.6

PT-Invoices 2010 | PT-Salesperson By Country

Drag to Cut and Insert cell contents, use Alt key to switch sheets

	A	B	C	D	E
3	Sum of ExtendedPrice	Column Labels			
4	Row Labels	Andrew Fuller	Anne Dodsworth	Janet Leverling	Laura Callahan
5	Argentina		12.5	319.2	225.5
6	Brazil	5524.4		3389.64	4983.6
7	Austria	6129.45	344	14595.45	5422.09
8	Belgium		1505.18		
9	Canada	57.5	966.8	8922.35	1278.4
10	Denmark	1405.2		1684.27	48.75
11	Finland	5292.03	1590.56		4131.8
12	France	5279.51	1761	8907.52	3062.57
13	Germany	25984.1	7800.6	22430.68	11220.47

Apply It

Excel offers a third method for moving row and column items to apply a custom sort order, and this method uses a rather surprising trick. To move a particular row or column item, first click the row or column item that is currently in the position where you want the moved item to end up. For example, if you want to move the item to the top of the items in the row area, click the first item in the row area. Now type the text of the item you want Excel to move. For example, if the item you want to move is "Brazil," type **Brazil**. When you press Enter to confirm the text, Excel switches the two items. That is, Excel moves the item you typed to the current cell, and Excel moves the item that was previously in the cell to the cell where the moved item used to appear.

What makes this technique even more convenient is that Excel monitors your typing and its AutoComplete feature should fill in the text of the item you want to move after just a few keystrokes. For example, after you type **Br**, Excel should fill in Brazil automatically.

Group Numeric Values

Most PivotTable reports have just a few items in the row and column fields, which makes the report easy to read and analyze. However, it is not unusual to have row or column fields that consist of dozens of items, which makes the report much harder to work with. One solution is to cut the report down to size by hiding items; see Chapter 5 for more. Unfortunately, this solution is not appropriate if you need to work with all the PivotTable data.

To make a report with a large number of row or column items easier to work with, you can group the items together. For example, you could group months into quarters, thus reducing the number of items from 12 to four. Similarly, a report that lists dozens of countries could group those countries by continent, thus reducing the number of items to four or five, depending on where

the countries are located. Finally, if you use a numeric field in the row or column area, you may have hundreds of items, one for each numeric value. You can improve the report by creating just a few numeric ranges.

Excel enables you to group three types of data: numeric (discussed in this section), date and time (see the section "Group Date and Time Values"), and text (see the section "Group Text Values"). Grouping numeric values is useful when you use a numeric field in a row or column field. Excel enables you to specify numeric ranges into which the field items are grouped. For example, suppose you have a PivotTable of invoice data that shows the extended price (the row field) and the salesperson (the column field). It would be useful to group the extended prices into ranges and then count the number of invoices each salesperson processed in each range.

Group Numeric Values

① Click any item in the numeric field you want to group.

② Click Options→ Group→Group Field.

The Grouping dialog box appears.

③ Type the starting numeric value.

● Select this check box to have Excel extract the minimum value of the numeric items and place that value in the text box.

④ Type the ending numeric value.

● Select this check box to have Excel extract the maximum value of the numeric items and place that value in the text box.

⑤ Type the size you want to use for each grouping.

⑥ Click OK.

● Excel groups the numeric values.

Grouping

Auto

Starting at: 1 ◄─③

Ending at: 11000 ◄─④

By: 1000 ◄─⑤

⑥► OK   Cancel

	A	B
1		
2		
3	**Count of ExtendedPrice**	Column Labels
4	**Row Labels**	Andrew Fuller
5	1-1001	83
6	1001-2001	11
7	2001-3001	6
8	3001-4001	
9	4001-5001	1
10	5001-6001	1
11	6001-7001	
12	7001-8001	
13	8001-9001	
14	10001-11001	
15	**Grand Total**	102
16		
17		
18		

PT-Salesperson By Country   PT-Ext Pr

Ready

Extra

The ranges that Excel creates after you apply the grouping to a numeric field are not themselves numeric values; they are, instead, text values. Unfortunately, this means it is not possible to use Excel's AutoSort feature to switch the ranges from ascending order to descending order; see the section "Sort PivotTable Data with AutoSort," earlier in this chapter. If you try, Excel sorts the ranges as text, which usually results in improper sort orders. For example, in a descending sort, the range 2001–3001 would come before the range 10001–11001 because 2 (the first character of the text "2001–3001") has a higher value than 1 (the first character of the text "10001–11001"). To sort the ranges, you must move the items by hand. See the section "Move Row and Column Items" earlier in this chapter.

Similarly, the text nature of the range items means that you also cannot use Excel's Top 10 Filter feature, which only works properly with numeric values. See Chapter 5 for more. The only way to simulate this feature would be to hide those ranges you do not want to view in your report; see Chapter 5 for more.

Group Date and Time Values

If your PivotTable includes a field with date or time data, you can use Excel's grouping feature to consolidate that data into more manageable or useful groups.

For example, a PivotTable based on a list of invoice data might show the total dollar amount, which is the Sum of ExtendedPrice in the date area, of the orders placed on each day, which is the Date field in the row area. Tracking daily sales is useful, but a manager might need a report that shows the bigger picture. In that case, you can use the Grouping feature to consolidate the dates into weeks, months, or even quarters. Excel even allows you to choose multiple date groupings. For example, if you have several years' worth of invoice data, you could group the data into years, the years into quarters, and the quarters into months.

Excel also enables you to group time data. For example, suppose you have data that shows the time of day that an assembly line completes each operation. If you want to analyze how the time of day affects productivity, you could set up a PivotTable that groups the data into minutes — for example, 30-minute intervals — or hours.

Group Date and Time Values

① Click any item in the date field you want to group.

② Click Options→ Group→Group Field.

The Grouping dialog box appears.

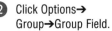

③ Type the starting date or time.

● Select this check box to have Excel extract the earliest date or time from the data and place that value in the text box.

④ Type the ending date or time.

● Select this check box to have Excel extract the latest date or time from the data and place that value in the text box.

⑤ Click the type of grouping you want.

To use multiple groupings, click each type of grouping you want to use.

● If you clicked only Days in step **5**, you can type the number of days to use as the group interval.

⑥ Click OK.

● Excel groups the date or time values.

	A	B
1	ProductName	(All)
2		
3	**Row Labels**	**Sum of ExtendedPrice**
4	Jan	$61,258.06
5	Feb	$38,483.63
6	Mar	$38,547.21
7	Apr	$53,032.95
8	May	$53,781.28
9	Jun	$36,362.79
10	Jul	$51,020.83
11	Aug	$47,287.66
12	Sep	$55,629.24
13	Oct	$66,749.23
14	Nov	$43,533.79
15	Dec	$71,398.41
16	**Grand Total**	**$617,085.08**
17		
18		

PT-Extended Price By Date

Ready

Apply It

In a factory or other manufacturing facility, it is often useful to analyze how productivity varies according to the day of the week. For example, which day of the week is the most productive? Which day is the least productive? Unfortunately, Excel does not have a "weekday" grouping type. To work around this limitation, create a new field in your source data and give it the heading Weekday. To derive the weekday for a given day, start with Excel's WEEKDAY() function, which returns a number from 1 to 7, where 1 corresponds to Sunday and 7 corresponds to Saturday. To convert the WEEKDAY() result into the day of the week, use the CHOOSE() function. If the cell with the date value is A1, use the following formula to derive the corresponding day of the week:

Example:

```
=CHOOSE(WEEKDAY(A1),"Sunday","Monday","Tuesday","Wednesday","Thursday","Friday","Saturday")
```

When you fill this formula for all the dates in your source data, build a new PivotTable and use the Weekday field in the row or column area. Excel automatically consolidates the Weekday items into the days of the week.

Group Text Values

You can use Excel's PivotTable Grouping feature to create custom groups from the text items in a row or column field.

One common problem that arises when you work with PivotTables is that you often need to consolidate items, but you have no corresponding field in the data. For example, the data may have a Country field, but what if you need to consolidate the PivotTable results by continent? It is unlikely that your source data includes a Continent field. Similarly, your source data may include employee names, but you may need to consolidate the employees according to the people they report to. What

do you do if your source data does not include a Supervisor field?

The solution in both cases is to use the Grouping feature to create custom groups. For the country data, you could create custom groups named North America, South America, Europe, and so on. For the employees, you could create a custom group for each supervisor. You select the items that you want to include in a particular group, create the custom group, and then change the new group name to reflect its content. This section shows you the steps to follow to create such a custom grouping for text values.

Group Text Values

① Select the items that you want to include in the group.

To select multiple cells in Excel, click the first cell, hold down Ctrl, and then click each of the other cells.

② Click Options→ Group→Group Selection.

Excel creates a new group named Group*n* (where *n* means this is the *n*th group you have created) and restructures the PivotTable.

③ Click the group label.

④ Type a new name for the group.

⑤ Press Enter.

Excel renames the group.

⑥ Repeat steps **1** to **5** for the other items in the field until you have created all your groups.

⑦ Rename the group label to reflect the contents of the group.

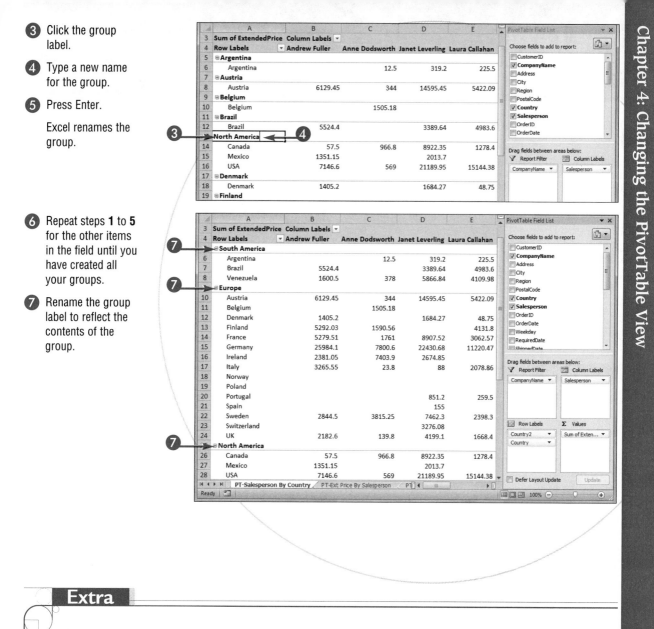

Extra

By default, Excel does not add subtotals for each custom group. To add the subtotals, click the custom group label, and then click Options→Field Settings. In the Field Settings dialog box, select Automatic and then click OK. This tells Excel to use the Sum function for the subtotals. If you want to use a different function, see Chapter 8.

Note, as well, that the values in the custom grouping — the group names — act as regular PivotTable text items. This means you can sort the groups either by applying an AutoSort or by moving the items by hand; see the sections "Sort PivotTable Data with AutoSort" and "Move Row and Column Items" earlier in this chapter. You can also filter the items to hide or show only specific groups, as seen in Chapter 5.

Hide Group Details

W hen you consolidate a row or column field into groups, Excel reconfigures the PivotTable. For example, when you group a row field, Excel reconfigures the PivotTable to show two row fields: The groups appear in the outer row field and the items that comprise each group appear in the inner row field. The latter are called the *group details*. To make your report easier to read or manage, you can hide the details for a specific group. In this case, Excel collapses the group to a single line and displays just the group name and, in the data area, the group's subtotals. You can quickly toggle between hiding a group's details and showing them. For the latter, see the next section, "Show Group Details."

The following VBA macro hides the details for all the groups in a PivotTable's row area (see Chapter 16 for more on VBA basics):

Example:
```
Sub HideAllGroupDetails()
    Dim objPT As PivotTable
    Dim objRowField As PivotField
    Dim objItem As PivotItem
    '
    ' Work with the first PivotTable
    Set objPT = ActiveSheet.PivotTables(1)
    '
    ' Work with the outermost row field
    Set objRowField = objPT.RowFields(objPT.
RowFields.Count)
    '
    ' Hide the details for each item
    For Each objItem In objRowField.PivotItems
        objItem.ShowDetail = False
    Next 'objItem
End Sub
```

Hide Group Details

① In the cell containing the name of the group, click the Collapse button (⊟).

You can also double-click the group name.

● Excel hides the group's details.

Show Group Details

If you have hidden the details for a group using the Hide Detail command — see the previous section, "Hide Group Details" — you can use the Show Detail command to redisplay the group's details. This enables you to quickly and easily display whatever level of detail you prefer in a PivotTable report.

The following VBA macro shows the details for all the groups in a PivotTable's row area (see Chapter 16 for more on VBA basics):

Example:

```
Sub ShowAllGroupDetails()
    Dim objPT As PivotTable
    Dim objRowField As PivotField
    Dim objItem As PivotItem
    '
    ' Work with the first PivotTable
    Set objPT = ActiveSheet.PivotTables(1)
    '
    ' Work with the outermost row field
    Set objRowField = objPT.RowFields(objPT.
RowFields.Count)
    '
    ' Hide the details for each item
    For Each objItem In objRowField.PivotItems
        objItem.ShowDetail = True
    Next 'objItem
End Sub
```

Show Group Details

1 In the cell containing the name of the group, click the Expand button ([+]).

You can also double-click the group name.

● Excel shows the group's details.

Ungroup Values

Grouping is a very useful PivotTable feature and you will likely find that you make groups a permanent part of many of your PivotTables. On the other hand, you can also use grouping as a temporary data-analysis tool. That is, you build your PivotTable, organize a field into groups, and then analyze the results. At this point, if you no longer need the groupings, then you need to reverse the process. With Excel's Ungroup command, you can remove the groupings from your PivotTable.

Excel gives you two ways to use the Ungroup command. For numeric, date, and time groups, running the Ungroup command ungroups all the values in the row or column area, thus returning the PivotTable to its normal layout. If you are working with text groupings, as seen in the section "Group Text Values," Excel also enables you to ungroup a single grouping of values, while leaving the other text groupings intact. In this case, Excel displays the group values in both the outer and the inner fields. This can be a bit confusing, so you should only use this technique on occasion.

Ungroup Values

Ungroup a Numeric, Date, or Time Grouping

1. Click any cell within the group field.

2. Click Options→ Group→Ungroup.

   You can also press Shift+Alt+Left arrow.

● Excel ungroups all the values.

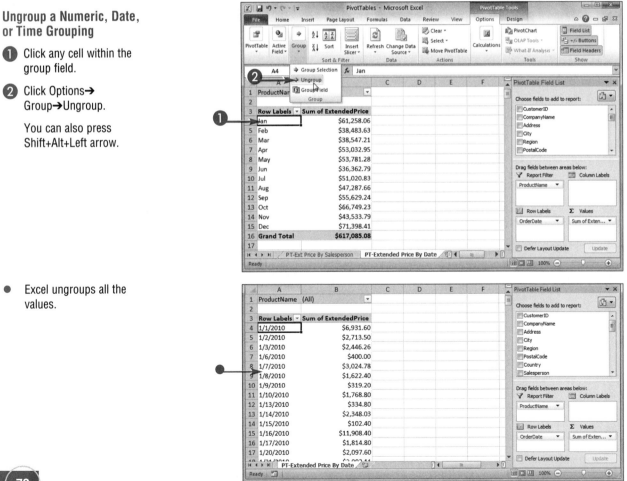

Ungroup a Text Grouping

① Click the label of the text grouping.

② Click Options→ Group→Ungroup.

You can also press Shift+Alt+Left arrow.

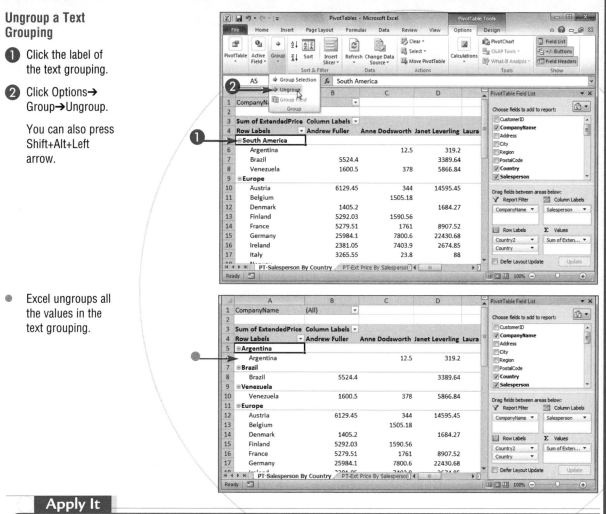

● Excel ungroups all the values in the text grouping.

Apply It

Here is a VBA macro that ungroups the row values in a PivotTable (for more on VBA basics, see Chapter 16):

Example:

```
Sub UngroupAll()
    Dim objPT As PivotTable
    Dim objRowField As PivotField
    Dim objItem As PivotItem
    '
    ' Work with the first PivotTable on the active worksheet
    Set objPT = ActiveSheet.PivotTables(1)
    '
    ' Work with the outermost row field
    Set objRowField = objPT.RowFields(objPT.RowFields.Count)
    '
    ' Select the row
    objPT.PivotSelect objRowField.Name & "[All]"
    '
    ' Ungroup it
    Selection.Ungroup
End Sub
```

Apply a Report Filter

By default, each PivotTable report displays a summary for all the records in your source data. This is usually what you want to see. However, there may be situations in which you need to focus more closely on some aspect of the data. You can focus on a specific item from one of the source data fields by taking advantage of the PivotTable's report filter field.

For example, suppose you are dealing with a PivotTable that summarizes data from thousands of customer invoices over some period of time. A basic PivotTable might tell you the total amount sold for each product that you carry. That is interesting, but what about if you want to see the total amount sold for each product in a specific country? If the Product field is in the PivotTable's row area, then you can add the Country field to the column

area. However, there may be dozens of countries, so that is not an efficient solution. Instead, you can add the Country field to the report filter. You can then tell Excel to display the total sold for each product for the specific country that you are interested.

As another example, suppose you ran a marketing campaign in the previous quarter and you set up an incentive plan for your salespeople whereby they could earn bonuses for selling at least a specified number of units. Suppose, as well, that you have a PivotTable showing the sum of the units sold for each product. To see the numbers for a particular employee, you can add the Salesperson field to the report filter, and then select the employee you want to work with.

Apply a Report Filter

Apply A Report Filter

Note: This chapter uses the PivotTables05.xlsm spreadsheet, available at www.wiley.com/go/pivottablesvb2e, or you can create your own sample file.

1 Click here (🔽) in the report filter field.

Excel displays a list of the report filter field values.

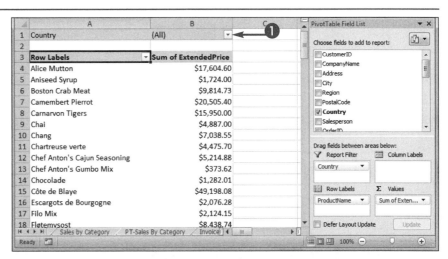

2 Click the report filter you want to view.

● If you want to display data for two or more report filters, click the Select Multiple Items check box and then repeat step **2** to select the other report filters.

3 Click OK.

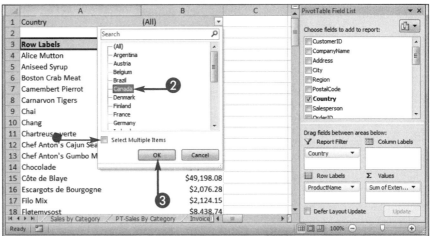

- Excel filters the PivotTable to show only the data for the report filter you selected.

Display All Report Filters

1. Click ⊤ in the report filter field.

   Excel displays a list of the report filter field values.

2. Click All.

3. Click OK.

   Excel adjusts the PivotTable to show the data for all the report filters.

Apply It

You can add multiple fields to the report filter, as described in Chapter 3. This enables you to apply multiple filters to the data. For example, suppose you have a PivotTable that summarizes invoice data by showing the total amount sold for each product that you carry, and that you have a report filter field with Country data that enables you to isolate the sales by product for a specific country. You might then want to extend your analysis to look at the country-specific sales by product for individual salespersons.

To do this, you would add the Salesperson field as a second field in the report filter. You could then use the steps shown in this section to choose a specific country and a specific salesperson. Remember that it does not matter which order the fields appear in the report filter, because the filtering comes out the same in the end.

When you filter your PivotTables using multiple report filter fields, be aware that not all combinations of items from the fields will produce PivotTable results. For example, a particular salesperson may not have sold any products to customers in a specific country, so combining those filters produces a PivotTable without any data.

Change the Report Filter Layout

In Chapter 3, you learned how to add multiple fields to the PivotTable's report filter. When you add a second field to the report filter, Excel displays one field below the other, which is the basic report filter layout. However, many PivotTable applications require a large number of report filter fields, sometimes half a dozen or more, so displaying these fields vertically, one on top of another, may not be the best way to display your report. You can alter this default configuration by changing the report filter layout to one that suits the layout of the rest of the PivotTable.

Excel gives you two ways to change the report filter layout. The most basic change is to reconfigure how the report filter fields appear on the worksheet. That is,

instead of displaying the fields vertically (one on top of another), you can display the fields horizontally (one beside another).

After you select the basic orientation, you can change whether Excel displays the fields in multiple columns or rows. For example, if you choose the vertical orientation (Excel calls it Down, Then Over), you can also specify the number of fields that appear in each column. If you have, say, six report filter fields and you specify two columns, Excel displays the first three fields in one column, and the other three fields in the next column. Similarly, if you choose the horizontal orientation (called Over, Then Down), you can also specify the number of fields that appear in each row.

Change the Report Filter Layout

1 Click any cell in the PivotTable.

2 Click Options→ PivotTable→Options.

The PivotTable Options dialog box appears.

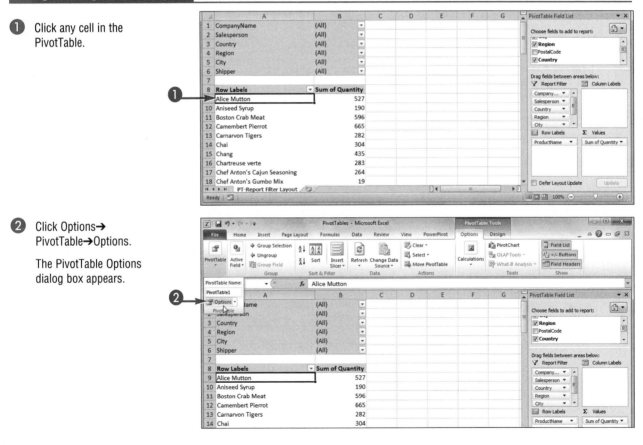

③ Click ▾ and then select the orientation.

④ Specify the maximum number of fields that you want Excel to display in each column.

If you select the Over, Then Down report filter layout in step **3**, specify the maximum number of fields that you want Excel to display in each column.

Note: If you type **0** in the Report filter fields per column (or Report filter fields per row) box, Excel displays the report filter fields in a single row (or column).

⑤ Click OK.

● Excel reconfigures the layout of the report filter.

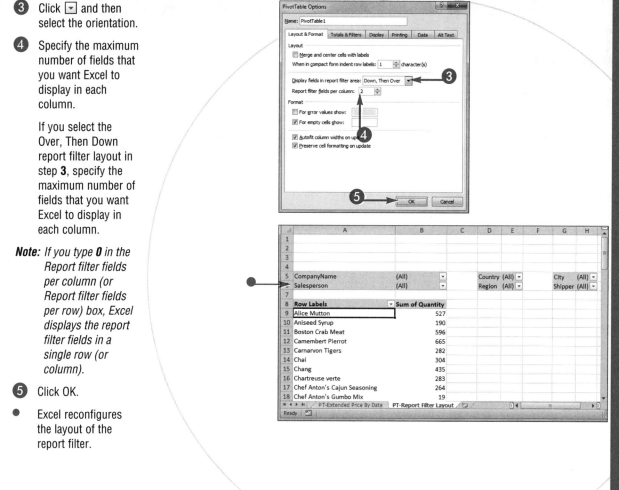

Apply It

If you want to use VBA to control the report filter layout, the PivotTable object has two properties you can work with: Report filterFieldOrder and Report filterFieldWrapCount. Use the Report filterFieldOrder property to set the report filter orientation (to either xlDownThenOver or xlOverThenDown); and use the Report filterFieldWrapCount property to set the number of rows or columns you want in the report filter layout. The following code sets these properties for a PivotTable object:

Example:
```
Set objPT = ActiveSheet.PivotTables(1)
With objPT
    .Report filterFieldOrder = xlOverThenDown
    .Report filterFieldWrapCount = 2
End With
```

Filter Row or Column Items

By default, your PivotTable shows all the items in whatever row and column fields you added to the report layout. This is usually what you want because the point of a PivotTable is to summarize all the data in the original source. However, you may not always want to see every item. For example, in a PivotTable report that includes items from the ProductName field in the row area, you might only want to see those products with names that begin with the letter G or that contain the word *tofu*.

When you modify a PivotTable report to show only a subset of the row or column items, you are applying

a field filter to the report, which is different than filtering the entire PivotTable as described earlier (see the section "Apply a Report Filter"). Excel offers a number of text filters, including Equals, Does Not Equal, Begins With, Ends With, Contains, Greater Than, and Less Than.

If your PivotTable report includes a date field in the row or column area, you can apply a date filter to that field. Excel offers many different date filters, including Before, After, Between, Today, Yesterday, Last Week, Last Month, Last Quarter, This Year, and Year to Date.

Filter Row or Column Items

Apply a Row or Column Filter

① Click ▾ in the header of the field you want to filter.

② Click Label Filters.

③ Select the filter type you want to apply, such as Begins With.

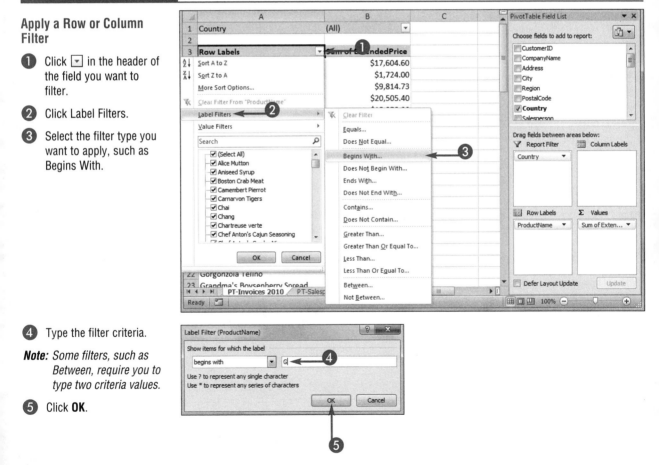

④ Type the filter criteria.

Note: *Some filters, such as Between, require you to type two criteria values.*

⑤ Click **OK**.

- Excel filters the PivotTable report.

Remove a Row or Column Filter

1 Click ⊤ in the header of the filtered field.

2 Click Clear Filter from *Field*, where *Field* is the name of the filtered field.

Excel removes the filter from the field.

Apply It

You can also apply a filter to a row or column field that includes date items. Click ▼ in the header of the date field, click Date Filters, and then select the filter type you want to apply. For filters such as Yesterday, Last Week, and This Quarter, Excel needs no input from you and filters the PivotTable directly. Other filters such as Before, After, and Between require you to type one or more dates. For specific quarters or months, click All Dates in the Period and then select the quarter or month you want to use as a filter.

Extra

When you are working with label filters, Excel enables you to generalize the filter criteria by using wildcard characters. You use the question mark (?) to represent any single character. For example, in a Begins With filter, the criteria ?ine matches items that end with ine, such as wine, dine, fine, and so on. You use the asterisk (*) to represent any number of consecutive characters. For example, in an Equals filter, the criteria i*land matches items such as Iceland and Ireland.

Filter PivotTable Values

T he previous section showed you how to apply a filter to the row or column items to see only a subset of a particular PivotTable field. Excel also enables you to apply value filters that restrict the values you see in the data area. For example, you may only want to see those values that are larger than some amount or that fall between two specified amounts. Excel offers several value filters, including Equals, Does Not Equal, Greater Than, Greater Than or Equal To, Less Than, Less Than or Equal To, Between, and Not Between.

Similarly, you may only be interested in the highest or lowest values that appear in the PivotTable. For example, you might want to see just the top ten values. You can

generate such a report by using Excel's Top 10 Filter, which filters the PivotTable to show just the top ten items based on the values in the data field.

For example, suppose you have a PivotTable report based on a database of invoices that shows the total sales for each product. The basic report shows all the products, but if you are only interested in the top performers for the year, you can activate the Top 10 Filter feature to see the ten products that sold the most. Despite its name, the Top 10 Filter can display more than just the top ten data values. You can specify any number between 1 and 2,147,483,647, and you can also ask Excel to show the bottommost values.

Filter PivotTable Values

Apply a Value Filter

1 Click ▾ in the header of any row or column field.

2 Click Value Filters.

3 Select the filter type you want to apply, such as Top 10.

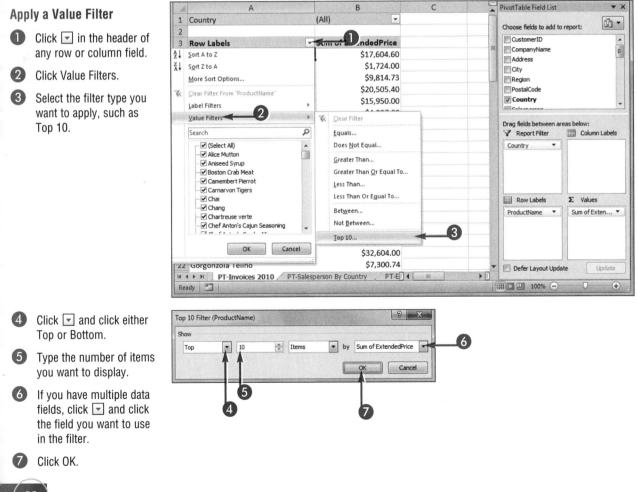

4 Click ▾ and click either Top or Bottom.

5 Type the number of items you want to display.

6 If you have multiple data fields, click ▾ and click the field you want to use in the filter.

7 Click OK.

- Excel filters the PivotTable report.

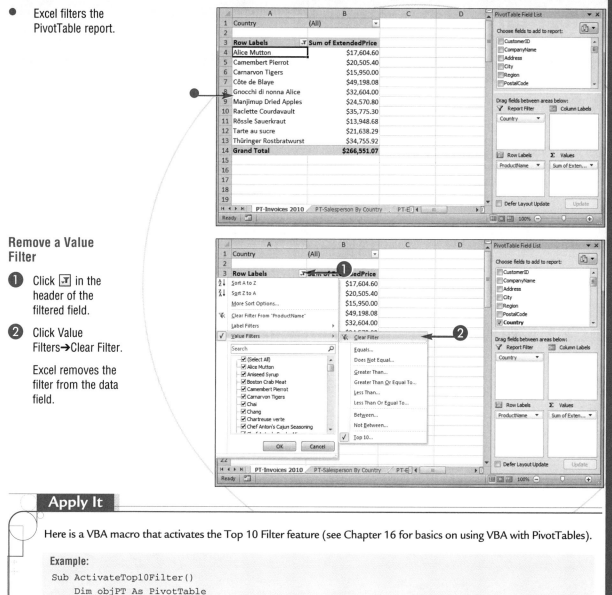

Remove a Value Filter

1 Click ▾ in the header of the filtered field.

2 Click Value Filters→Clear Filter.

Excel removes the filter from the data field.

Here is a VBA macro that activates the Top 10 Filter feature (see Chapter 16 for basics on using VBA with PivotTables).

Example:

```
Sub ActivateTop10Filter()
    Dim objPT As PivotTable
    Dim objPTRowField As PivotField
    Dim objPTDataField As PivotField
    '
    ' Work with the first PivotTable on the active worksheet
    Set objPT = ActiveSheet.PivotTables(1)
    '
    ' Work with the first row field
    Set objPTRowField = objPT.RowFields(1)
    '
    ' Get the data field
    Set objPTDataField = objPT.DataFields(1)
    '
    ' Set the Top 10 Filter
    objPTRowField.PivotFilters.Add xlTopCount, objPTDataField, 10
End Sub
```

Hide Items in a Row or Column Field

When you view a PivotTable report, it may contain items in a row or column field that you do not need to see. For example, in a report showing employee sales or other data, you may prefer to see only those employees who work for or with you. Similarly, if you are a product manager, you might want to customize the report to show only those items in the Product field that you are responsible for.

If you have a PivotTable that contains row or column items you do not need or want to see, you can remove those items from the report. Excel enables you to change

the PivotTable view to exclude one or more items in any row or column field. After you have hidden the items, Excel reconfigures the report to display without them, and also updates the totals to reflect the excluded items. Note, too, that the items remain hidden even if you update the PivotTable, move the field to a different area, and delete the field and add it back into the PivotTable.

After you have hidden one or more items, you should also know how to show them again. See the section "Show Hidden Items in a Row or Column Field."

Hide Items in a Row or Column Field

1 Click ☑ in the header of the field you want to work with.

- Excel displays a list of the items in the field.

2 Deselect an item you want to hide.

③ Repeat step **2** for any other items you want to hide.

④ Click OK.

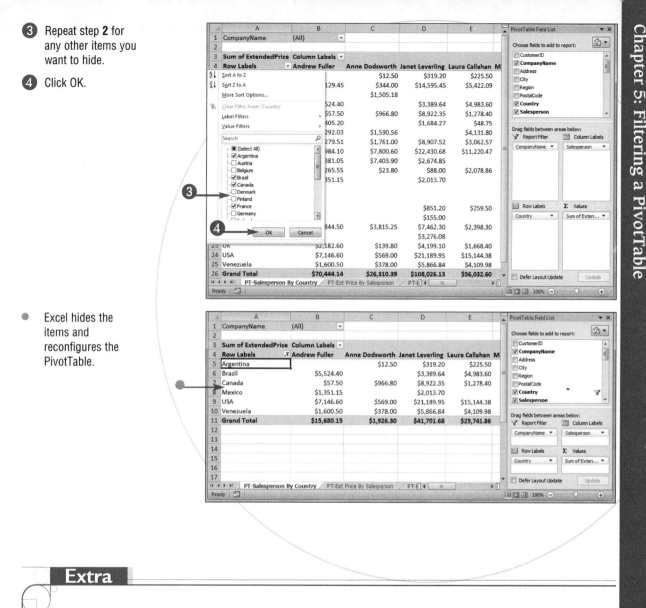

● Excel hides the items and reconfigures the PivotTable.

Use Search to Display Multiple Items

In a tip in the previous section, you learned how to set up a field filter to show only one or two items in any row or column field. This is a useful technique for reducing a large field down to a more manageable size. However, it is not uncommon for a field to contain an extremely large number of items — hundreds, perhaps even thousands of items. In this scenario it can be time consuming to scroll through the list of items to find the ones you want to display in the report.

To make it easier to locate items in a field, Excel 2010 includes a new feature that lets you search for the item or items you want to use. The filter list includes a Search box, and whatever text you type in that box, Excel replaces the complete list of field items with just those items that contain the search text. Excel also gives you the option of adding matching items to an existing field filter so you can use search to filter on multiple items.

Use Search to Display Multiple Items

1. Click ▾ in the header of the field you want to work with.

2. Click the Select All check box.

● Excel deselects all the check boxes.

3. Type a word or part of a word that matches the item you want to show.

4. Click the check box beside each item you want to display.

5. Click OK.

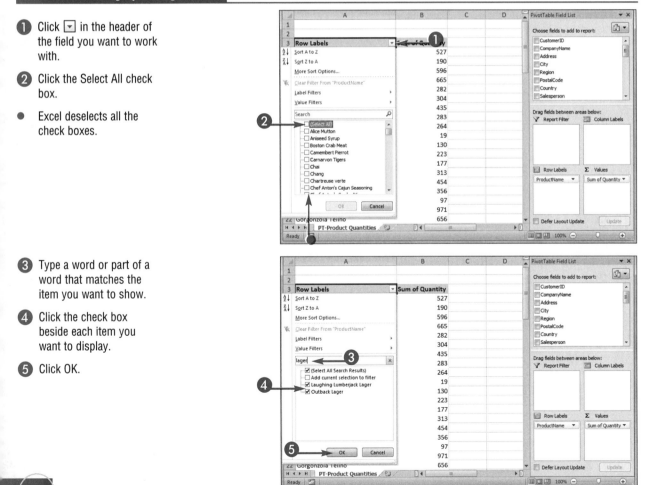

- Excel displays only the selected items and reconfigures the PivotTable.

6 Click ⏷ in the header of the field you want to work with.

7 Type a word or part of a word that matches the item you want to show.

8 Click the check box beside each item you want to display.

9 Click the Add Current Selection to Filter check box.

10 Click OK.

- Excel adds the selected items and reconfigures the PivotTable.

11 Repeat steps **6** to **10** to search for any other items you want to display.

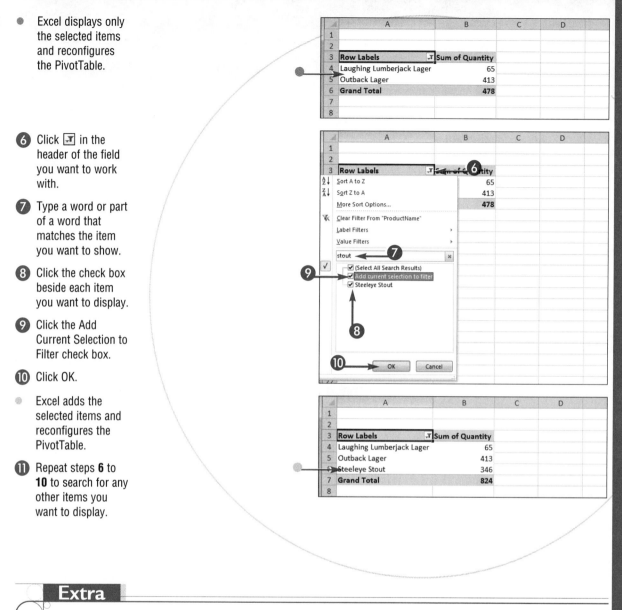

Extra

For more advanced searches, Excel offers the asterisk (*) wildcard character, which you use to represent one or more characters at the beginning or end of the field, or between any search term. Here are some examples:

SEARCH EXPRESSION	DESCRIPTION
*ale	Matches only those items that end with *ale*
acme*	Matches only those items that begin with *acme*
laughing*lager	Matches only those items that begin with *laughing* and end with *lager*
*pinot*france*	Matches only those items that contain the words *pinot* and *france*, in that order

Show Hidden Items in a Row or Column Field

In the previous two sections, you learned how to adjust the PivotTable view by hiding one or more items in any row or column field. The opposite case is when you have one or more hidden items and you want to show some or all of them again. For example, if you have hidden product items that are outside your division, you might want to show products from other divisions that are comparable to one or more of yours. This enables you to use the PivotTable report to compare product results between divisions.

As you see in this section, the procedure for showing hidden items is the opposite of the procedure you used to hide them in the first place.

Show Hidden Items In a Row or Column Field

① Click ▾ in the header of the field you want to work with.

Excel displays a list of the items in the field.

② Select an item you want to show.

● If you want to show all the items in the field, you can click Select All.

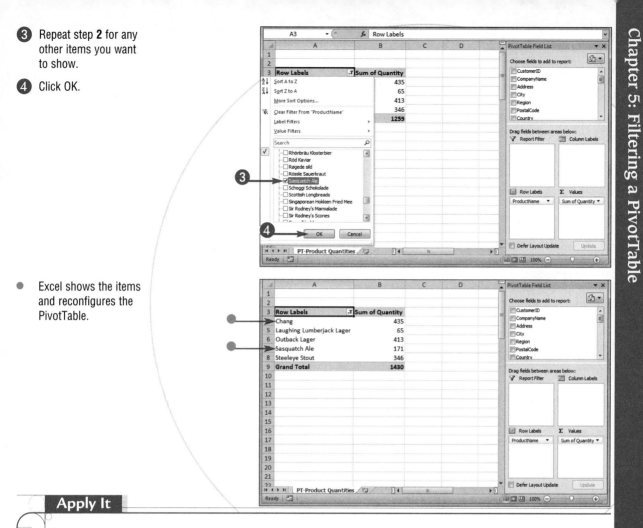

③ Repeat step **2** for any other items you want to show.

④ Click OK.

● Excel shows the items and reconfigures the PivotTable.

Apply It

Here is a VBA macro that shows all the hidden items in a PivotTable row and column areas (see Chapter 16 for basics on using VBA with PivotTables):

Example:
```
Sub ShowAllItems()
    Dim objPT As PivotTable, objPTField As PivotField
    Dim objPTItem As PivotItem
    Set objPT = ActiveSheet.PivotTables(1)
    ' Run through all the row fields
    For Each objPTField In objPT.RowFields
        ' Get the hidden items and make them visible
        For Each objPTItem In objPTField.HiddenItems
            objPTItem.Visible = True
        Next 'objPTItem
    Next 'objPTField
    ' Run through all the column fields
    For Each objPTField In objPT.ColumnFields
        ' Get the hidden items and make them visible
        For Each objPTItem In objPTField.HiddenItems
            objPTItem.Visible = True
        Next 'objPTItem
    Next 'objPTField
End Sub
```

Filter a PivotTable with a Slicer

S o far in this chapter you have learned how to filter a PivotTable either by using the report filter, which applies to the entire PivotTable report, or by using row or column items or data field values, which apply only to the filter field. In both cases, the filter is usable only with the PivotTable in which it is defined. However, it is not unusual to require the same filter in multiple PivotTable reports. For example, if you are a sales manager responsible for sales in a particular set of countries, then you might often need to filter a PivotTable to show data from just those countries. Similarly, if you work with a subset of your company's product line, you might often have to filter PivotTable reports to show the results from just those products.

Applying these kinds of filters to one or two PivotTables is not difficult or time consuming, but if you have to apply the same filter over and over again, then the process becomes frustrating and inefficient. To combat this, Excel 2010 introduces a new PivotTable feature called the *slicer*. A slicer is very similar to a report filter, except that it is independent of any PivotTable. This means that you can apply the same slicer to multiple PivotTables. This section shows you how to create a slicer, and the next two sections show you how to connect them to other PivotTables.

Filter a PivotTable with a Slicer

① Click a cell inside the PivotTable you want to work with.

② Click Options→Insert Slicer.

The Insert Slicers dialog box appears.

③ Select the check box beside each field for which you want to create a slicer.

④ Click OK.

- Excel displays one slicer for each field you selected.

- The Slicer Tools contextual tab appears when a slicer has the focus.

- You can use the controls in the Options tab to customize each slicer.

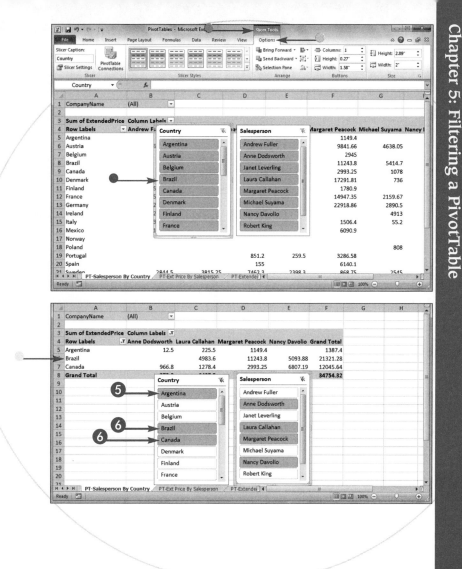

5 Click a field item that you want to include in your filter.

6 If you want to include multiple items in your filter, hold down Ctrl, click each item, and then release Ctrl.

- Excel filters the PivotTable based on the field items you selected in each slicer.

Extra

If a field contains many items, you may have to scroll a long way in the slicer to locate the item you want. It is often easier in this case to configure the slicer to display its items in multiple columns. Click the title of the slicer to select it, click the Options tab, and then use the Column spin box to set the number of columns.

If you find that you no longer need to use a slicer, you should remove it to avoid cluttering the PivotTable window. Right-click the slicer and then click Remove *Slicer*, where *Slicer* is the name of the slicer (which is usually the field name). If you only want to temporarily hide the slicer, click any slicer, click Options→Selection Pane to display the Selection and Visibility task pane, and then click the eye icon beside the slicer to hide it.

Connect a PivotTable to an Existing Slicer

In the previous section, you learned how to create a slicer to filter a PivotTable based on the items in a field. Although you used a specific PivotTable to create the slicer, that slicer is independent of the PivotTable in the sense that you can apply the same filter to a completely different report, as long as that report is based on the same data source. This is a tremendous timesaver because it means you only have to create a single slicer and you can then apply that filter to any number of PivotTables. In this section you learn how to connect a PivotTable to an existing slicer.

It is important to remember that although you can connect multiple PivotTable reports to a single slicer, that slicer only appears with the PivotTable report that you used originally to define the slicer. This means that if you want to format, edit, configure, or remove the slicer, you must use the original PivotTable.

Connect a PivotTable to an Existing Slicer

1 Click a cell inside the PivotTable you want to filter.

2 Click Options→Insert Slicer→Slicer Connections.

The Slicer Connections dialog box appears.

③ Select the check box beside each slicer you want to connect to the PivotTable.

④ Click OK.

● Excel filters the PivotTable based on the slicer or slicers you selected.

● In the PivotTable Field List, Excel displays a filter icon beside each field that has a connected slicer.

Extra

You can connect a PivotTable to an existing slicer using VBA. Before doing so, you might want to adjust the slicer name that you use in macros. The default is `Slicer_Field`, where `Field` is the slicer's source field name. Switch to the PivotTable you used to define the slicer, click the slicer, and then click Options→Slicer Settings. In the Slicer Settings dialog box, use the Name text box to set the name you prefer to use, and then click OK.

Apply It

Here is a VBA macro that connects a PivotTable to a slicer (see Chapter 16 for basics on using VBA with PivotTables).

Example:
```
Sub ConnectSlicer()
    Dim objSC As SlicerCache
    '
    ' Specify the slicer
    Set objSC = ActiveWorkbook.SlicerCaches("Slicer_Salesperson")
    '
    ' Connect the slicer to the first PivotTable on the active sheet
    objSC.PivotTables.AddPivotTable (ActiveSheet.PivotTables(1))
End Sub
```

Connect a Slicer to Multiple PivotTables

In the previous section, you learned how to add a slicer to a PivotTable to filter that report based on the filter defined in the slicer. That is a useful technique if you only need to associate one or two PivotTables with a particular slicer. However, it is possible that you may need to apply a slicer to many PivotTables. For example, your workbook may contain many PivotTables that show the complete sales data for all the countries that your company serves. If you are responsible for just a few of those countries, then you most likely want to filter all those PivotTables to show just the data from your countries.

Instead of repeating the steps from the previous section over and over, Excel gives you an easier method. You can use the slicer's PivotTable Connections list to quickly connect the slicer to multiple PivotTables.

Connect a Slicer to Multiple PivotTables

① Click the tab of the worksheet that contains the slicer you want to work with.

② Click the slicer.

③ Click Options→PivotTable Connections.

The PivotTable Connections dialog box appears.

④ Select the check box beside each PivotTable you want to connect to the slicer.

⑤ Click OK.

● Excel filters each selected PivotTable based on the slicer.

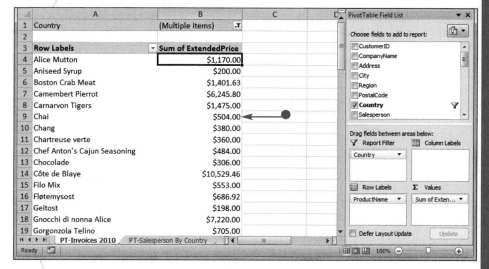

Apply It

Here is a VBA macro that disconnects a slicer from the active PivotTable (see Chapter 16 for basics on using VBA with PivotTables).

Example:

```
Sub DisconnectSlicer()
    Dim objSC As SlicerCache
    '
    ' Specify the slicer
    Set objSC = ActiveWorkbook.SlicerCaches("Slicer_Salesperson")
    '
    ' Disconnect the slicer from the first PivotTable on the active sheet
    objSC.PivotTables.RemovePivotTable (ActiveSheet.PivotTables(1))
    '
    ' Refresh the PivotTable
    ActiveSheet.PivotTables(1).PivotCache.Refresh
End Sub
```

Rename a PivotTable Field

PivotTable field names come from the column headings used in the original source data. However, if you are using an external data source, the field names come from the names used in the data source's fields. The exception is when you are using the Compact report layout. In this case, for the row and column areas, Excel uses the names Row Labels and Column Labels. If you do not like some or all of the field names in your PivotTable, you can rename them. Excel will remember the new names you specify and even preserve them when you refresh or rebuild the PivotTable. Note, however, that Excel does not change the corresponding headings in the source data.

You usually rename a field because the original name is not suitable in some way. For example, many field names

consist of multiple words that have been joined to avoid spaces, so you might have field names such as CategoryName and UnitsInStock. Renaming these fields to Category Name and Units In Stock makes them easier to read. Similarly, if you have field names that are all uppercase letters, you might prefer to use title case instead. Finally, if you are using the Compact report layout, you might want to change the names Row Labels and Column Labels to something more meaningful. Also, many PivotTable users prefer to change the name of the data field. Excel's default is Sum of *Field*, where *Field* is the name of the field used in the summary calculation. A better name might use the form *Field* Total, or something similar.

Rename a PivotTable Field

Note: *This chapter uses the PivotTables06.xlsm spreadsheet, available at www.wiley.com/go/ pivottablesvb2e, or you can create your own sample file.*

① Click any cell in the field you want to rename.

② Click Design→Report Layout→Show in Outline Form.

● Excel displays the field name.

③ Click Options→Active Field.

④ Click inside the Active Field text box.

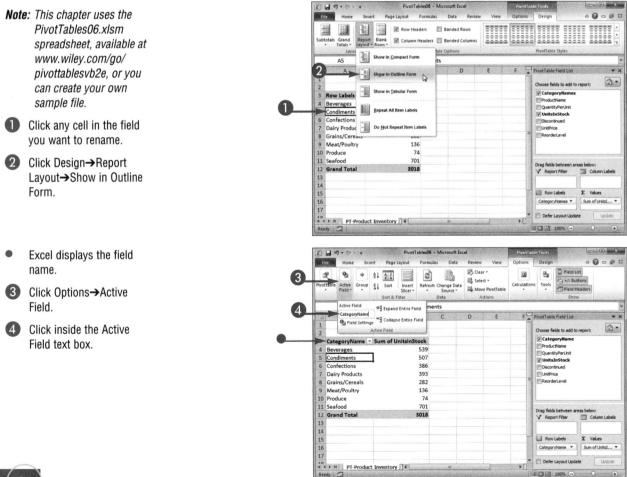

⑤ Change the text to the new field name.

Note: Make sure that the new name you use does not conflict with an existing field name.

⑥ Press Enter.

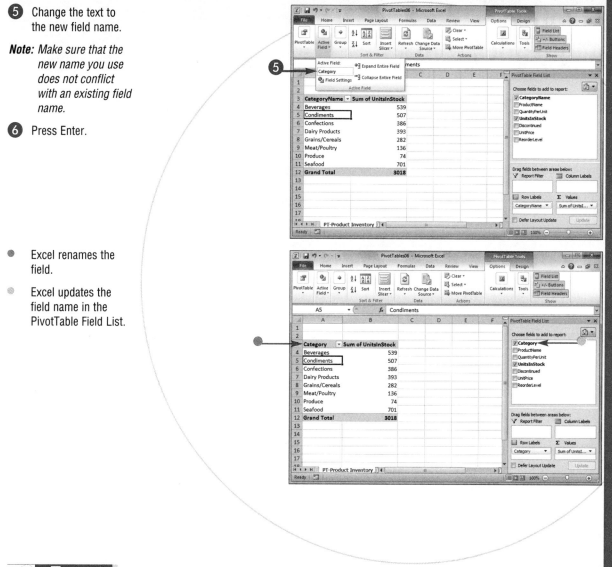

● Excel renames the field.

● Excel updates the field name in the PivotTable Field List.

Extra

The field headings you see in a PivotTable are really just worksheet cells that have had special formatting applied. This means that when you click a field heading, the button text appears inside Excel's formula bar. So an easier way to rename a PivotTable field is to click its button and then edit the button text that appears in the formula bar. You can also press F2 and edit the text directly in the cell.

Alternatively, you can right-click anywhere inside the field, and then click Field Settings to open the Field Settings dialog box. Edit the text in the Custom Name text box, and then click OK.

Rename a PivotTable Item

The names of the items that appear in the PivotTable's row or column area are the unique values that Excel extracts from the source data fields you have added to each area. Therefore, because the items come from the data itself, you might think that their names would be unchangeable. That is not true, however. You can rename any field item and Excel "remembers" that the new name corresponds with the original item. Excel preserves your new names even after you refresh or rebuild the PivotTable.

As with field names, you will usually want to rename an item when its existing name is unsuitable. For example,

the original name might not be very descriptive, it might be obscure, or it may come from a data source that uses all uppercase or (more rarely) all lowercase letters.

You should exercise a bit of caution when you rename items, however. If the people reading your report are familiar with the underlying data, they could become confused if you use names that differ significantly from the originals.

Remember, too, that renaming one or more items might cause the field to lose its current sort order. After you have finished renaming items in the field, you might need to re-sort the field, as described in Chapter 4.

Rename a PivotTable Item

① Click the cell of the item you want to rename.

② Press F2.

● Excel opens the cell for editing.

③ Type the new item name in the cell.

Note: Make sure that the new name you use does not conflict with an existing item name in the same field. If you enter an existing name, Excel switches the position of the two items. See Chapter 4 for more.

④ Press Enter.

● Excel renames the item.

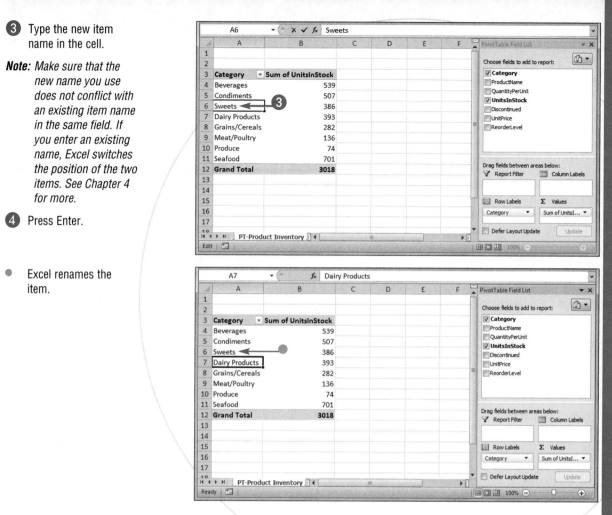

Apply It

The technique you learned in this section applies to items in the row and column areas. For obvious reasons, Excel does not allow you to edit any of the cells in the data area because they are all calculated values. That leaves only the report filter area. So how can you rename report filter items if they do not reside in worksheet cells?

The solution is to pivot the report filter you want to work with over to either the row or column area. Excel displays the field's items in cells, so you can then edit the item or items you want to rename. After you finish renaming the items, pivot the field back to the report filter area. Excel preserves your new names in the report filter drop-down list. Moreover, Excel sets up a correspondence between your new name and the item's original name in the source data. Therefore, when you select the renamed item in the report filter drop-down list, Excel filters the PivotTable results appropriately.

Format a PivotTable Cell

I f you will be sharing your PivotTables with other people, via a network, e-mail, the Web, or a presentation, your report will have much more impact if it is nicely formatted and presented in a readable, eye-catching layout. You can use Excel's cell-formatting tools to apply a wide variety of formats to your PivotTable cells.

By default, Excel applies almost no formatting to PivotTable cells. The only exceptions are the bold text and background colors it applies to field labels and Grand Total cells, and the borders it applies below the column area and above the column Grand Total. However, you are free to modify the formatting for any cell in the PivotTable. For example, you can apply a numeric or date format, or create

a custom format, as discussed in detail in the next three sections in this chapter. You can also change the cell alignment to the left, center, or right; or you can wrap text within the cell. For the cell font, you can change the typeface, style, size, color, and more. You can also change the cell borders and apply background shading, either as a solid color or with a fill pattern.

By the way, the default format that Excel applies to a new PivotTable is a Quick Style called Pivot Style Light 16. Excel offers more than 80 PivotTable Quick Styles that enable you to apply a uniform format to an entire PivotTable. For the details, see Chapter 8. Excel also has a feature that preserves your formatting when you refresh your PivotTable; see Chapter 8 for more.

Format a PivotTable Cell

① Click the cell you want to format.

You can also select a range or a PivotTable area.

Note: To learn how to select PivotTable areas, see Chapter 3.

② Click the Home tab.

③ Use the controls in the Font group to apply font options to the cell text (see the table on the next page).

● You can also click the Font dialog launcher or press Ctrl+Shift+F to display the Font tab of the Format Cells dialog box.

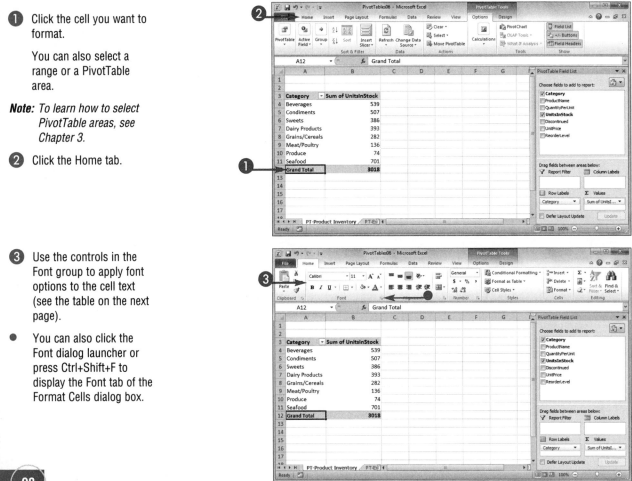

④ Use the controls in the Alignment group to align data within the cell (see the table below).

● You can also click the Alignment dialog launcher to display the Alignment tab of the Format Cells dialog box.

Note: For the details on using the Number group, see the sections "Apply a Numeric Format to PivotTable Data" and "Apply a Date Format to PivotTable Data" later in this chapter.

● Excel applies the formatting to the cell.

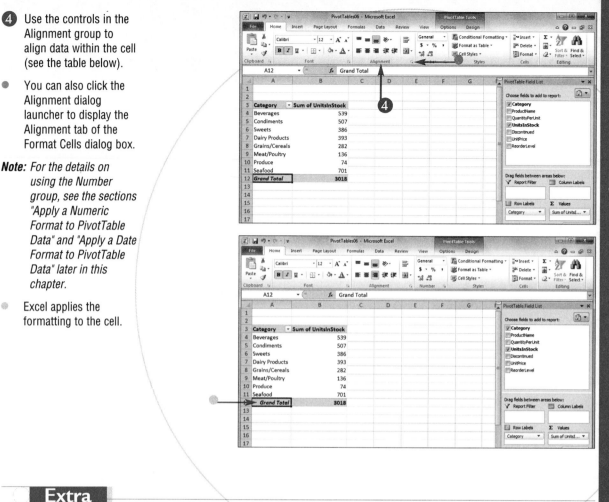

Extra

Here are the buttons to use in the Font and Alignment groups to format PivotTable cell text:

BUTTON	DESCRIPTION
Calibri ▾	Applies a typeface
11 ▾	Sets the font size
B	Formats text as bold
I	Formats text as italics
U̲	Formats text as underlined
▦	Applies a border
◇	Applies a background color
A	Applies a text color
▤	Left-aligns text
▥	Centers text
▤	Right-aligns text

Apply a Numeric Format to PivotTable Data

One of the best ways to improve the readability of your PivotTable is to display the report in a format that is logical, consistent, and straightforward. Formatting currency amounts with leading dollar signs, percentages with trailing percent signs, and large numbers with commas are a few of the ways you can improve your PivotTable style.

When you create a PivotTable, Excel applies the General number format to the data area. If you want your numbers to appear differently, you can choose from among Excel's six categories of numeric formats:

- **Number.** Enables you to specify three components: the number of decimal places (0 to 30), whether or not the thousands separator (,) is used, and how negative numbers are displayed. For negative numbers, you can display the number with a leading minus sign, in red, surrounded by parentheses, or in red surrounded by parentheses.

- **Currency.** Similar to the number format, except that the thousands separator is always used, and you have the option of displaying the numbers with a leading dollar sign ($) or other currency symbol.

- **Accounting.** Enables you to select the number of decimal places and whether to display a leading currency symbol, which Excel displays flush-left in the cell. All negative entries are displayed surrounded by parentheses.

- **Percentage.** Displays the number multiplied by 100 with a percent sign (%) to the right of the number. For example, .506 is displayed as 50.6%. You can display 0 to 30 decimal places.

- **Fraction.** Enables you to express decimal quantities as fractions. There are nine fraction formats in all, including displaying the number as halves, quarters, eighths, sixteenths, tenths, and hundredths.

- **Scientific.** Displays the most significant number to the left of the decimal, 2 to 30 decimal places to the right of the decimal, and then the exponent. For example, 123000 is displayed as 1.23E+05.

Apply a Numeric Format to PivotTable Data

1. Click the cell or select the range you want to format.

- If you want to apply a numeric format to an entire field, click Options→Active Field→Field Settings, and then click Number Format.

2. Click the Home tab.

3. Click Number Format→More Number Formats.

- You can also click a numeric format in the list to apply the format with the default options.

Excel displays the Format Cells dialog box with the Number tab displayed.

④ Click the numeric format you want to use.

⑤ Use the controls on the right side of the tab to select the format options.

● The Sample area shows what your formatting will look like.

⑥ Click OK.

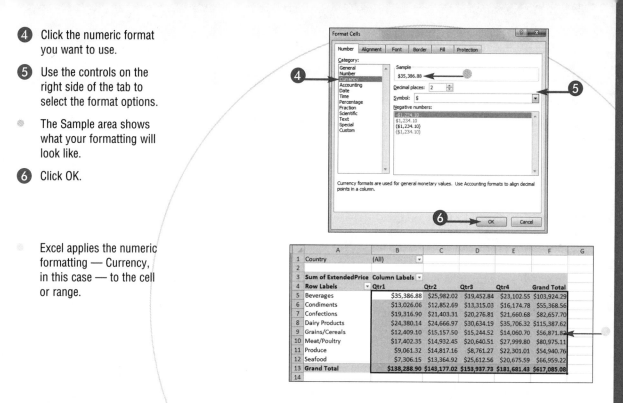

● Excel applies the numeric formatting — Currency, in this case — to the cell or range.

Extra

You can set the numeric format of the selected range by applying a style. Click Home➔Cell Styles and then click the numeric style you want: Comma, Comma [0], Currency, Currency [0], or Percent. You can also set the numeric format using the following buttons in the Home tab's Number group:

BUTTON	DESCRIPTION
$	Applies the Currency style
%	Applies the Percent style
,	Applies the Comma style
.0↑	Increases the number of decimal places
.00↓	Decreases the number of decimal places

There are also a few shortcut keys you can use to set the numeric format:

PRESS	TO APPLY THE FORMAT
Ctrl+~	General
Ctrl+!	Number (Two decimal places, using the thousands separator)
Ctrl+$	Currency (Two decimal places, using the dollar sign and negative numbers surrounded by parentheses)
Ctrl+%	Percentage (Zero decimal places)
Ctrl+^	Scientific (Two decimal places)

Apply a Date Format to PivotTable Data

If you include dates or times in your PivotTables, you need to make sure that they are presented in a readable, unambiguous format. For example, most people would interpret the date 1/5/11 as January 5, 2011. However, in some countries this date would mean May 1, 2011. Similarly, if you use the time 2:45, do you mean AM or PM? To avoid these kinds of problems, you can apply Excel's built-in date and time formats to a PivotTable cell or range.

The Date format specifies how Excel displays the date components — the day, month, and year — as well as which symbol to use to separate the components. For the month component of the date, Excel can display any of the following: the number (where January is 1, February is 2, and so on) with or without a leading 0; the first letter of the month name (for example, M for March); the

abbreviated month name (for example, Mar for March); or the full month name. For the year component, Excel can display either the final two digits (for example, 11 for 2011) or all four digits. You can also choose either a slash (/) or a hyphen (–) to separate the date components. Depending on the location you choose, such as the United States or Canada, you may also be able to include the day of the week or use a period (.) as the date separator.

The Time format specifies which time components — hours, minutes, and seconds — Excel displays. You can also choose whether Excel uses regular time (for example, 1:30:55 PM) or military time (for example, 13:30:55). When you select a regular time format, Excel always includes either AM or PM; when you choose a military time format, Excel does not include AM or PM.

You can also create custom date formats. See Chapter 11 for more details.

Apply a Date Format to PivotTable Data

1 Click the cell or select the range you want to format.

● If you want to apply a date or time format to an entire field, click Options→Active Field→Field Settings, and then click Number Format.

2 Click the Home tab.

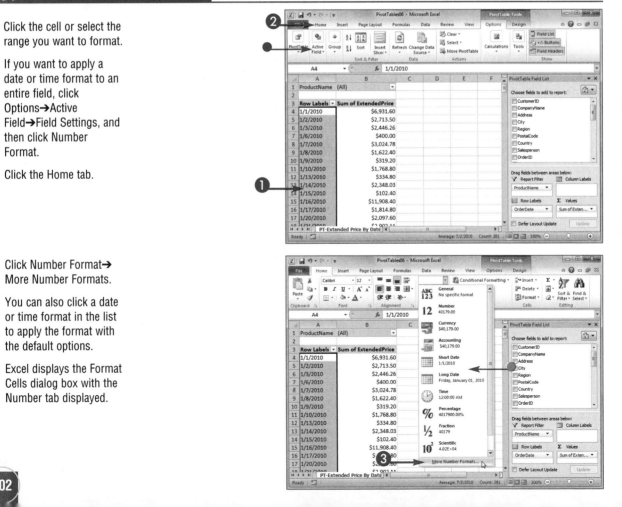

3 Click Number Format→ More Number Formats.

● You can also click a date or time format in the list to apply the format with the default options.

Excel displays the Format Cells dialog box with the Number tab displayed.

④ Click Date.

If you are formatting times, click Time instead.

⑤ Click the format type you want to apply.

⑥ Click the drop-down arrow ( ) and click the location.

◉ The Sample area shows what your formatting will look like.

⑦ Click OK.

◉ Excel applies the date or time formatting to the cell or range.

Extra

There are a few shortcut keys you can use to set the date or time format as well as to add the current date or time:

PRESS	TO
Ctrl+#	Apply the date format 14–Mar–08
Ctrl+@	Apply the time format 1:30 PM
Ctrl+;	Enter the current date using the format 3/14/2008
Ctrl+:	Enter the current time using the format 1:30 PM

In the Number tab of the Format Cells dialog box, if you click the Date format and choose English (United States) in the Locale list, Excel shows two date formats at the top of the Type list:

```
*3/14/2001
```

```
*Wednesday, March 14, 2001
```

The asterisks tell you that the order of the date components may change if someone opening the worksheet is using a different locale. For example, if you select the *3/14/2001 format, a user in the United Kingdom will likely see the date as 14/3/2001. If you want to make sure that other users always see the dates as you format them, choose a format that does not have a leading asterisk.

Apply a Conditional Format to PivotTable Data

Formatting numbers with thousands separators, decimals, or currency symbols is useful because a PivotTable is, in the end, a report, and reports should always look their best. However, the main purpose of a PivotTable is to perform data analysis, and regular numeric formatting achieves that goal only insofar as it helps you and others read and understand the report. However, if you want to extend the analytic capabilities of your PivotTables, you need to turn to a more advanced technique called *conditional formatting*.

The idea behind conditional formatting is that you want particular values in your PivotTable results to stand out from the others. For example, if your PivotTable tracks product inventory, you might want to be alerted when the inventory of any item falls below some critical value. Similarly, you might want to track the total amount sold by

your salespeople and be alerted when an employee's results exceed some value so that, say, a bonus can be awarded.

Conditional formatting enables you to achieve these and similar results. With a conditional format rule applied to some or all of the PivotTable's data area, Excel examines the numbers and then applies formatting — a font, border, and pattern that you specify — to any cells that match your criteria. By applying, say, a bold font, thick cell border, and a background color to results that satisfy your criteria, you can find those important results with a quick glance at your PivotTable.

In versions of Excel prior to 2007, the conditional formatting was a property of the cells to which you applied it, so it did not move when you pivoted the report. In Excel 2007 and 2010, however, the conditional formatting is a property of the PivotTable, so it stays with the data as the report changes.

Apply a Conditional Format to PivotTable Data

① Select some or all of the PivotTable's data area.

② Click Home→Conditional Formatting→New Rule.

● You can also click these commands to work with predefined rules, as described in the Apply It section on the next page.

The New Formatting Rule dialog box appears.

③ Click Format only cells that contain.

④ Click the drop-down arrow (🔽) and then click Cell Value.

⑤ Click 🔽 and then click a comparison operator.

⑥ Type or select the value you want to use with the comparison operator.

⑦ If the comparison operator requires a second value, type or select that value.

⑧ Click Format.

Excel displays the Format Cells dialog box.

⑨ Use the Font tab to apply font options to the conditional format.

⑩ Use the Border tab to apply a border to the conditional format.

⑪ Use the Fill tab to apply a fill pattern to the conditional format.

⑫ Click OK.

Excel returns you to the New Formatting Rule dialog box.

⑬ Click OK in the New Formatting Rule dialog box.

● Excel applies the conditional formatting to the range.

	A	B	C	D	E	F
1						
2						
3	Sum of ExtendedPrice	Column Labels				
4	Row Labels	Qtr1	Qtr2	Qtr3	Qtr4	Grand Total
5	Andrew Fuller	$7,488.78	$24,374.17	$17,309.15	$21,272.04	$70,444.14
6	Anne Dodsworth	$2,471.98	$4,187.10	$10,245.95	$9,405.36	$26,310.39
7	Janet Leverling	$28,793.05	$33,901.93	$10,469.46	$34,861.69	$108,026.13
8	Laura Callahan	$18,684.31	$7,465.81	$10,800.40	$19,082.08	$56,032.60
9	Margaret Peacock	$41,088.53	$24,474.10	$29,947.73	$33,299.42	$128,809.78
10	Michael Suyama	$3,899.44	$13,806.01	$5,481.65	$19,939.27	$43,126.37
11	Nancy Davolio	$14,402.07	$14,824.31	$32,077.16	$31,844.50	$93,148.04
12	Robert King	$18,940.34	$12,605.92	$25,520.43	$3,404.50	$60,471.19
13	Steven Buchanan	$2,520.40	$7,537.67	$12,085.80	$8,572.57	$30,716.44
14	Grand Total	$138,288.90	$143,177.02	$153,937.73	$181,681.43	$617,085.08
15						
16						
17						
18						

PT-Employee Sales By Quarter

Ready

Apply It

When you click Home→Conditional Formatting, Excel displays several commands that enable you to work with predefined conditional formatting rules. Click Highlight Cells Rules to have Excel format cells that meet criteria such as being greater than or less than a particular value; click Top/Bottom Rules to have Excel format cells that are the highest or lowest *N* values in the range (where *N* is a number or a percentage), or that are above or below the range average; click Data Bars to have Excel format all the cells in the range with background data bars that reflect the relative size of each cell value compared to the highest value in the range; click Color Scales to have Excel format all the cells in the range with background color gradients, where the lowest values are one color, the highest values are another, and the intermediate values are shades between these colors; and click Icon Sets to have Excel format all the cells in the range with icons that represent the relative values. For example, if you choose stoplight icons, the highest values get the green light, the lowest values get the red light, and the intermediate values get the yellow light.

Show Items with No Data

A PivotTable report is meant to be a succinct summary of a large quantity of data. One way that Excel increases the succinctness of a PivotTable is to exclude from the report any items that have no data. This is usually the behavior that you want, but it can cause some problems with certain kinds of reports.

One of the problems that appears when some items have no data concerns filtering the PivotTable using a report filter. For example, suppose there are two items in the report filter field, and that a particular row item has data for the first report filter item, but it has no data for the second report filter item. When you switch report filters,

your PivotTable layout will change because Excel removes the row field item from the report when you filter on the second report filter.

Another problem occurs when you group the PivotTable results. If no results fall within a particular grouping, Excel does not display the grouping.

In both cases, the exclusion of a field item or grouping can be confusing and, in any case, you may be interested in seeing items or groupings that have no data.

You can work around these problems by forcing Excel to always show field items that have no data, as described in this section.

Show Items with No Data

1 Click any cell in the field you want to work with.

2 Click Options→Active Field→Field Settings.

The Field Settings dialog box appears.

③ Click the Layout & Print tab.

④ Select the Show Items with No Data check box.

⑤ Click OK.

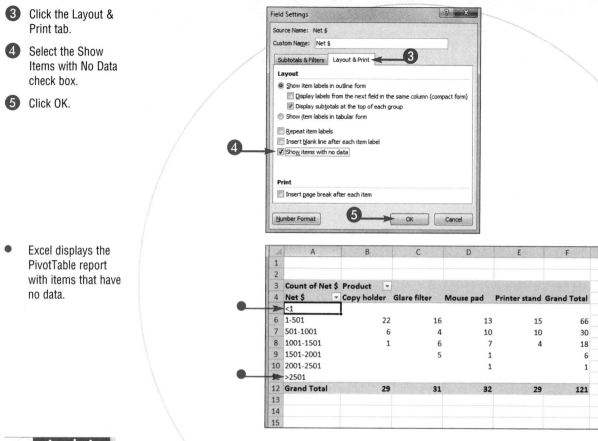

● Excel displays the PivotTable report with items that have no data.

Apply It

One PivotTable problem that comes up more often than you might think is when you end up with phantom field items, or items that no longer exist in the source data. This occurs when an item appears originally in the source data, appears in a PivotTable report, and is then subsequently renamed in or deleted from the source data. When you refresh the PivotTable, the item disappears. However, if you activate the Show Items with No Data check box for the field, Excel displays the item again. Even if you refresh or rebuild the PivotTable, the phantom item still appears in the report.

The only way to solve this problem is to use VBA to delete the PivotTable item. Here is a VBA macro that deletes the PivotTable item in the active worksheet cell (see Chapter 16 for basics on using VBA with PivotTables):

Example:
```
Sub DeletePivotTableItem()
    Dim nResult As Integer

    '
    ' Work with the PivotItem object in the active cell
    With ActiveCell.PivotItem

        '
        ' Confirm the deletion
        nResult = MsgBox("Are you sure you want " & _
                  "to delete the """ & _
                  .Value & """ item?", vbYesNo)

        '
        ' If Yes, delete the PivotItem object
        If nResult = vbYes Then .Delete
    End With
End Sub
```

Exclude Items from a Report Filter

Y ou can configure your PivotTable to hide multiple report filter items and thus display a subset of the report filter in your PivotTable results.

In a default PivotTable that includes a report filter, Excel displays the results for all items in the report filter field. In Chapter 4, you learned how to display the results for a single item. However, there may be times when you need to display the results for more than one report filter item, although not all the items. For example, you may know

that the results from one or more item are incomplete or inaccurate, and so should not be included in the report. Alternatively, your data analysis may require that you view the PivotTable results for only a subset of items.

For these and similar situations, Excel enables you to customize the report filter to exclude one or more items. Excel then redisplays the PivotTable without showing those items or including their results in the PivotTable totals.

Exclude Items from a Report Filter

① Click ▾ in the report filter.

② Click the Select Multiple Items check box.

- Excel displays check boxes beside each report filter item.

③ Click each item that you want to exclude from the PivotTable results.

④ Click OK.

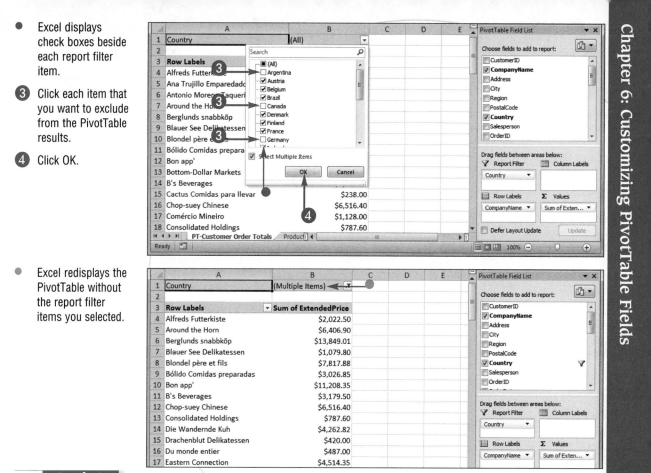

- Excel redisplays the PivotTable without the report filter items you selected.

Excel does not offer an easy way to add hidden page items back into the report filter list. You need to open the report filter's item list again and click each item that you hid earlier. To make this chore easier, you can include all report filter items via VBA by setting the `Visible` property of each report filter `PivotItem` object to `True`, as shown in the following macro (see Chapter 16 for basics on using VBA with PivotTables):

Example:
```
Sub ShowAllReportFilterItems()
    Dim objPT As PivotTable
    Dim objReportFilter As PivotField
    Dim objItem As PivotItem
    '
    ' Work with the first PivotTable on the active worksheet
    Set objPT = ActiveSheet.PivotTables(1)
    '
    ' Work with the first page field
    Set objReportFilter = objPT.PageFields(1)
    '
    ' Run through all the page field items
    For Each objItem In objReportFilter.PivotItems
        '
        ' Display the item
        objItem.Visible = True
    Next 'objItem
End Sub
```

Repeat Item Labels in Fields

You can better analyze your PivotTable using tools such as Excel's lookup and summary worksheet functions if you first configure one or more PivotTable fields to repeat their item labels.

Excel offers many analytical tools that are PivotTable-specific. These tools include summary functions, custom calculations, report filters, and field filters, to name a few. However, there may be situations where you need to summarize, analyze, or extract values from a PivotTable in ways that are not possible using Excel's built-in PivotTable tools. In such cases, you can create your own custom tools by building formulas that use Excel's worksheet functions.

For most PivotTables, you can apply the worksheet functions directly to the report. However, this can be problematic if you have multiple fields in the row or column area, because in the outer field Excel only displays the item label once for each unique value in the field. This makes the table easier to read, but it prevents you from using worksheet functions such as SUMIF(), COUNTIF(), VLOOKUP(), HLOOKUP(), and MATCH(), which do not work correctly if you have blank cells in a range.

To fix this problem, you can configure the outer field to repeat its unique labels so that the field does not display any blank cells.

Repeat Item Labels in Fields

Repeat Item Labels in a Single Field

1. Click any cell in the field you want to work with.

2. Click Options→Active Field→Field Settings.

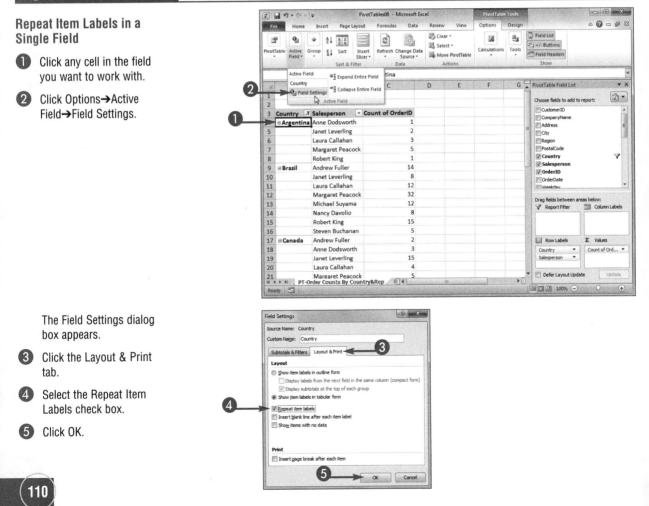

The Field Settings dialog box appears.

3. Click the Layout & Print tab.

4. Select the Repeat Item Labels check box.

5. Click OK.

- Excel reconfigures the PivotTable report to repeat the item labels in the field.

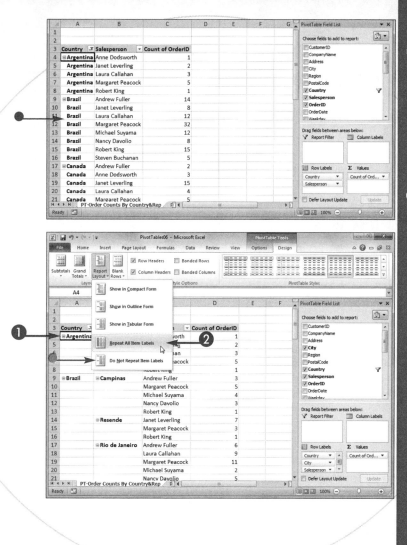

Repeat Item Labels in All Fields

1. Click any cell in the PivotTable.

2. Click Design→Report Layout→Repeat All Item Labels.

   Excel reconfigures the PivotTable report to repeat the item labels in all the row and column fields.

- You can click Do Not Repeat Item Labels to turn off label repeats in all fields.

Extra

If you plan on applying worksheet functions such as SUMIF(), COUNTIF(), VLOOKUP(), HLOOKUP(), and MATCH() directly to a PivotTable, it helps if you configure the report design to display the data optimally. For example, the compact report layout does not display the repeated field items, and the outline report layout displays an extra label for each unique field item that enables you to collapse and expand the item. The best layout choice is the tabular layout, which you choose by clicking any cell in the PivotTable and then selecting Design→Report Layout→Show in Tabular Form.

After you configure a field to repeat its item labels, you might notice that the field still includes extra rows for the subtotals associated with each unique item in the field. These subtotals can also throw off your results when you use worksheet functions such as SUMIF(), COUNTIF(), VLOOKUP(), HLOOKUP(), and MATCH(). To work around this problem, turn off subtotals by clicking any cell in the PivotTable and then clicking Design→Subtotals→Do Not Show Subtotals.

Understanding PivotChart Limitations

A *PivotChart* is a graphical representation of the values in a PivotTable report. However, a PivotChart goes far beyond a regular chart because a PivotChart comes with many of the same capabilities as a PivotTable. These capabilities include hiding items, filtering data via the report filter, refreshing the PivotChart to account for changes in the underlying data, and more. Also, if you move fields from one area of the PivotTable to another, the PivotChart changes accordingly. You also have access to most of Excel's regular charting capabilities, so PivotCharts are a powerful addition to your data-analysis toolkit.

However, PivotCharts are not a perfect solution. Excel has fairly rigid rules for which parts of a PivotTable report correspond to which parts of the PivotChart layout. Moving a field from one part of the PivotChart to another can easily result in a PivotChart layout that is either difficult to understand or that does not make any sense at all.

Similarly, you also face a number of other limitations that control the types of charts you can make and the formatting options you can apply. For example, you cannot configure a PivotChart to use the Stock chart type, which can be a significant problem for some applications.

This section outlines these and other PivotChart limitations. Note, however, that most of these limitations are not onerous in most situations, so they should in no way dissuade you from taking advantage of the analytical and visualization power of the PivotChart.

If you have any trouble with the terminology or concepts in this chapter, be sure to refer to Chapter 1 for the appropriate background.

PivotTables Versus PivotCharts

One of the main sources of PivotChart confusion is the fact that Excel uses different terminology with PivotCharts and PivotTables. In both, you have a data area that contains the numeric results, and you have a report filter that you can use to filter the data. However, it is important to understand how Excel maps the PivotTable's row and column areas to the PivotChart.

Row Area Versus Category Area

In a PivotTable, the row area contains the unique values — the items — that Excel has extracted from a particular field in the source data. The PivotChart equivalent is the category area, which corresponds to the chart's X-axis. That is, each unique value from the source data field has a corresponding category axis value.

Column Area Versus Series Area

In a PivotTable, the column area contains the unique values — the items — that Excel has extracted from a particular field in the source data. The PivotChart equivalent is the series area, which corresponds to the chart's data series. That is, each unique value from the source data field has a corresponding data series.

PivotChart Limitations

Chart Types

Excel offers a large number of chart types, and you can change the default PivotChart type to another that more closely suits your needs; see the section "Change the PivotChart Type" later in this chapter. However, there are three chart types that you cannot apply to a PivotChart: Bubble, XY (Scatter), and Stock.

Adding and Removing Fields

Unlike in versions of Excel prior to 2007, you cannot add or remove fields directly to or from a PivotChart in Excel 2007 or 2010. Once you create the PivotChart, as long as you are working with the chart itself, you cannot add or remove fields. If you want to reconfigure the PivotChart's fields, you must add or remove the fields in the underlying PivotTable.

Pivoting Fields

In previous versions of Excel, each PivotChart field had its own button, and you could use those buttons to pivot the fields from one part of the PivotChart to another. Unfortunately, you cannot do this directly in Excel 2010 PivotCharts. If you want to pivot a field from one part of PivotChart to another, you must pivot the field using the underlying PivotTable.

Create a PivotChart from a PivotTable

You can create a PivotChart directly from an existing PivotTable. This saves times because you do not have to configure the layout of the PivotChart or any other options.

You have seen elsewhere in this book that the pivot cache that Excel maintains for each PivotTable saves time, memory, and hard drive space. For example, if you attempt to create a new PivotTable using the same source data as an existing PivotTable, Excel enables you to share the source data between them.

The pivot cache also comes in handy when you want to create a PivotChart. If the layout of an existing PivotTable is the same as what you want for a PivotChart, you can create the PivotChart directly from the PivotTable. You can use this method to create a PivotChart using just one keystroke.

Extra

You can also create a chart directly from an existing PivotTable using Visual Basic for Applications (VBA). Select the `PivotTable` object using the `PivotSelect` method and then run the `Chart` object's `Add` method, as shown in the following example (see Chapter 16 for basics on using VBA with PivotTables):

Example:
```
Sub CreatePivotChart()
    ' Select the first PivotTable
    ActiveSheet.PivotTables(1).PivotSelect ""
    ' Add the chart
    Charts.Add
End Sub
```

Create a PivotChart from a PivotTable

Note: *This chapter uses the PivotCharts07. xlsm spreadsheet, available at www. wiley.com/go/ pivottablesvb2e, or you can create your own sample file.*

① Click any cell in the PivotTable.

② Press F11.

Excel creates a new chart sheet and displays the PivotChart and the PivotChart Filter Pane.

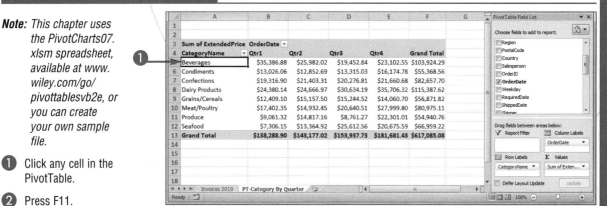

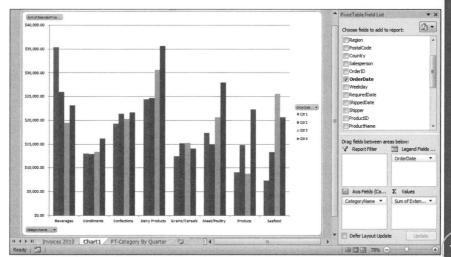

Create a PivotChart beside a PivotTable

Y ou can create a PivotChart on the same worksheet as its associated PivotTable. This enables you to easily compare the PivotTable and the PivotChart.

When you create a PivotChart directly from an existing PivotTable by pressing F11, as described in the section "Create a PivotChart from a PivotTable," Excel places the chart on a new chart sheet. This is usually the best solution because it gives you the most room to view and manipulate the PivotChart. However, it is often useful to view the PivotChart together with its associated PivotTable. For example, when you change the PivotTable view, Excel

automatically changes the PivotChart view in the same way. Rather than switching from one sheet to another to compare the results, having the PivotChart on the same worksheet enables you to compare the PivotChart and PivotTable immediately.

This section shows you how to create a new PivotChart on the same worksheet as an existing PivotTable. This is called *embedding* the PivotChart on the worksheet. If you already have a PivotChart, you can move it to the PivotTable's worksheet; see the section "Move a PivotChart to Another Sheet."

Create a PivotChart beside a PivotTable

① Click any cell in the PivotTable.

② Click Options→ PivotChart.

The Insert Chart dialog box appears.

③ Click the chart type you want.

Note: *You cannot use the XY (Scatter), Bubble, or Stock chart type with a PivotChart.*

④ Click the chart subtype you want.

⑤ Click OK.

● Excel embeds the PivotChart on the PivotTable's worksheet.

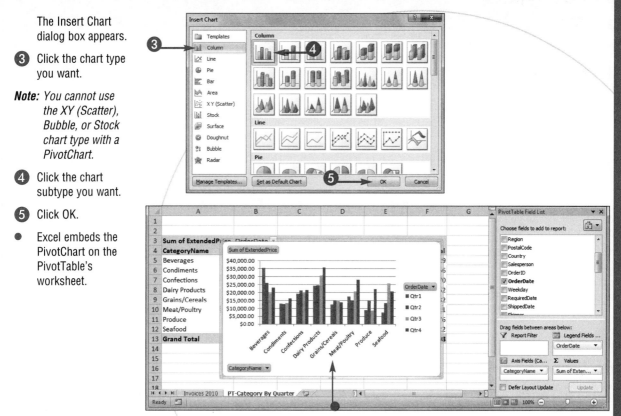

Excel embeds the PivotChart in the center of the visible worksheet area. In most cases, this means the new PivotChart overlaps your existing PivotTable, which makes it more difficult to compare them. To fix this problem, you can move or resize the PivotChart. To move the PivotChart, move the mouse pointer over an empty part of the chart area, and then click and drag the chart object to the new position. To resize the PivotChart, first click the chart to select it. Then move the mouse pointer over any one of the selection handles that appear on the chart area's corners and sides. Click and drag a handle to the size you require.

In the section "Create a PivotChart from a PivotTable" earlier in this chapter, you saw a macro that created a new PivotChart from a PivotTable. You can modify that macro to embed the PivotChart on the PivotTable's worksheet by using the Shapes object's AddChart method. In the previous macro, you need to replace the Charts.Add statement with the following statement:

Example:
```
ActiveSheet.Shapes.AddChart.Select
```

Create a PivotChart from an Excel Table

If the data you want to summarize and visualize exists as an Excel table, you can build a PivotChart directly from that data. Note, however, that Excel does not allow you to create just a PivotChart on its own. Instead, it enables you to create a PivotTable and an embedded PivotChart at the same time. If you know how to analyze your data using both a PivotTable and a PivotChart, then this method will save you time because it does not require any extra steps to embed the PivotChart along with the PivotTable.

The steps you follow to create a PivotChart from an Excel table are nearly identical to those you follow to create a

PivotTable by itself using a range as the data source, as described in Chapter 2. When you run the Insert PivotChart command, Excel prompts you to select the table you want to use as the data source, and it asks you to specify the location of the new PivotTable and PivotChart — on a new worksheet or an existing worksheet. You then use the PivotTable Field List to define the row and column fields, the data fields, and the filter field, if you need one.

Note, too, that this method also works if your data exists as an Excel range instead of a table.

Create a PivotChart from an Excel Table

① Click a cell within the table or range that you want to use as the source data.

② Click Insert→PivotTable→ PivotChart.

The Create PivotTable with PivotChart dialog box appears.

③ Select the New Worksheet option.

● If you want to place the PivotTable in an existing location, select Existing Worksheet and then use the Location range box to select the worksheet and cell where you want the PivotTable to appear.

④ Click OK.

- Excel creates a blank PivotTable.

- Excel creates a blank PivotChart.

- Excel displays the PivotTable Field List.

5 Select the check box of the field you want to add to the PivotChart's Axis Fields (Categories) area.

6 Select the check box of the field you want to add to the PivotChart's Values area.

- Excel creates the PivotChart.

- You can click and drag the PivotChart to a new location to see the complete chart.

7 If desired, click and drag fields and drop them in the Legend Field (Series) area and the Report Filter area.

Each time you drop a field in an area, Excel updates the PivotChart to include the new data.

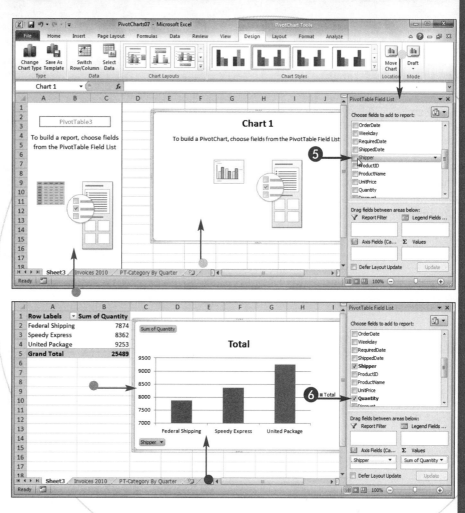

Extra

If your PivotChart includes just a category field, then Excel displays the results using a standard bar chart. If the PivotChart includes both a category field and a series field, then Excel displays the results using a clustered column chart. To learn how to view the PivotChart using a different type of chart, see the section "Change the PivotChart Type" later in this chapter.

The clustered column chart is a great way to visualize two-dimensional PivotTable results, but it is not always easy to decipher the chart. This is particularly true if you have a large number of data series, which usually means that most of the columns in each category are quite small. To get a better understanding of the chart, you might want to know what data is represented by specific columns.

You can find the specifics related to each column by moving the mouse pointer over the column in the plot area. Excel then displays a banner with data in the following format:

```
Series "SeriesItem" Point "CategoryItem" Value: Value
```

Here, SeriesItem is an item from the series field, CategoryItem is an item from the category field, and Value is the value of the data point. For example, if the Shipper field has an item named United Package, the Salesperson field has an item named Steven Buchanan, and the value is 488, the banner shows the following:

```
Series "United Package" Point "Steven Buchanan" Value: 488
```

Move a PivotChart to another Sheet

I f you have an existing PivotChart that resides in a separate chart sheet, you can move the PivotChart to a worksheet. This reduces the number of sheets in the workbook and, if you move the chart to the PivotTable's worksheet, it makes it easier to compare the PivotChart with its associated PivotTable.

In the section "Create a PivotChart from a PivotTable" earlier in this chapter, you learned how to create a new PivotChart on a separate chart sheet. However, there may be situations where this separate chart sheet is not convenient. For example, if you want to compare the

PivotChart and its associated PivotTable, that comparison is more difficult if the PivotChart and PivotTable reside in separate sheets. Similarly, you may prefer to place all your PivotCharts on a single sheet so that you can compare them or so that they are easy to find. Finally, if you plan on creating a number of PivotCharts, you might not want to clutter your workbook with separate chart sheets.

The solution in all these cases is to move your PivotChart or PivotCharts to the worksheet you prefer. This section shows you how to move a PivotChart to a new location.

Move a PivotChart to another Sheet

① Click the PivotChart you want to move.

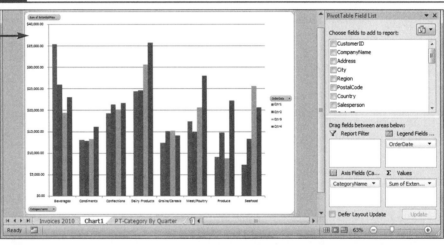

② Click Design→Move Chart.

You can also right-click the chart area or plot area and then click Move Chart.

The Move Chart dialog box appears.

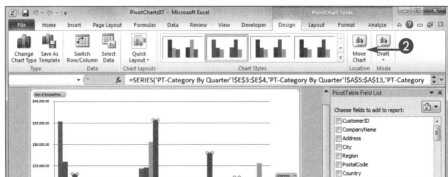

③ Select Object in.

④ Click ▾ and then click the sheet where you want the PivotChart moved.

⑤ Click OK.

● Excel moves the PivotChart to the location you specified.

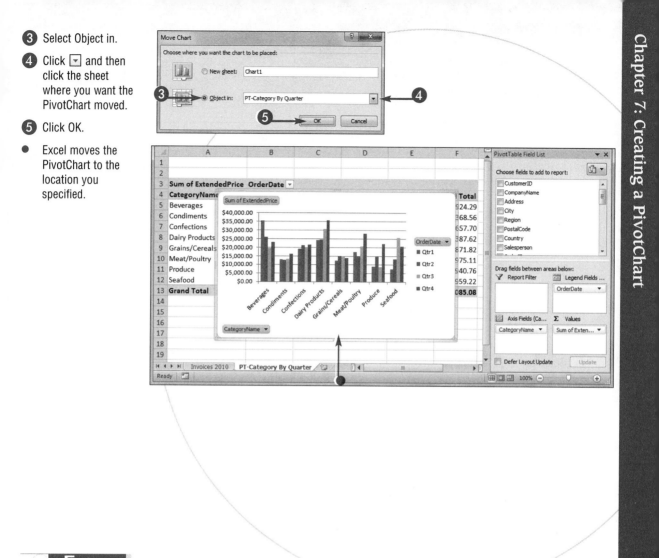

Extra

The steps you learned in this section apply both to PivotCharts embedded in separate chart sheets and to PivotChart objects floating on worksheets. For the latter, however, there is a second technique you can use. First, click the PivotChart object to select it. Then click Home→Cut to remove the PivotChart and store it in the Windows Clipboard. Display the sheet where you want the PivotChart moved. If you are moving the PivotChart to a worksheet, click the cell where you want the upper-left corner of the chart to appear. Click Home→Paste. Excel pastes the PivotChart object to the sheet. Move and resize the PivotChart object as needed.

Filter a PivotChart

B y default, each PivotChart report displays a summary for all the records in your source data. This is usually what you want to see. However, there may be situations where you need to focus more closely on some aspect of the data. You can focus on a specific item from one of the source data fields by taking advantage of the PivotChart's report filter.

For example, suppose you are dealing with a PivotChart that summarizes data from thousands of customer invoices over some period of time. A basic PivotChart might tell you the total units sold for each product category. However, what if you want to see the units sold for each product in a specific country? If the Product field is in the PivotChart's Axis Fields (Categories) area, then you could add the Country field to the Legend Fields

(Series) area. However, there may be dozens of countries, so that is not an efficient solution. Instead, you could add the Country field to the Report Filter area. You can then tell Excel to display the total sold for each product for the specific country in which you are interested.

As another example, suppose you ran a marketing campaign in the previous quarter and you set up an incentive plan for your salespeople whereby they could earn bonuses for selling at least a specified number of units. Suppose, as well, that you have a PivotChart showing the sum of the units sold for each product. To see the numbers for a particular employee, you could add the Salesperson field to the Report Filter area, and then select the employee you want to work with.

Display Selected Items

1 Click the PivotChart's Report Filter button.

Excel displays a list of the report filter field items.

2 Click the item you want to view.

● If you want to display data for two or more items, click Select Multiple Items and then repeat step **2** to select the other items.

3 Click OK.

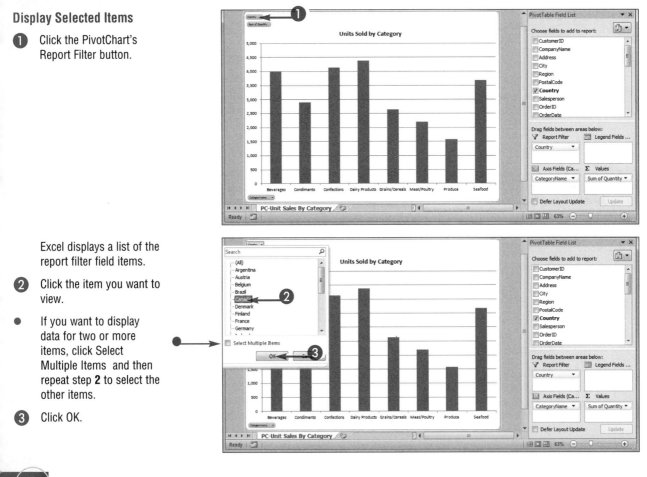

- Excel filters the PivotChart to show only the data for the item (or items) you selected.

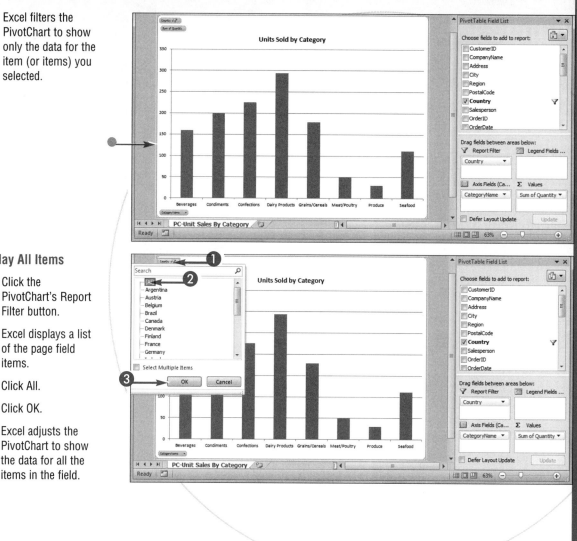

Display All Items

① Click the PivotChart's Report Filter button.

Excel displays a list of the page field items.

② Click All.

③ Click OK.

Excel adjusts the PivotChart to show the data for all the items in the field.

Extra

You can also filter the items in the Axis Fields (Categories) area. For example, in a PivotChart that includes items from the ProductName field in the row area, you might only want to see those products with names that begin with the letter G or that contain the word *tofu*. You can do that by applying a filter to a category field. Excel offers a number of text filters, including Equals, Does Not Equal, Begins With, Ends With, Contains, Greater Than, and Less Than. If the field uses dates, you can apply a date filter such as Before, Yesterday, Last Month, and This Year.

In the PivotChart, click the button for the field you want to work with, and then click either Label Filters or Date Filters. In the list that appears, select the filter type you want to apply, such as Begins With. Then type your filter criteria and click OK.

Change the PivotChart Type

You can modify your PivotChart to use a chart type that is more suitable for displaying the report data.

When you create a PivotChart, Excel uses a clustered column chart by default. If you do not include a series field in the PivotChart, Excel displays the report using regular columns, which is useful for comparing the values across the category field's items. If you include a series field in the PivotChart, Excel displays the report using clustered columns, where each category shows several different-colored columns grouped beside one another, one for each item in the series field. This is useful for comparing the series values for each item in the category.

Although this default chart type is fine for many applications, it is not always the best choice. For example, if you do not have a series field and you want to see the relative contribution of each category item to the total, a pie chart would be a better choice. If you are more interested in showing how the results trend over time, then a line chart is usually the ideal type.

Whatever your needs, Excel enables you to change the default PivotChart type to any of the following types: Column, Bar, Line, Pie, Area, Doughnut, Radar, Surface, Cylinder, Cone, or Pyramid. Remember that Excel does not allow you to use the following chart types with a PivotChart: XY (Scatter), Bubble, or Stock.

Change the PivotChart Type

1 Click the PivotChart.

2 Click Design→Change Chart Type.

The Change Chart Type dialog box appears.

3 Click the chart type you want to use.

Excel displays the available chart subtypes.

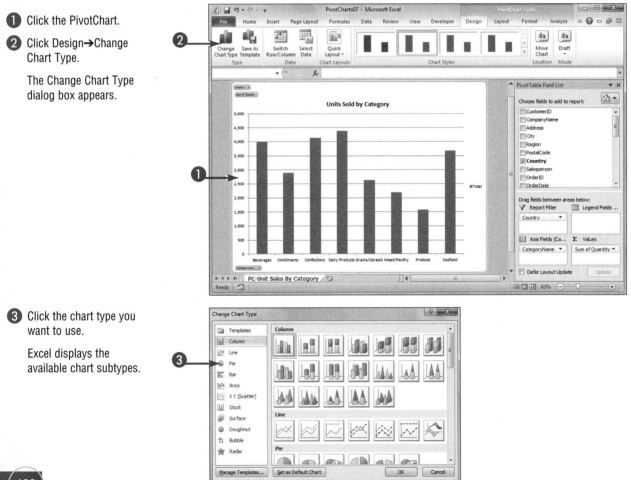

④ Click the Chart subtype you want to use.

⑤ Click OK.

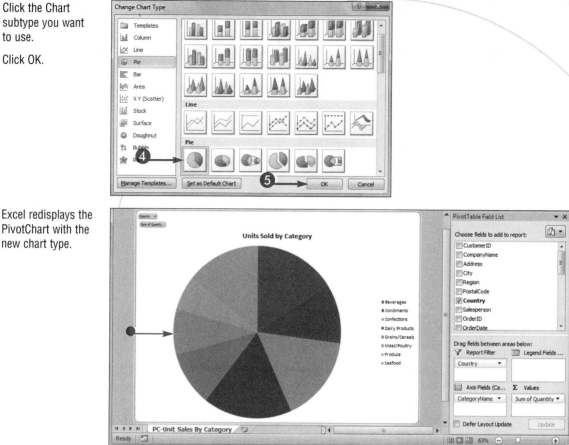

● Excel redisplays the PivotChart with the new chart type.

Extra

Depending on the chart type you choose, it is often useful to augment the chart with the actual values from the report. For example, with a pie chart, you can add to each slice the value as well as the percentage the value represents of the grand total. In most cases, you can also add the series name and the category name.

To add these data labels to your PivotChart, click the chart and then click Layout→Data Labels. In the menu that appears, select the data label position you want to use: Center, Inside End, Inside Base, Outside End, or Best Fit (available only with certain chart types). You can also click More Data Label Options to open the Format Data Labels dialog box and then activate the Value check box. Depending on the data, you may also be able to activate the Series name, Category name, and Percentage check boxes.

If there is a particular chart type that you would prefer to use for all your future PivotCharts, you can set that chart type as the default. Follow steps 1 to 4 in this section to open the Change Chart Type dialog box and choose your chart type and subtype. Then click the Set as Default Chart button. Click OK or Cancel to close the Change Chart Type dialog box.

Sort the PivotChart

You can customize the PivotChart to display the data series and the categories in a different order.

When you create a PivotChart and include a series field, Excel displays the data series based on the order of the field's items as they appear in the PivotTable. That is, as you move left to right through the items in the PivotTable's column field, the data series moves left to right in the PivotChart's series field (or top to bottom if you're looking at the PivotChart legend). This default series order is fine in most applications, but you may prefer to change the order. In the default clustered column chart, for example, you may prefer to reverse the data series so that they appear from right to left.

Similarly, the PivotChart categories appear in the same order as they appear in the underlying PivotTable's row field. In this case, you may prefer to display the categories in some custom order. For example, you may want to rearrange employee names so that those who have the same supervisor or who work in the same division appear together.

In this section, you learn how to sort the data series items and categories, but Excel also gives you the option of rearranging the series items and categories manually. See the tip on the next page for information on sorting data series items and categories by hand.

Sort the PivotChart

Sort the Data Series Items

1 Click the PivotChart.

2 Click the PivotChart's Legend Fields (Series) button.

Excel displays a list of sort options for the field.

Note: The sort options you see vary depending on the field's data type. The options you see here are for a date field.

3 Click the sort order you want to use.

● Excel redisplays the PivotChart using the new series order.

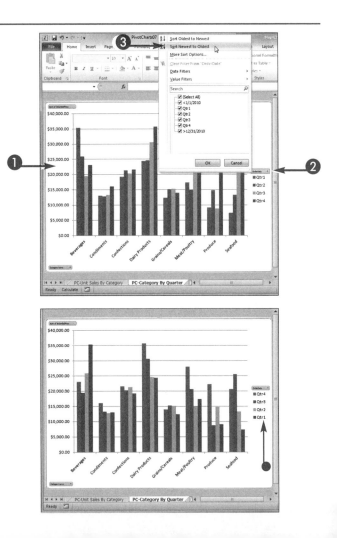

124

Sort the Categories

1 Click the PivotChart.

2 Under Axis Fields (Categories), click ⊡ for the field you want to sort.

Excel displays a list of sort options for the field.

Note: *The sort options you see vary depending on the field's data type. The options you see here are for a text field.*

3 Click the sort order you want to use.

● Excel redisplays the PivotChart using the new field order.

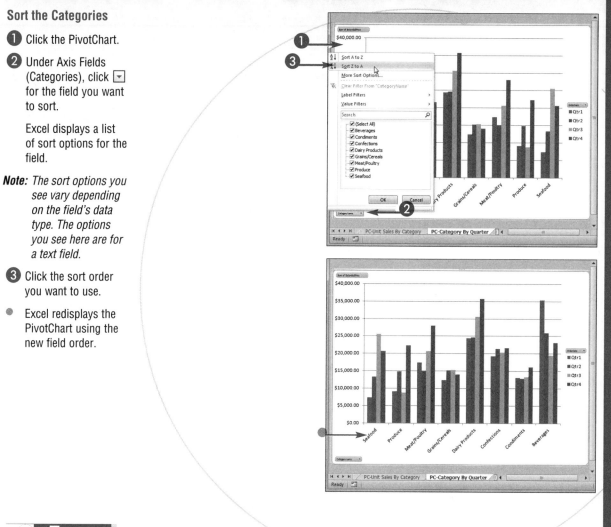

Extra

Besides the standard ascending or descending sort orders shown in this section, Excel also enables you to sort the data series items or categories by hand. Unfortunately, Excel does not offer a method for manually sorting series items or categories directly on the PivotChart. Instead, you must manually sort the data on the PivotTable itself. When you do this, Excel automatically applies the new sort order to the PivotChart.

To manually sort the data series items, display the PivotChart's underlying PivotTable, and select the label of the column field item you want to move (such as Qtr1 or Qtr2 in the example shown in this section). Move the mouse pointer to the bottom edge of the label cell (the pointer changes into a four-headed arrow), and then click and drag the label left or right to the new position.

To manually sort the categories, display the PivotChart's underlying PivotTable, and select the label of the row field item you want to move (such as Beverages or Condiments in the example shown in this section). Move the mouse pointer to the bottom edge of the label cell (the pointer changes into a four-headed arrow), and then click and drag the label up or down to the new position.

When you return to the PivotChart, you see that the data series items or categories now appear in the new sort order.

Add PivotChart Titles

Y ou can add one or more titles to your PivotChart to make the report easier to understand.

By default, Excel does not add any titles to your PivotChart. This is not a concern for most PivotCharts because the field names and item labels often provide enough context to understand the report. However, the data you use may have cryptic field names or it may have coded item names, so the default PivotChart may be difficult to decipher. In that case, you can add titles to the PivotChart that make the report more comprehensible.

Excel offers three PivotChart titles: an overall chart title that sits either above the chart's plot area or is overlaid on the plot area; a category (X) axis title that sits below the category items; and a value (Y) axis title that sits to

the left of the value axis labels. You can add one or more of these titles to your PivotChart. And although Excel does not allow you to move these titles to a different location, you can adjust the font, border, background, and text alignment.

The downside to adding PivotChart titles is that most of them take up some space within the chart area, which means there is less space to display the PivotChart itself. (The exception is an overall chart title overlaid on the plot area.) This is not usually a problem with a simple PivotChart, but if you have a complex chart — particularly if you have a large number of category items — then you may prefer not to display titles at all, or you may prefer to display only one or two.

Add PivotChart Titles

Add the Overall Chart Title

1. Click the PivotChart.

2. Click Layout→Chart Title.

3. Click the type of chart title you want to add.

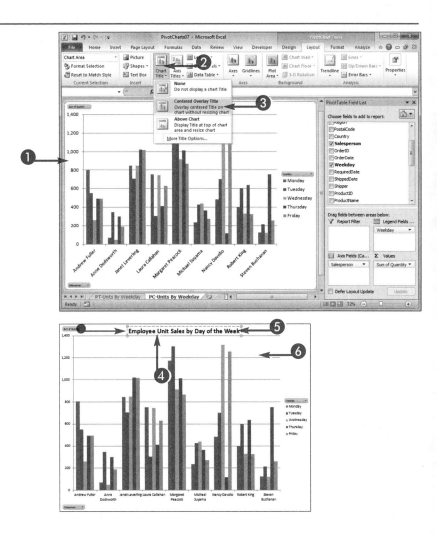

● Excel adds the title to the PivotChart.

4. Click inside the chart title.

5. Type the title you want to use.

6. Click outside the chart title.

   Excel removes the selection handles from the title.

Add Axis Titles

1 Click the PivotChart.

2 Click Layout→Axis Titles.

3 Click the axis to which you want to add the title.

4 Click the type of axis title you want to add.

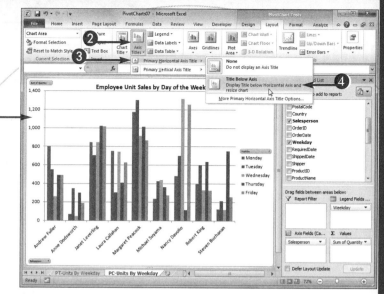

● Excel adds the title to the PivotChart axis.

5 Click inside the axis title.

6 Type the title you want to use.

7 Click outside the axis title.

Excel removes the selection handles from the title.

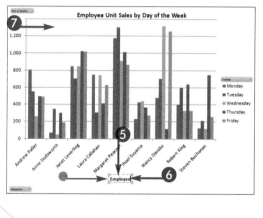

Extra

To format the chart title, right-click the title and then click Format Chart Title. To format an axis title, right-click the title and then click Format Axis Title. You can also click the title and then click Layout→Format Selection. In the dialog box that appears, use the Fill tab to apply a background color or fill effect; use the Border Color and Border Styles tabs to format the title border; use the Shadow tab to apply a shadow effect to the title; use the 3-D Format tab to add a 3-D effect to the title; and use the Alignment tab to configure the alignment and orientation of the text within the title. Click Close when you are done. Note, too, that you can also format a title by clicking it and then clicking the buttons in Excel's Home tab.

To edit a title, right-click the title and then click Edit Text. Excel gives you three methods for removing a title from a PivotChart:

● Follow the steps in this section, and in the menu of title options, click None.

● Right-click the title you want to remove and then click Delete.

● Click the title you want to remove and then press Delete.

Move the PivotChart Legend

You can change the placement of the PivotChart legend to give the chart more room or to better display the data series within the legend.

The PivotChart legend displays the series field items along with a colored box that tells you which series belongs to which item. By default, Excel displays the legend to the right of the plot area. This is usually the best position because it does not interfere with other chart elements such as titles — see the previous section, "Add PivotChart Titles" — or the value (Y) axis labels.

However, displaying the legend on the right does mean that it takes up space that would otherwise be used by

your PivotChart. If you have a number of category items in your PivotChart report, you may prefer to display the legend above or below the plot area to give the PivotChart more horizontal room.

Excel enables you to move the legend to one of five positions with respect to the plot area: right, left, bottom, top, and upper-right corner. Excel also gives you the option of having the legend overlapping the chart, which means that Excel does not resize the plot area to accommodate the legend. This is useful if you have some white space on the chart (for example, at the top) where you can place the legend so that it does not hide any chart data.

Move the PivotChart Legend

① Click the PivotChart.

② Click Layout→Legend.

● You can select a predefined legend position here.

③ Click More Legend Options.

The Format Legend dialog box appears.

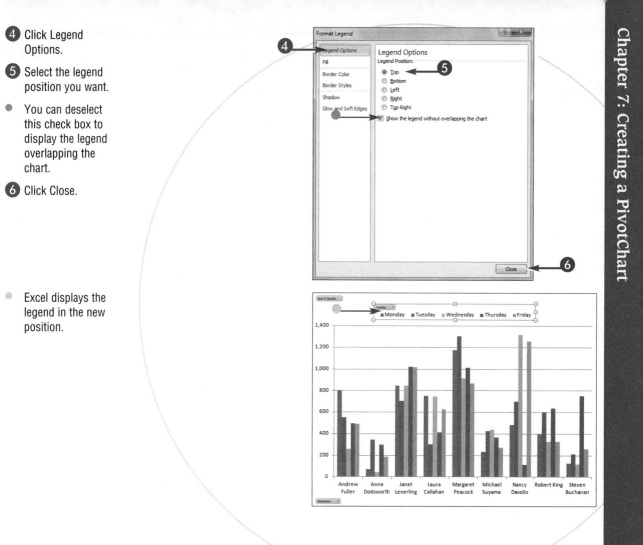

4 Click Legend Options.

5 Select the legend position you want.

● You can deselect this check box to display the legend overlapping the chart.

6 Click Close.

● Excel displays the legend in the new position.

Extra

In some cases, you might prefer to not display the legend at all. For example, if your PivotChart does not have a series field, Excel still displays a legend for the default "series" named Total. This is not particularly useful, so you can gain some extra chart space by hiding the legend. To do this, follow steps 1 and 2 to display the Legend menu, and then click None. Alternatively, right-click the legend and then click Delete.

To format the legend, right-click the legend and then click Format Legend; you can also click the legend and then click Layout→Format Selection. In the Format Legend dialog box, use the Fill tab to apply a background color or fill effect; use the Border Color and Border Styles tabs to format the legend border; and use the Shadow tab to apply a shadow effect to the legend. You can also format a legend by clicking it and then clicking the buttons in Excel's Home tab.

You can also format individual legend entries. Click the legend to select it, and then click the legend entry you want to work with. Right-click the entry, click Format Legend Entry, and then, in the dialog box that appears, use the tabs to apply the formatting you want. You can also use Excel's Home tab to format the entry.

Display a Data Table
with the PivotChart

To augment your PivotChart and make the chart report easier to understand and analyze, you can display a data table that provides the values underlying each category and data series.

The point of a PivotChart is to combine the visualization effects of an Excel chart with the pivoting and filtering capabilities of a PivotTable. The visualization part helps your data analysis because it enables you to make at-a-glance comparisons between series and categories, and it enables you to view data points relative to other parts of the report.

However, while visualizing the data is often useful, it lacks a certain precision because you do not see the underlying data. Excel offers several ways to overcome

this, including creating the PivotChart on the same worksheet as the PivotTable (see the section "Create a PivotChart Beside a PivotTable"); moving a chart to the PivotTable worksheet (see the section "Move a PivotChart to Another Sheet"); and displaying data labels (see the first tip in the section "Change the PivotChart Type"), all earlier in this chapter.

Yet another method is to display a data table along with the PivotChart. A *PivotChart data table* is a table that displays the chart's categories as columns and its data series as rows, with the cells filled with the actual data values. Because these values appear directly below the chart, the data table gives you an easy way to combine a visual report with the specifics of the underlying data.

Display a Data Table with the PivotChart

1. Click the PivotChart.

2. Click Layout→Data Table.

● You can select a predefined data table here.

3. Click More Data Table Options.

   The Format Data Table dialog box appears.

④ Click Data Table Options.

● You can use the Table Borders check boxes to control which data table borders Excel displays.

● You can deselect this check box if you do not want to see the colored boxes that identify each data series.

⑤ Click Close.

● Excel displays the data table below the PivotChart.

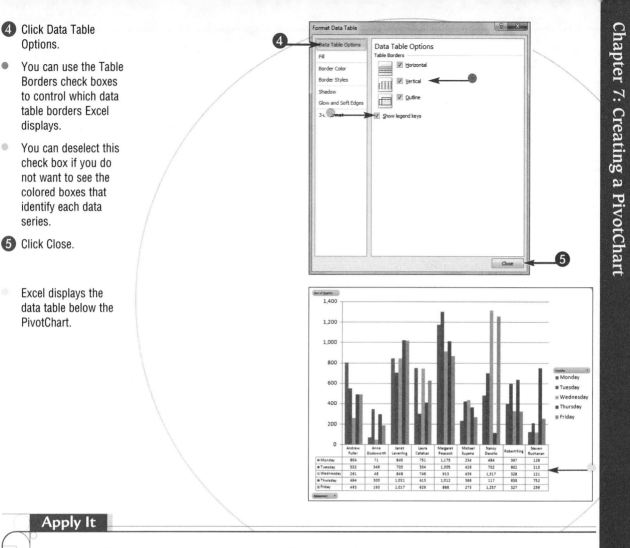

Apply It

You can use a VBA macro to control the display of a PivotChart's data table. You do this by setting the Chart object's HasDataTable property to True with the data table displayed, or False with the data table hidden. The following macro toggles the data table on and off for the active PivotChart (see Chapter 16 for basics on using VBA with PivotTables):

Example:
```
Sub TogglePivotChartDataTable()
    '
    ' Work with the active chart
    With ActiveChart
        '
        ' Toggle the HasDataTable property
        .HasDataTable = Not .HasDataTable
        '
        ' Display the current state
        MsgBox "The PivotChart's data table is " & _
            IIf(.HasDataTable, "visible.", "hidden.")
    End With
End Sub
```

Apply a PivotTable Quick Style

I n Chapter 6, you learned how to apply formatting options such as alignments and fonts to portions of a PivotTable. This works well, particularly if you have custom formatting needs. For example, you may have in-house style guidelines that you need to follow. Unfortunately, applying formatting can be time consuming, particularly if you are applying a number of different formatting options. And the total formatting time can become onerous if you need to apply different formatting options to different parts of the PivotTable. You can greatly reduce the time you spend formatting your PivotTables if you apply a Quick Style instead.

A Quick Style is a collection of formatting options — fonts, borders, and background colors — that Excel defines for different areas of a PivotTable. For example,

a Quick Style might use bold, white text on a black background for labels and grand totals, and white text on a dark blue background for items and data. Defining all these formats by hand might take half an hour to an hour. But with the Quick Style feature, you choose the one you want to use for the PivotTable as a whole, and Excel applies the individual formatting options automatically.

Excel defines more than 80 Quick Styles, divided into three categories: Light, Medium, and Dark. The Light category includes Pivot Style Light 16, the default formatting applied to PivotTable reports you create; and None, which removes all formatting from the PivotTable. You can also create your own Quick Style formats, as described in the next section, "Create a Custom PivotTable Quick Style."

Apply a PivotTable Quick Style

Note: *This chapter uses the PivotTables08.xlsm spreadsheet, available at www.wiley.com/go/pivottablesvb2e, or you can create your own sample file.*

1 Click any cell within the PivotTable you want to format.

2 Click the Design tab.

3 In the PivotTable Styles group, click the More button ().

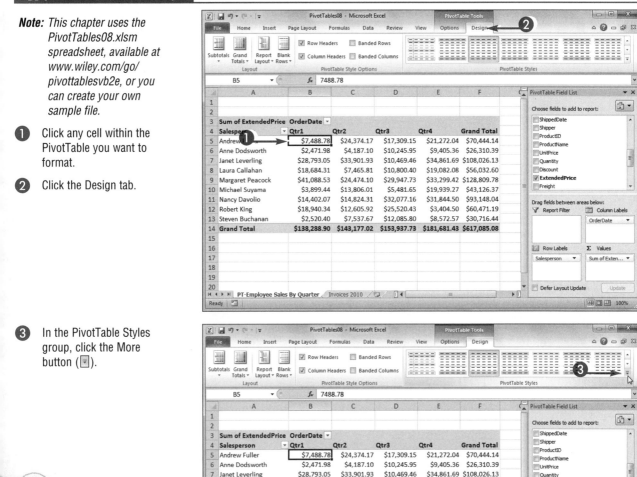

The Quick Style gallery appears.

④ Click the Quick Style you want to apply.

Excel applies the Quick Style.

Apply It

In VBA, each `PivotTable` object has a `TableStyle2` property that you can set to a string value that corresponds to the Quick Style you want to apply. The strings are PivotStyleLight1 to PivotStyleLight28, PivotStyleMedium1 to PivotStyleMedium28, and PivotStyleDark1 to PivotStyleDark28. Here is a macro that applies a random Quick Style (see Chapter 16 for basics on using VBA with PivotTables):

Example:

```
Sub ApplyRandomQuickStyle()
    Dim strStyleCategory As String
    Dim nStyleNumber As Integer, n As Integer
    '
    ' Generate a random number between 1 and 3 to choose the category
    Randomize
    n = Int(Rnd * 3) + 1
    strStyleCategory = Choose(n, "Light", "Medium", "Dark")
    '
    ' Generate a random number between 1 and 28 for the style number
    nStyleNumber = Int(Rnd * 28) + 1
    '
    ' Work with the first PivotTable on the active worksheet
    With ActiveSheet.PivotTables(1)
        '
        ' Apply the Quick Style
        .TableStyle2 = "PivotStyle" & strStyleCategory & nStyleNumber
    End With
End Sub
```

Create a Custom PivotTable Quick Style

You may find that none of the predefined PivotTable Quick Styles gives you the exact look that you want. In that case, you can define that look yourself by creating a custom PivotTable Quick Style from scratch.

Excel offers you tremendous flexibility when you create custom PivotTable Quick Styles. There are 25 separate PivotTable elements that you can format. These elements include the entire table, the page field labels and values, the first column, the header row, the Grand Total row, and the Grand Total column. You can also define *stripes*, which are separate formats applied to alternating rows or columns. For example, the First Row Stripe applies formatting to rows 1, 3, 5, and so on; while the Second Row Stripe applies formatting to rows 2, 4, 6, and so on.

Stripes can make a long or wide report easier to read.

Having control over so many elements enables you to create a custom Quick Style to suit your needs. For example, you might need your PivotTable to match your corporate colors. Similarly, if the PivotTable will appear as part of a larger report, you might need the PivotTable formatting to match the theme used in the larger report.

The only downside to creating a custom PivotTable Quick Style is that you must do so from scratch. Excel does not enable you to customize an existing Quick Style. So if you need to define formatting for all 25 PivotTable elements, creating a custom Quick Style can be time consuming.

Create a Custom PivotTable Quick Style

1 Click the Design tab.

2 In the PivotTable Styles group, click ⬇ (not shown).

The Quick Style gallery appears.

3 Click New PivotTable Style.

The New PivotTable Quick Style dialog box appears.

4 Type a name for your custom Quick Style.

5 Click the table element you want to format.

6 Click Format.

The Format Cells dialog box appears.

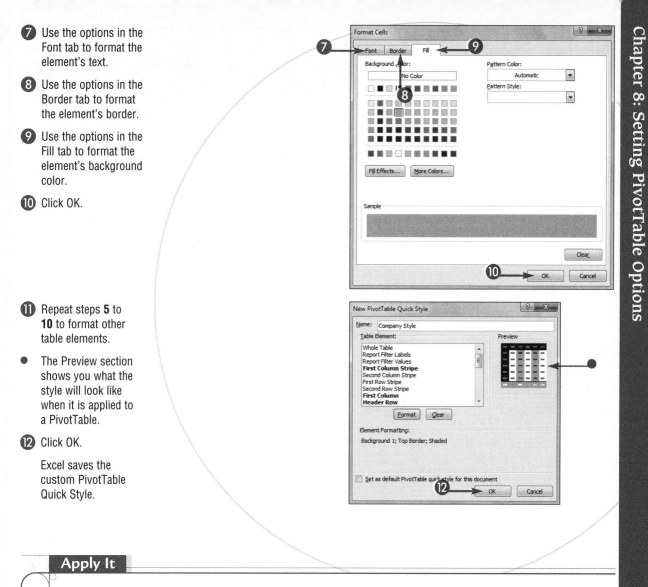

7 Use the options in the Font tab to format the element's text.

8 Use the options in the Border tab to format the element's border.

9 Use the options in the Fill tab to format the element's background color.

10 Click OK.

11 Repeat steps **5** to **10** to format other table elements.

● The Preview section shows you what the style will look like when it is applied to a PivotTable.

12 Click OK.

Excel saves the custom PivotTable Quick Style.

Apply It

After you close the New PivotTable Quick Style dialog box, Excel does not apply the new style to the current PivotTable. To apply the style, select any cell within the PivotTable, click Design, click ▼ in the PivotTable Styles group to open the Quick Style gallery, and then click your style in the Custom section.

If you need to make changes to your custom Quick Style, open the Quick Style gallery, right-click your custom style, and then click Modify. Use the Modify PivotTable Quick Style dialog box to make your changes, and then click OK.

If you find that you need to create another custom Quick Style that is similar to an existing custom style, you do not need to create the new style from scratch. Instead, open the Quick Style gallery, right-click the existing custom style, and then click Duplicate. In the Modify PivotTable Quick Style dialog box, adjust the style name and formatting, and then click OK.

If you no longer need a custom Quick Style, you should delete it to reduce clutter in the Quick Style gallery. Open the gallery, right-click the custom style you no longer need, and then click Delete. When Excel asks you to confirm, click OK.

Preserve PivotTable Formatting

You may find that Excel does not preserve your custom formatting when you refresh or rebuild the PivotTable. For example, if you applied a bold font to some labels, that text may revert to regular text after a refresh. Excel has a feature called Preserve Formatting that enables you to preserve such formatting during a refresh; you can retain your custom formatting by activating it.

The Preserve Formatting feature is always activated in default PivotTables. However, it is possible that another user could have deactivated this feature. For example, you may be working with a PivotTable created by another person and he or she may have deactivated the Preserve Formatting feature.

Note, however, that when you refresh or rebuild a PivotTable, Excel reapplies the report's current Quick Style formatting. If you have not specified a Quick Style, Excel reapplies the default PivotTable Quick Style (named Pivot Style Light 16); if you have specified a Quick Style — as described in the earlier section "Apply a PivotTable Quick Style" — Excel reapplies that Quick Style.

Also, Excel always preserves your numeric formats and date formats. In Chapter 6, see the sections "Apply a Numeric Format to PivotTable Data" and "Apply a Date Format to PivotTable Data" for more.

Preserve PivotTable Formatting

① Click any cell within the PivotTable you want to work with.

② Click Options→ PivotTable→Options.

The PivotTable Options dialog box appears.

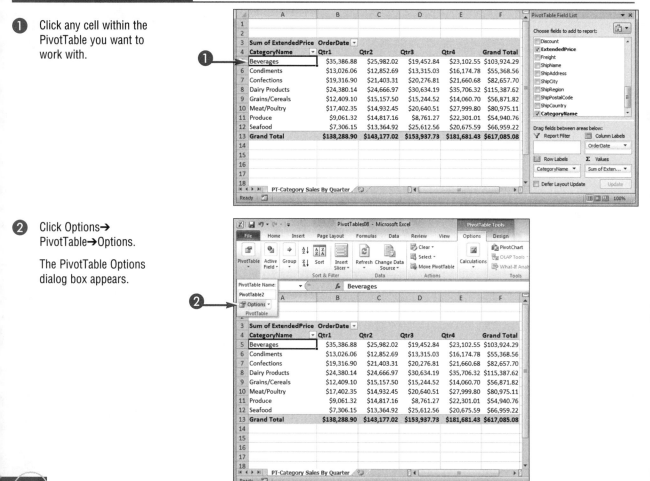

③ Click the Layout & Format tab.

④ Deselect Autofit Column Widths on Update.

Note: Deselecting this option prevents Excel from automatically formatting things such as column widths when you pivot fields.

⑤ Select Preserve Cell Formatting on Update.

⑥ Click OK.

Excel preserves your custom formatting each time you refresh the PivotTable.

Apply It

In VBA, you use the `PivotTable` object's `PreserveFormatting` property to turn the Preserve Formatting feature on (`True`) or off (`False`). Here is a VBA procedure that toggles the value of this property between `True` and `False` (see Chapter 16 for basics on using VBA with PivotTables):

Example:
```
Sub TogglePreserveFormatting()
    Dim objPT As PivotTable
    '
    ' Work with the first PivotTable on the active worksheet
    Set objPT = ActiveSheet.PivotTables(1)
    With objPT
        '
        ' Toggle the PreserveFormatting property
        .PreserveFormatting = Not .PreserveFormatting
        '
        ' Display the new setting
        MsgBox "The Preserve Formatting feature is now " & _
            IIf(.PreserveFormatting, "activated.", "deactivated.")
    End With
End Sub
```

Rename the PivotTable

When you create the first PivotTable in a workbook, Excel gives it the default name PivotTable1. Subsequent PivotTables are named sequentially: PivotTable2, PivotTable3, and so on. However, Excel also repeats these names when you build new PivotTables based on different data sources. If your workbook contains a number of PivotTables, you can make them easier to distinguish by giving each one a unique and descriptive name.

Why do you need to provide your PivotTables with descriptive names? The main benefit occurs if you use VBA to manipulate PivotTables. In most of the examples you have seen so far in this book, the PivotTable operations have been performed on the active PivotTable, usually referenced as follows:

```
ActiveSheet.PivotTables(1)
```

However, your work with PivotTables via VBA will be much more powerful if you can apply statements to *any* PivotTable. However, given a typical workbook may contain several PivotTables named, say, PivotTable1, you need to apply a unique name to each PivotTable.

Using unique names to reference PivotTable objects can also make your code easier to read. For example, to reference a PivotTable named "Budget Summary" that exists in a worksheet named "Sheet1," you use the following statement:

```
Worksheets("Sheet1").PivotTables("Budget
  Summary")
```

This makes it easy to know exactly which PivotTable your code is working with.

Rename the PivotTable

① Click any cell within the PivotTable you want to work with.

② Click Options→ PivotTable→Options.

● You can also rename the PivotTable directly using the PivotTable Name text box.

The PivotTable Options dialog box appears.

③ Type the new name for the PivotTable.

Note: *The maximum length for a PivotTable name is 255 characters.*

④ Click OK.

Excel renames the PivotTable.

Apply It

What happens if your workbook contains a large number of PivotTables? Rather than renaming each one by hand, you can use the following macro to rename each one automatically using the worksheet name:

Example:

```
Sub RenameAllPivotTables()
    Dim objWS As Worksheet
    Dim objPT As PivotTable
    Dim i As Integer
    '
    ' Run through all the worksheets
    For Each objWS In ThisWorkbook.Worksheets
        i = 1
        '
        ' Run through all the PivotTables
        For Each objPT In objWS.PivotTables
            '
            ' Rename it to the sheet name plus the value of i
            objPT.Name = objWS.Name & " " & i
            i = i + 1
        Next 'objPT
    Next 'objWS
End Sub
```

Turn Off Grand Totals

You can configure your PivotTable to not display the Grand Total row or the Grand Total column (or both). This is useful if you want to save space in the PivotTable or if the grand totals are not relevant in your data analysis.

A default PivotTable that has at least one row field contains an extra row at the bottom of the table. This row is labeled Grand Total and it includes the total of the values associated with the row field items. However, the value in the Grand Total row may not actually be a sum. For example, if the summary calculation is Average, then the Grand Total row includes the average of the values associated with the row field items. To learn how to use a different summary calculation, see Chapter 9.

Similarly, a PivotTable that has at least one column field contains an extra column at the far right of the table. This column is also labeled "Grand Total" and it includes the total of the values associated with the column field items. If the PivotTable contains both a row and a column field, the Grand Total row also has the sums for each column item, and the Grand Total column also has the sums for each row item.

Besides taking up space in the PivotTable, these grand totals are often not necessary for data analysis. For example, suppose you want to examine quarterly sales for your salespeople to see which amounts are over a certain value for bonus purposes. Because your only concern is the individual summary values for each employee, the grand totals are useless. In such a case, you can tell Excel not to display the grand totals.

Turn Off Grand Totals

① Click any cell within the PivotTable you want to work with.

② Click Options→ PivotTable→Options.

The PivotTable Options dialog box appears.

③ Click the Totals & Filters tab.

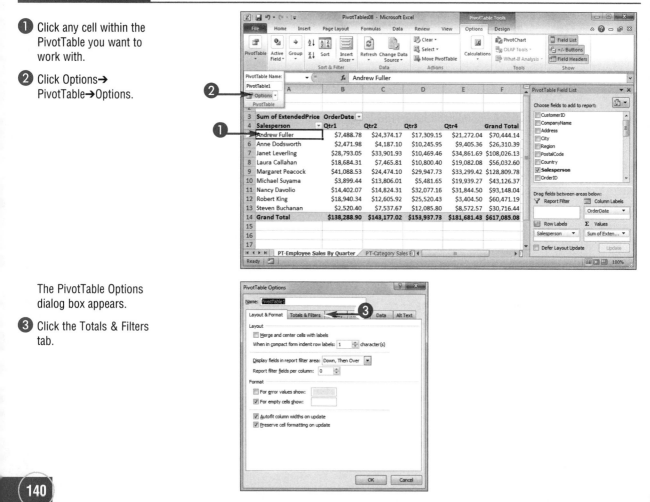

④ Deselect this option to turn off the row grand totals.

⑤ Deselect this option to turn off the column grand totals.

⑥ Click OK.

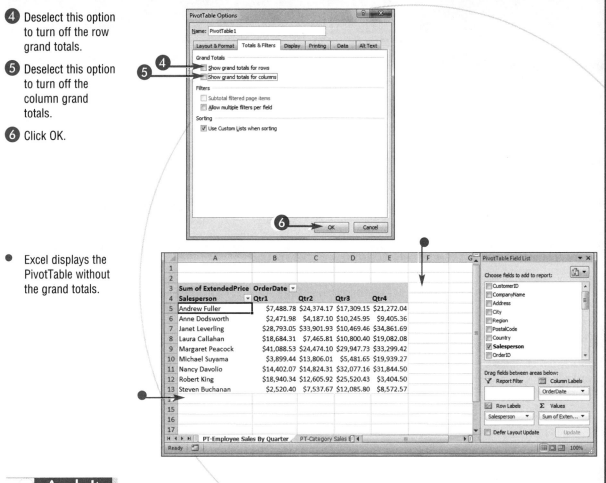

● Excel displays the PivotTable without the grand totals.

You can work with grand totals via VBA using the `PivotTable` object's `ColumnGrand` and `RowGrand` properties, which are Boolean values that hide (`False`) and display (`True`) the grand totals. The following macro toggles these properties on and off (see Chapter 16 for basics on using VBA with PivotTables):

Example:

```
Sub ToggleGrandTotals()
    Dim objPT As PivotTable
    '
    ' Work with the first PivotTable on the active worksheet
    Set objPT = ActiveSheet.PivotTables(1)
    With objPT
        '
        ' Toggle the ColumnGrand and RowGrand properties
        .ColumnGrand = Not .ColumnGrand
        .RowGrand = Not .RowGrand
        '
        ' Display the new setting
        MsgBox "The grand totals are now " & _
            IIf(.ColumnGrand, "displayed.", "hidden.")
    End With
End Sub
```

141

Merge Item Labels

I f you have a tabular PivotTable with multiple fields either in the row area or the column area, you can make the outer field easier to read by merging the cells associated with each of the field's item labels.

When you configure a PivotTable with two fields in the row area, Excel displays the outer field on the left and the inner field on the right. If you display the report using the tabular layout (see Chapter 4) for each item in the outer field, Excel displays the item label in the left column and the associated inner field items in the right column. If the inner field has two or more associated items, there will be one or more blank cells below the outer field item. This

makes the PivotTable report less attractive and harder to read because the outer field items appear just below the subtotals.

A similar problem occurs when you have multiple fields in the column area. In this case, you can end up with one or more blank cells to the right of each outer field item.

To fix these problems, you can activate a PivotTable option that tells Excel to merge the cells associated with each outer field item. Excel then displays the item label in the middle of these merged cells, which makes the PivotTable report more attractive and easier to read.

Merge Item Labels

1 Click any cell within the PivotTable you want to work with.

2 Click Options→ PivotTable→Options.

You can also right-click any PivotTable cell and then click Table Options.

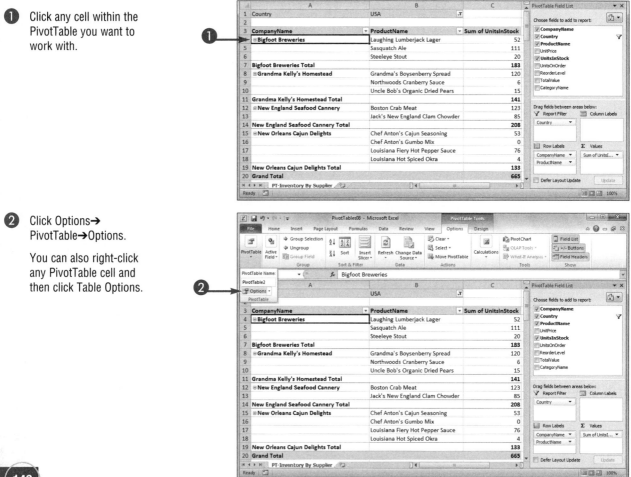

The PivotTable Options dialog box appears.

3 Click the Layout & Format tab.

4 Select Merge and Center Cells with Labels.

5 Click OK.

Excel merges the cells associated with each item in the outer row and outer column fields.

● Excel displays the item labels centered within the merged cells.

Apply It

In VBA, you use the `PivotTable` object's `MergeLabels` property to turn the Merge Labels feature on (`True`) or off (`False`). Here is a VBA procedure that toggles the value of this property between `True` and `False` (see Chapter 16 for basics on using VBA with PivotTables):

Example:
```
Sub ToggleMergeLabels()
    Dim objPT As PivotTable
    '
    ' Work with the first PivotTable on the active worksheet
    Set objPT = ActiveSheet.PivotTables(1)
    With objPT
        '
        ' Toggle the MergeLabels property
        .MergeLabels = Not .MergeLabels
        '
        ' Display the new setting
        MsgBox "The Merge Labels feature is now " & _
            IIf(.MergeLabels, "activated.", "deactivated.")
    End With
End Sub
```

Specify Characters for Errors and Empty Cells

You can improve the look of a PivotTable report by specifying alternative text to appear in place of error values and blank cells.

Excel has seven error values: #DIV/0!, #N/A, #NAME?, #NULL!, #NUM!, #REF!, and #VALUE!. These errors are almost always the result of improperly constructed formulas, and because a basic PivotTable has no formulas, you rarely see error values in PivotTable results. There are two exceptions, however. First, if the source data field you are using for the PivotTable summary calculation contains an error value, Excel reproduces that error value within the PivotTable results. Second, you can add a custom calculated field to the PivotTable, and that field's values will be based on a formula. For the details about calculated fields, see Chapter 10. If that formula generates an error, Excel displays the corresponding error value in the PivotTable results. For example, if your formula divides by 0, the #DIV/0! error appears. Seeing these errors is usually a good thing because it alerts you to problems in the data or the report. However, if the error is caused by something temporary, you may prefer to hide any errors by displaying a blank or some other text instead.

A related PivotTable concern is what to do with data area cells where the calculation results in a 0 value. By default, Excel displays nothing in the cell. This can make the report slightly easier to read, but it may also cause confusion for readers of the report. In an inventory PivotTable, for example, does an empty cell mean that the product has no stock or that it was not counted? To avoid this problem, you can specify that Excel display the number 0 or some other text instead of an empty cell.

Specify Characters for Errors and Empty Cells

1 Click any cell within the PivotTable you want to work with.

2 Click Options→ PivotTable→Options.

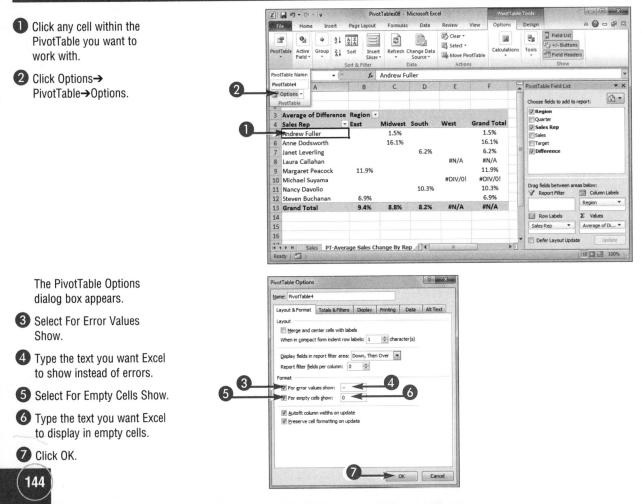

The PivotTable Options dialog box appears.

3 Select For Error Values Show.

4 Type the text you want Excel to show instead of errors.

5 Select For Empty Cells Show.

6 Type the text you want Excel to display in empty cells.

7 Click OK.

- Excel replaces the PivotTable's errors with the text you specified.

- Excel replaces the PivotTable's empty cells with the text you specified.

Apply It

In VBA you use the `PivotTable` object's `ErrorString` property to set the text to replace error values, and you use the `DisplayErrorString` property to turn this feature on and off. Also, you use the `PivotTable` object's `NullString` property to set the text to use in empty cells, and you use the `DisplayNullString` property to turn this feature on and off. Here is an example macro that uses these properties (see Chapter 16 for basics on using VBA with PivotTables):

Example:

```
Sub SetTextForErrorsAndEmptyCells()
    Dim objPT As PivotTable
    '
    ' Work with the first PivotTable on the active worksheet
    Set objPT = ActiveSheet.PivotTables(1)
    With objPT
        '
        ' Set ErrorString and activate it
        .ErrorString = "--"
        .DisplayErrorString = True
        '
        ' Set NullString and activate it
        .NullString = "0"
        .DisplayNullString = True
        '
        ' Display the new settings
        MsgBox "The ErrorString text is " & _
               "now """ & .ErrorString & """" & _
               vbCrLf & _
               "The NullString text is " & _
               "now """ & .NullString & """"
    End With
End Sub
```

Protect a PivotTable

If you have a PivotTable that you will share with other people, but you do not want those people to make any changes to the report, you can activate protection for the worksheet that contains the PivotTable. This prevents unauthorized users from changing the PivotTable results.

If you have put a lot of work into the layout and formatting of a PivotTable, you most likely want to avoid having any of your work undone if you allow other people to open the PivotTable workbook. The easiest way to do this is to enable Excel's worksheet protection feature. When this feature is activated for a worksheet that contains a PivotTable, no user can modify any cells in the PivotTable. If needed, you can also apply a password to the protection, so that only authorized users can make changes to the worksheet.

Excel's default protection options affect PivotTables in two ways:

- Unauthorized users cannot edit or format PivotTable cells. However, it is possible to configure the protection to allow editing of particular cells, such as the labels of a PivotTable report. See the tip on the next page to learn how to configure protection to allow this.

- Unauthorized users cannot add, remove, pivot, filter, or group the PivotTable. However, it is possible to configure the protection to allow users to perform these PivotTable actions.

Protect a PivotTable

1 Display the worksheet that contains the PivotTable you want to protect.

2 Click Home→Format→ Protect Sheet.

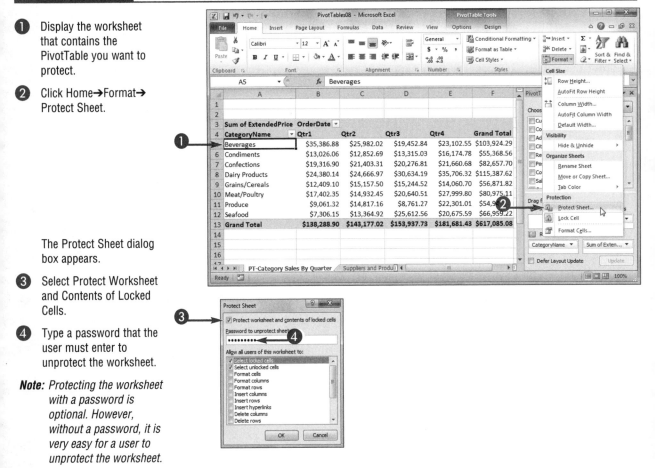

The Protect Sheet dialog box appears.

3 Select Protect Worksheet and Contents of Locked Cells.

4 Type a password that the user must enter to unprotect the worksheet.

Note: *Protecting the worksheet with a password is optional. However, without a password, it is very easy for a user to unprotect the worksheet.*

⑤ Select Use PivotTable Reports.

⑥ Click OK.

Protect Sheet

☑ Protect worksheet and contents of locked cells

Password to unprotect sheet:

••••••••

Allow all users of this worksheet to:

- Insert columns
- Insert rows
- Insert hyperlinks
- Delete columns
- Delete rows
- Sort
- Use AutoFilter
- ☑ Use PivotTable reports
- Edit objects
- Edit scenarios

⑤

⑥ → OK   Cancel

If you specified a password in step **4**, Excel asks you to confirm the password.

⑦ Retype the password.

⑧ Click OK.

Excel protects the worksheet.

Confirm Password

Reenter password to proceed.

•••••••••| ← ⑦

Caution: If you lose or forget the password, it cannot be recovered. It is advisable to keep a list of passwords and their corresponding workbook and sheet names in a safe place. (Remember that passwords are case-sensitive.)

⑧ OK   Cancel

Extra

When you want to make changes to a PivotTable on a protected worksheet, you must first unprotect the worksheet. Display the protected worksheet and then click Home➔Format➔Unprotect Sheet. If you protected the worksheet with a password, Excel displays a dialog box that asks you for the password. Type the password and then click OK. Excel unprotects the worksheet.

When you protect a worksheet, you may be willing to let users modify certain cells on the worksheet. In a PivotTable, for example, you may want to allow users to rename the PivotTable fields or items. You can set this up by unlocking those cells before you activate worksheet protection. Begin by unprotecting the worksheet if it is currently protected. Next, select the cells that you will allow users to edit. Click Home➔Format➔Lock Cell to deactivate this command, and then protect the worksheet.

Change the PivotTable Summary Calculation

If you add a numeric field to the data area, Excel uses Sum as the default summary calculation. If, instead, you use a text field in the data area, Excel uses Count as the default summary calculation. If your data analysis requires a different calculation, you can configure the data field to use any one of Excel's 11 built-in summary calculations:

- **Sum.** Adds the values in a numeric field
- **Count.** Displays the total number of cells in the source field
- **Average.** Calculates the mean value in a numeric field
- **Max.** Displays the largest value in a numeric field
- **Min.** Displays the smallest value in a numeric field

- **Product.** Multiplies the values in a numeric field
- **Count Numbers.** Displays the total number of numeric values in the source field
- **StdDev.** Calculates the standard deviation of a population sample, which tells you how much the values in the source field vary with respect to the average
- **StdDevp.** Calculates the standard deviation when the values in the data field represent the entire population
- **Var.** Calculates the variance of a population sample, which is the square of the standard deviation
- **Varp.** Calculates the variance when the values in the data field represent the entire population

Change the PivotTable Summary Calculation

Note: This chapter uses the PivotTables09.xlsm spreadsheet, available at www.wiley.com/go/pivottablesvb2e, or you can create your own sample file.

① Click any cell in the data field.

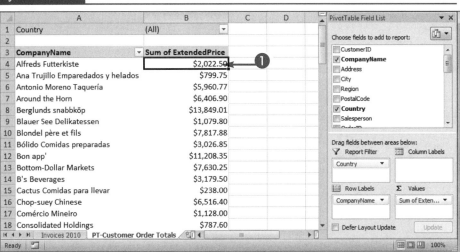

② Click Options→ Summarize Values By.

- If you see the calculation you want to use, click it and skip the rest of these steps.

③ Click More Options.

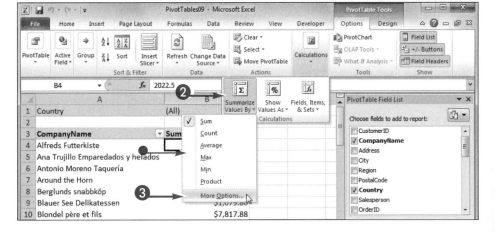

The Value Field Settings dialog box appears with the Summarize Values By tab displayed.

④ Click the summary calculation you want to use.

⑤ Click OK.

Value Field Settings

Source Name: ExtendedPrice

Custom Name: Max of ExtendedPrice

Summarize Values By | Show Values As

Summarize value field by

Choose the type of calculation that you want to use to summarize data from the selected field

Sum
Count
Average
Max
Min
Product

Number Format | OK | Cancel

Excel recalculates the PivotTable results.

● Excel renames the data field label to reflect the new summary calculation.

	A	B	C
1	Country	(All)	
2			
3	**CompanyName**	**Max of ExtendedPrice**	
4	Alfreds Futterkiste	$878.00	
5	Ana Trujillo Emparedados y helados	$340.00	
6	Antonio Moreno Taquería	$945.00	
7	Around the Horn	$1,060.00	
8	Berglunds snabbköp	$3,557.25	
9	Blauer See Delikatessen	$294.00	
10	Blondel père et fils	$1,379.00	
11	Bólido Comidas preparadas	$1,856.85	
12	Bon app'	$1,500.00	
13	Bottom-Dollar Markets	$1,700.00	
14	B's Beverages	$720.00	
15	Cactus Comidas para llevar	$96.50	
16	Chop-suey Chinese	$1,520.00	
17	Comércio Mineiro	$912.00	
18	Consolidated Holdings	$278.00	

Invoices 2010 | PT-Customer Order Totals

Ready

Extra

When you build your PivotTable, you may find that the results do not look correct. For example, the number may appear to be far too small. In that case, check the summary calculation that Excel has applied to the field to see if it is using Count instead of Sum. If the data field includes one or more text cells or one or more blank cells, Excel defaults to the Count summary function instead of Sum. If your field is supposed to be numeric, check the data to see if there are any text values or blank cells.

When you add a second field to the row or column area — see the Chapter 3 section "Add Multiple Fields to the Row or Column Area" — Excel displays a subtotal for each item in the outer field. (If you do not see the subtotals, click Design→Subtotals→Show Subtotals at Bottom of Group.) By default, that subtotal shows the sum of the data results for each outer field item. However, the same 11 summary calculations — from Sum to Varp — are also available for subtotals.

To change the subtotal summary calculation, click any cell in the outer field and then click Options→Active Field→Field Settings to display the Field Settings dialog box. Select Custom, and then click the summary calculation you want to use for the subtotals. Click OK.

Create a Difference Summary Calculation

You can use Excel's difference calculations to compare the items in a numeric field and return the difference between them.

The built-in summary calculations — Sum, Count, and so on — apply over an entire field. However, a major part of data analysis involves comparing one item with another. If you are analyzing sales to customers, for example, it is useful to know how much you sold this year, but it is even more useful to compare this year's sales with last year's. Are the sales up or down? By how much? Are the sales up or down with all customers or only some? These are fundamental questions that help managers run departments, divisions, and companies.

Excel offers two difference calculations that can help with this kind of analysis:

- **Difference From.** Compares one numeric item with another and returns the difference between them
- **% Difference From.** Compares one numeric item with another and returns the percentage difference between them

Before you set up a difference calculation, you need to decide which field in your PivotTable you will use as the comparison field, or *base field*, and which item within that field you will use as the basis for all the comparisons, which is called the *base item*. For example, if you are comparing the sales in 2010 to the sales in 2009, the date field is the base field and 2009 is the base item.

Create a Difference Summary Calculation

① Click any cell in the data field.

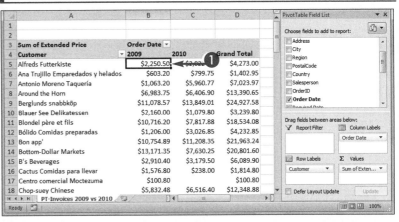

② Click Options→ Calculations→Show Values As.

③ Click Difference From.

● If you want to see the difference in percentage terms, click % Difference From instead.

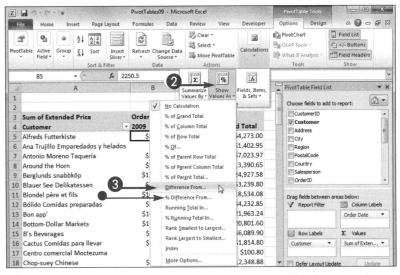

The Show Values As dialog box appears.

4 Click the field from which you want Excel to calculate the difference.

5 Click a base item.

6 Click OK.

● Excel recalculates the PivotTable results to show the difference summary calculation.

Show Values As (Sum of Extended Price)

Calculation: Difference From

Base Field: Order Date — 4

Base Item: 2009 — 5

6 → OK   Cancel

	A	B	C	D
1				
2				
3	**Sum of Extended Price**	Order Date		
4	**Customer**	2009	2010	Grand Total
5	Alfreds Futterkiste		-$228.00	
6	Ana Trujillo Emparedados y helados		$196.55	
7	Antonio Moreno Taquería		$4,897.57	
8	Around the Horn		-$576.85	
9	Berglunds snabbköp		$2,770.44	
10	Blauer See Delikatessen		-$1,080.20	
11	Blondel père et fils		-$2,898.32	
12	Bólido Comidas preparadas		$1,820.85	
13	Bon app'		$453.46	
14	Bottom-Dollar Markets		-$5,541.10	
15	B's Beverages		$269.10	
16	Cactus Comidas para llevar		-$1,338.80	
17	Centro comercial Moctezuma		-$100.80	
18	Chop-suey Chinese		$683.92	

PT-Invoices 2009 vs 2010

Ready

Apply It

It is sometimes handy to toggle between the Difference From and % Difference From calculations, and this is most easily handled with a macro. The following procedure uses the `PivotField` object's `Calculation` property to toggle the Sum of Extended Price field between the two calculations:

Example:
```
Sub ToggleDifferenceCalculations()
    ' Work with the first data field
    With Selection.PivotTable.DataFields(1)
        ' Is the calculation currently Difference From?
        If .Calculation = xlDifferenceFrom Then
            ' If so, change it to % Difference From
            .Calculation = xlPercentDifferenceFrom
            .BaseField = "Order Date"
            .BaseItem = "2009"
            .NumberFormat = "0.00%"
        Else
            ' If not, change it to Difference From
            .Calculation = xlDifferenceFrom
            .BaseField = "Order Date"
            .BaseItem = "2009"
            .NumberFormat = "$#,##0.00"
        End If
    End With
End Sub
```

Create a Percentage Summary Calculation

You can use Excel's percentage calculations to view data items as a percentage of some other item or of the total in the current row, column, or PivotTable. Percentage calculations are useful data-analysis tools because they enable you to make apples-to-apples comparisons between values. Excel offers seven percentage calculations:

- **% Of.** Returns the percentage of each value with respect to a selected base item.
- **% of Row Total.** Returns the percentage that each value in a row represents of the total value of the row.
- **% of Column Total.** Returns the percentage that each value in a column represents of the total value of the column.
- **% of Grand Total.** Returns the percentage that each value represents of the PivotTable grand total.

- **% of Parent Row Total.** If you have multiple fields in the row area, this calculation returns the percentage that each value in an inner row represents with respect to the total of the parent item in the outer row.
- **% of Parent Column Total.** If you have multiple fields in the column area, this calculation returns the percentage that each value in an inner column represents with respect to the total of the parent item in the outer column.
- **% of Parent Total.** If you have multiple fields in the row or column area, this calculation returns the percentage of each value with respect to a selected base field in the outer row or column.

If you use the % Of or the % of Parent Total calculation, you must also choose a base field and a base item upon which Excel will calculate the percentages.

Create a Percentage Summary Calculation

① Click any cell in the data field.

② Click Options→ Calculations→Show Values As.

③ Click the percentage calculation you want to use.

If you clicked % Of or % of Parent Total, the Show Values As dialog box appears.

④ Click the field from which you want Excel to calculate the difference.

⑤ Click the base item.

⑥ Click OK.

● Excel recalculates the PivotTable results and applies the percentage summary calculation.

Show Values As (Sum of Sales)

Calculation: % Of

Base Field: Quarter ◄———④

Base Item: 1st ◄———⑤

⑥———► OK   Cancel

	A	B	C	D	E	F
1						
2						
3	Sum of Sales	Quarter ▾				
4	Region ▾	1st	2nd	3rd	4th	Grand Total
5	East	100.00%	91.03%	97.50%	99.12%	
6	Midwest	100.00%	95.88%	113.88%	115.25%	
7	South	100.00%	95.57%	108.75%	102.66%	
8	West	100.00%	94.86%	87.72%	76.44%	
9	Grand Total	100.00%	94.26%	101.02%	97.11%	
10						
11						
12						
13						
14						
15						
16						
17						

Sales | **PT-Sales By Region & Qtr**

Ready

Apply It

If you want to use VBA to set the percentage calculation for a data field, set the `PivotField` object's `Calculation` property to one of the following constants: `xlPercentOf`, `xlPercentOfRow`, `xlPercentOfColumn`, or `xlPercentOfTotal`. Here is a macro that switches the Sum of Sales field between the % of Row and % of Column calculations (see Chapter 16 for basics on using VBA with PivotTables):

Example:
```
Sub TogglePercentageCalculations()
    ' Work with the first data field
    With Selection.PivotTable.DataFields(1)
        ' Is the calculation currently % of Row?
        If .Calculation = xlPercentOfRow Then
            ' If so, change it to % of Column
            .Calculation = xlPercentOfColumn
        Else
            ' If not, change it to % of Row
            .Calculation = xlPercentOfRow
        End If
    End With
End Sub
```

Create a Running Total Summary Calculation

You can use Excel's Running Total calculation to view the PivotTable results as values that accumulate as they run through the items in a row or column field.

A *running total* is the cumulative sum of the values that appear in a given set of data. Most running totals accumulate over a period of time. For example, suppose you have 12 months of sales figures. In a running total calculation, the first value is the first month of sales, the second value is the sum of the first and second months, the third value is the sum of the first three months, and so on.

You use a running total in data analysis when you need to see a snapshot of the overall data at various points. For example, suppose you have a sales budget for each month. As the fiscal year progresses, comparing the running total of the budget figures with the running total of the actual sales tells you how your department or company is doing with respect to the budget. If sales are consistently below budget, you might consider lowering prices, offering customers extra discounts, or increasing your product advertising.

Excel offers a Running Total summary calculation that you can apply to your PivotTable results. Note, too, that the Running Total applies not just to the Sum calculation, but also to related calculations such as Count and Average. Before you configure your PivotTable to use a Running Total summary calculation, you must decide the field on which to base the accumulation, or the *base field*. This will most often be a date field, but you can also create running totals based on other fields, such as customer, division, product, and so on.

Create a Running Total Summary Calculation

① Click any cell in the data field.

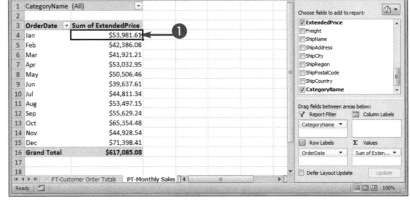

② Click Options→ Calculations→Show Values As.

③ Click Running Total In.

● If you want to see the running total in percentage terms, click % Running Total In instead.

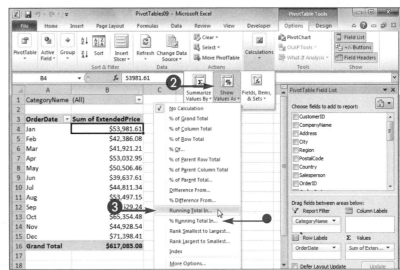

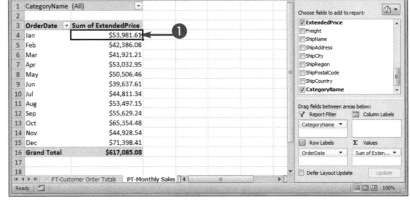

④ Click the base field you want to use.

⑤ Click OK.

● Excel recalculates the PivotTable results to show the running total calculation.

Show Values As (Sum of ExtendedPrice)

Calculation: Running Total In

Base Field: OrderDate ◄─── ④

⑤ ──► OK   Cancel

	A	B	C
1	CategoryName (All)	▼	
2			
3	**OrderDate** ▼	**Sum of ExtendedPrice**	
4	Jan	$53,981.61	
5	Feb	$96,367.69	
6	Mar	$138,288.90	
7	Apr	$191,321.85	
8	May	$241,828.31	
9	Jun	$281,465.92	
10	Jul	$326,277.26	
11	Aug	$379,774.41	
12	Sep	$435,403.65	
13	Oct	$500,758.13	
14	Nov	$545,686.67	
15	Dec	$617,085.08	
16	**Grand Total**		
17			
18			

PT-Customer Order Totals | **PT-Monthly Sales**

Ready

Apply It

You can use VBA to set the Running Total calculation for a data field. Set the `PivotField` object's `Calculation` property to the constant `xlRunningTotal`, and set the `BaseField` property to the name of the base field. Here is a macro that switches the Sum of ExtendedPrice field between the Running Total calculation and the normal calculation (see Chapter 16 for basics on using VBA with PivotTables):

Example:
```
Sub ToggleRunningTotalCalculation()
    ' Work with the first data field
    With Selection.PivotTable.DataFields(1)
        ' Is the calculation currently Running Total?
        If .Calculation = xlRunningTotal Then
            ' If so, turn it off
            .Calculation = xlNoAdditionalCalculation
        Else
            ' If not, change it to Running Total
            .Calculation = xlRunningTotal
            .BaseField = "OrderDate"
        End If
    End With
End Sub
```

Create an Index Summary Calculation

Y ou can use Excel's Index calculation to determine the relative importance of the results in your PivotTable, which is one of the most crucial aspects of data analysis. This is particularly true in a PivotTable, where the results summarize a large amount of data, but on the surface provide no clue as to the relative importance of the various data area values.

For example, suppose your PivotTable shows the units sold for various product categories broken down by state. Suppose further that in Oregon you sold 30 units of Produce and 35 units of Seafood. Does this mean that Seafood sales are relatively more important in the Oregon market than Produce sales? Not necessarily. To determine relative importance, you must take the larger picture into account. For example, you must look at the total units sold of both Produce and Seafood across all states. Suppose the

Produce total is 145 units and the Seafood total is 757 units. You can see that the 30 units of Produce sold in Oregon represents a much higher portion of total Produce sales than does Oregon's 35 units of Seafood. A proper analysis would also take into account the total units sold in Oregon and the total units sold overall (the Grand Total).

This sounds complex, but Excel's Index calculation handles everything easily. The Index calculation determines the *weighted average* — the average taking into account the relative importance of each value — of each cell in the PivotTable results. Here is the formula Excel uses:

```
(Cell Value) * (Grand Total) / (Row Total) *
  (Column Total)
```

In the resulting numbers, the higher the value, the more important the cell is in the overall results.

Create an Index Summary Calculation

Apply the Index Calculation

1. Click any cell in the data field.

2. Click Options→ Calculations→Show Values As→Index.

Format the Data Field for Easier Analysis

- Excel recalculates the PivotTable results to shown the Index calculation.

3. Right-click any cell in the data field.

4. Click Number Format.

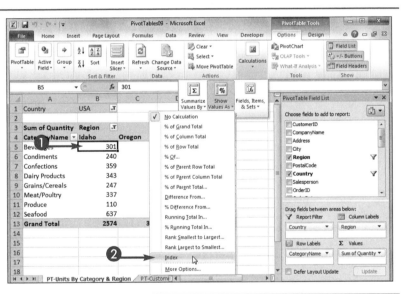

The Format Cells dialog box appears.

5 Click Number in the Category list.

6 Type **2** in the Decimal places field.

7 Click OK.

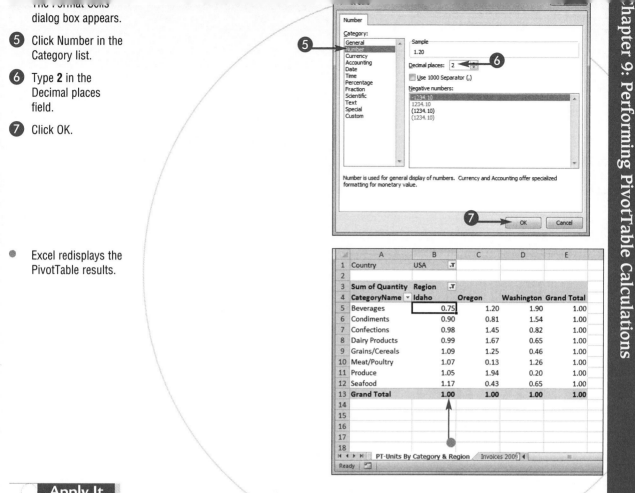

● Excel redisplays the PivotTable results.

Apply It

You can use VBA to apply the Index calculation for a data field by setting the `PivotField` object's `Calculation` property to the constant `xlIndex`. Here is a macro that switches the Sum of Quantity field between the Index calculation and the normal calculation (see Chapter 16 for basics on using VBA with PivotTables):

Example:
```
Sub ToggleIndexCalculation()
    ' Work with the first data field
    With Selection.PivotTable.DataFields(1)
        ' Is the calculation currently Index?
        If .Calculation = xlIndex Then
            ' If so, turn it off
            .Calculation = xlNoAdditionalCalculation
            .NumberFormat = "0"
        Else
            ' If not, change it to Index
            .Calculation = xlIndex
            .NumberFormat = "0.00"
        End If
    End With
End Sub
```

Turn Off Subtotals for a Field

Y ou can make a multiple-field row or column area easier to read by turning off the display of subtotals.

When you add a second field to the row or column area, as described in Chapter 3, and you view the PivotTable in tabular form, Excel automatically displays subtotals for the items in the outer field. This is a useful component of data analysis because it shows you not only how the data breaks down according to the items in the second (inner) field, but also the total of those items for each item in the first (outer) field.

If you add a third field to the row or column area, Excel displays *two* sets of subtotals: one for the second (middle) field and one for the first (outer) field. And for every extra field you add to the row or column area, Excel adds another set of subtotals.

A PivotTable displaying two or more sets of subtotals in one area can be quite confusing to read. You can reduce the complexity of the PivotTable layout by turning off the subtotals for one or more of the fields.

Turn Off Subtotals for a Field

① Click any cell in the field you want to work with.

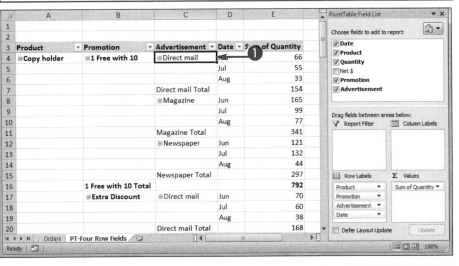

② Click Options→Active Field→Field Settings.

You can also right-click any field cell and then click Field Settings.

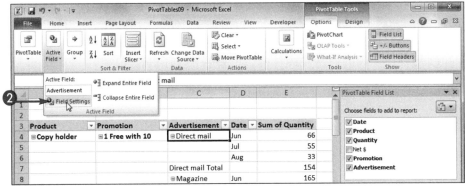

dialog box appears.

3 Click the Subtotals & Filters tab.

4 Select None.

5 Click OK.

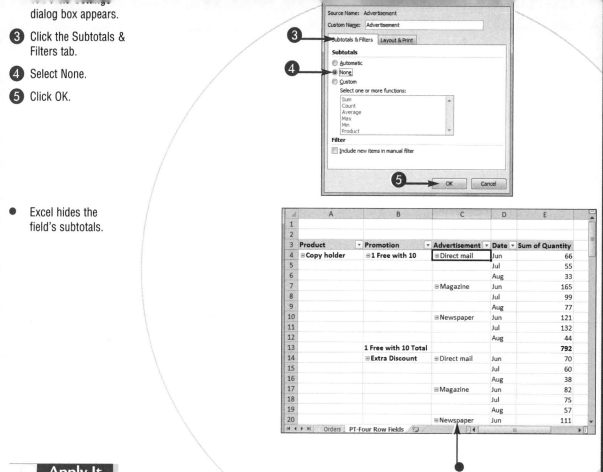

● Excel hides the field's subtotals.

Apply It

To learn how to work with subtotals via VBA, see the tip in the next section, "Display Multiple Subtotals for a Field." The following macro uses VBA to turn a field's subtotals on and off (see Chapter 16 for basics on using VBA with PivotTables):

Example:

```
Sub ToggleFieldSubtotals()
    ' Work with the Advertisement field
    With ActiveSheet.PivotTables(1).RowFields("Advertisement")
        ' Is the Automatic subtotal option turned on?
        If .Subtotals(1) = True Then
            ' If so, turn off all subtotals
            .Subtotals = Array(False, False, False, False, _
                               False, False, False, False, _
                               False, False, False, False)
        Else
            ' If not, turn on the Automatic subtotal option
            .Subtotals = Array(True, False, False, False, _
                               False, False, False, False, _
                               False, False, False, False)
        End If
    End With
End Sub
```

Display Multiple Subtotals for a Field

Y ou can extend your data analysis by reconfiguring your PivotTable results to show more than one type of subtotal for a given field.

When you add a second field to the row or column area, as described in Chapter 3, Excel displays a subtotal for each item in the outer field, and that subtotal uses the Sum calculation. If you prefer to see the Average for each item or the Count, you can change the field's summary calculation; see the section "Change the PivotTable Summary Calculation" earlier in this chapter.

However, it is a common data-analysis task to view items from several different points of view. That is, you may

want to study the results by seeing not just a single summary calculation, but also several: Sum, Average, Count, Max, Min, and so on. Unfortunately, it is not convenient to switch from one summary calculation to another. To avoid this problem, Excel enables you to view multiple subtotals for each field, where each subtotal uses a different summary calculation. You can use as many of Excel's 11 built-in summary calculations as you need. Note, however, that it does not make sense to use StdDev and StDevp at the same time, because the former is for sample data and the latter is for population data. The same is true for the Var and Varp calculations.

Display Multiple Subtotals for a Field

1 Click any cell within the field you want to work with.

2 Click Options→Active Field→Field Settings.

You can also right-click any field cell and then click Field Settings.

The Field Settings
dialog box appears.

③ Select Custom.

④ Click each
calculation that you
want to appear as a
subtotal.

⑤ Click OK.

● Excel recalculates
the PivotTable to
show the subtotals
you selected.

● You may need to
change the number
format for some of
the results.

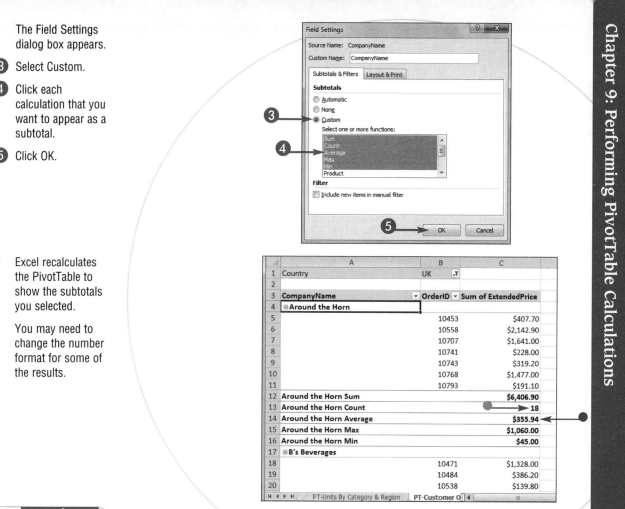

Apply It

To work with subtotals via VBA, use the `PivotField` object's `Subtotals` property, which is a 12-item array of
Boolean (`True` or `False`) values. In this array, the index numbers 1 through 12 correspond to the calculations
shown in the following table:

ARRAY INDEX	CALCULATION	ARRAY INDEX	CALCULATION
1	Automatic	7	Product
2	Sum	8	Count Nums
3	Count	9	StdDev
4	Average	10	StdDevp
5	Max	11	Var
6	Min	12	Varp

The following VBA statement activates the Sum, Count, Average, Max, and Min subtotals for the field represented
by the `objField` object (see Chapter 16 for basics on using VBA with PivotTables):

Example:
```
objField.Subtotals = Array(False, True, True, True, True, True, False, False, False, False,
    False, False)
```

Introducing Custom Calculations

A *custom calculation* is a formula that you define yourself to produce PivotTable values that would not otherwise appear in the report if you used only the source data fields and Excel's built-in summary calculations. Custom calculations enable you to extend your data analysis to include results that are specific to your needs.

For example, suppose your PivotTable shows employee sales by quarter and you want to award a 10 percent bonus to each employee with sales of more than $25,000 in any quarter. You can create a custom calculation that checks for sales greater than $25,000 and then multiplies those by 0.1 to get the bonus number.

A custom calculation is an Excel formula that is applied to your source data to produce a summary result. In other words, in most cases the custom calculation is just like Excel's built-in PivotTable summary calculations, except that you define the specifics of the calculation yourself. Because you are creating a formula, you can use most of Excel's formula power, which gives you tremendous flexibility to create custom calculations that suit your data-analysis needs. And by placing these calculations within the PivotTable itself — as opposed to, for example, adding them to your source data — you can easily update the calculations as needed and refresh the report results.

Formula Basics

Custom calculations are formulas with certain restrictions imposed; see the next section, "Understanding Custom Calculation Limitations." You need to understand the basics of an Excel formula before you can create your own calculations.

For much more detail on this topic, see Chapter 11. A formula always begins with an equals sign (=), followed by one or more operands and operators.

Operands

The *operands* are the values that the formula uses as the raw material for the calculation. In a custom PivotTable calculation, the operands can be numbers, worksheet functions, or fields from your data source.

Operators

The *operators* are the symbols that the formula uses to perform the calculation. In a custom PivotTable calculation, the available operators include addition (+), subtraction (−), multiplication (*), division (/), comparison operators such as greater than (>) and less than or equal to (<=), and more.

Custom Calculation Types

When building a custom calculation for a PivotTable, Excel offers two types: a calculated field and a calculated item.

Calculated Field

A *calculated field* is a new data field in which the values are the result of a custom calculation formula. You can display the calculated field along with another data field or on its own. A calculated field is really a custom summary calculation, so in almost all cases, the calculated field references one or more fields in the source data. See the section "Insert a Custom Calculated Field" later in this chapter.

Calculated Item

A *calculated item* is a new item in a row or column field in which the values are the result of a custom calculation. In this case, the calculated item's formula references one or more items in the same field. See the section "Insert a Custom Calculated Item."

Understanding Custom Calculation Limitations

C ustom calculations — whether they are calculated fields or calculated items — are powerful additions to your PivotTable analysis toolbox. However, although custom calculation formulas look like regular worksheet formulas, you cannot assume that everything you do with a worksheet formula you can also do with a custom PivotTable formula. In fact, there are a number of limitations that Excel imposes on custom formulas.

General Limitations

The major limitation is that, with the exception of constant values such as numbers, you cannot reference anything outside the PivotTable's source data:

- You cannot use a cell reference, range address, or range name as an operand in a custom calculation formula.

- You cannot use any worksheet function that requires a cell reference, range, or defined name. However, you can still use many of Excel's worksheet functions by substituting either a field or an item in place of a cell reference or range name. For example, if you want a calculated item that returns the average of items named Jan, Feb, and Mar, you could use the following formula:

    `=AVERAGE(Jan, Feb, Mar)`

- You cannot use the PivotTable's subtotals, row totals, column totals, or Grand Total as an operand in a custom calculation formula.

Calculated Item Limitations

Excel imposes the following limitations on the use of calculated items:

- A formula for a calculated item cannot reference items from any field except the one in which the calculated item resides.

- You cannot insert a calculated item into a PivotTable that has at least one grouped field. You must ungroup all the PivotTable fields before you can insert a calculated item.

- You cannot group a field in a PivotTable that has at least one calculated item.

- You cannot insert a calculated item into a page field. Also, you cannot move a row or column field that has a calculated item into the page area.

- You cannot insert a calculated item into a PivotTable in which a field has been used more than once.

- You cannot insert a calculated item into a PivotTable that uses the Average, StdDev, StdDevp, Var, or Varp summary calculations.

Calculated Field Limitations

When you are working with calculated fields, it is important to understand how references to other PivotTable fields work within your calculations and what limitations you face when using field references.

Field References

It is important to understand that when you reference a field in your formula, Excel interprets this reference as the *sum* of that field's values. For example, the formula `=Sales + 1` does not add 1 to each Sales value and return the sum of these results; that is, Excel does not interpret the formula as `=Sum of (Sales + 1)`. Instead, the formula adds 1 to the sum of the Sales values — Excel interprets the formula as `=(Sum of Sales) + 1`.

Field Reference Problems

The fact that Excel defaults to a Sum calculation when you reference another field in your custom calculation can lead to problems. The trouble is that it does not make sense to sum certain types of data. For example, suppose you have inventory source data with UnitsInStock and UnitPrice fields. You want to calculate the total value of the inventory, so you create a custom field based on the following formula:

`=UnitsInStock * UnitPrice`

Unfortunately, this formula does not work because Excel treats the UnitPrice operand as Sum of UnitPrice. Of course, it does not make sense to "add" the prices together, so your formula produces an incorrect result.

Insert a Custom Calculated Field

If your data analysis requires PivotTable results that are not available using just the data source fields and Excel's built-in summary calculations, you can insert a calculated field that uses a custom formula to derive the results you need.

A custom calculated field is based on a formula that looks much like an Excel worksheet formula; see the section "Introducing Custom Calculations" earlier in this chapter. However, you do not enter the formula for a calculated field into a worksheet cell. Instead, Excel offers the Calculated Field feature, which provides a dialog box

for you to name the field and construct the formula. Excel then stores the formula along with the rest of the PivotTable data in the pivot cache.

Having the calculated field stored in the pivot cache is handy because the pivot cache is often shared by other PivotTables that you have built using the same source data. When you build a second PivotTable based on the same source data as the first, Excel asks if you want to reuse the original data in the new PivotTable. Therefore, you can reuse calculated fields in other PivotTable reports, which can save time.

Insert a Custom Calculated Field

Note: This chapter uses the PivotTables10.xlsm spreadsheet, available at www.wiley.com/go/pivottablesvb2e, or you can create your own sample file.

1 Click any cell inside the PivotTable's data area.

2 Click Options→ Calculations→Fields, Items, & Sets→Calculated Field.

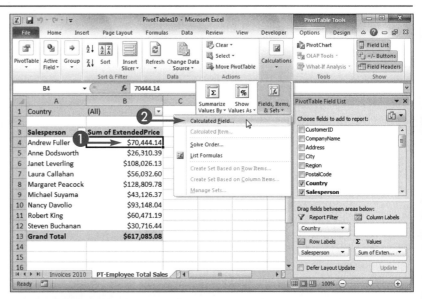

The Insert Calculated Field dialog box appears.

3 Type a name for the calculated field.

4 Start the formula for the calculated field.

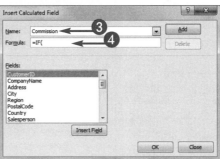

⑤ To insert a field into the formula at the current cursor position, click the field.

⑥ Click Insert Field.

⑦ When the formula is complete, click Add.

⑧ Click OK.

● Excel adds the calculated field to the PivotTable's data area.

● Excel adds the calculated field to the PivotTable Field List.

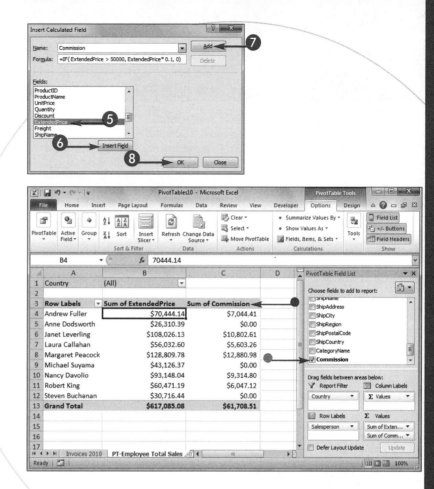

Extra

As pointed out previously, the new calculated field appears in the PivotTable Field List. However, the calculated field also appears in the PivotTable Field List for *every* PivotTable that uses the same pivot cache. Therefore, you can reuse calculated fields in other PivotTable reports. To do this, click inside the other report and then click the calculated field's check box in the PivotTable Field List. Note, however, that it may not make sense to use the calculated field in certain PivotTables. For example, you would not reuse a sales commission calculation in a PivotTable that provides an inventory summary.

When you add a calculated field to the PivotTable, Excel also applies the custom calculation to the Grand Total value. Unfortunately, this total is often inaccurate and you should be careful not to assume that it is correct. The problem is that it is *not* a sum of the values in the calculated field. Instead, Excel applies the calculated field's formula to the sum of whatever field or fields you referenced in the formula. In the example used in this section, Excel applies the formula to the Sum of ExtendedPrice field's Grand Total value, which is not the correct way to calculate the total commission. To work around this problem, you need to set up a formula outside the PivotTable that sums the commission values.

Insert a Custom Calculated Item

If your data analysis requires PivotTable results that are not available using just the data source fields and Excel's built-in summary calculations, you can insert a calculated item that uses a custom formula to derive the results you need.

As with a calculated field, a calculated item uses a formula much like an Excel worksheet formula; see the section "Introducing Custom Calculations" earlier in this chapter. Again, however, you do not enter the formula for a calculated item into a worksheet cell. Instead, Excel offers the Calculated Item command, which displays a dialog box where you name the item and construct the formula. Excel then stores the formula along with the rest of the PivotTable data in the pivot cache.

Remember that the Calculated Item feature creates just a single item in a field. However, you are free to add as many calculated items as you need. For example, suppose you want to compare the performance of male and female sales representatives. One way to do that would be to create one calculated item that returns the average sales of the men and a second calculated item that returns the average sales of the women.

Before you create a calculated item, be sure to remove all groupings from your PivotTable; see the section "Understanding Custom Calculation Limitations" earlier in this chapter. Note that it is not enough to simply remove the grouped field from the PivotTable. Instead, you must run the Ungroup command on the field, as described in Chapter 4.

Insert a Custom Calculated Item

① Click any cell inside the field to which you want to insert the item.

② Click Options→ Calculations→Fields, Items, & Sets→Calculated Item.

The Insert Calculated Item dialog box appears.

③ Type a name for the calculated item.

④ Start the formula for the calculated item.

⑤ To insert a field into the formula at the current cursor position, click the field.

⑥ Click Insert Field.

You can also double-click the field.

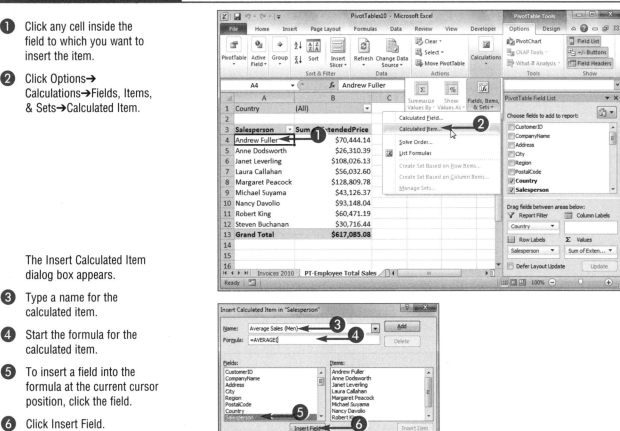

7 To insert an item into the formula at the current cursor position, click the field containing the item.

8 Click the item.

9 Click Insert Item.

You can also double-click the item.

10 When the formula is complete, click Add.

11 Repeat steps **3** to **10** to add other calculated items.

12 Click OK.

● Excel adds the calculated item to the field.

● The calculated item's formula appears in the formula bar when you click the result.

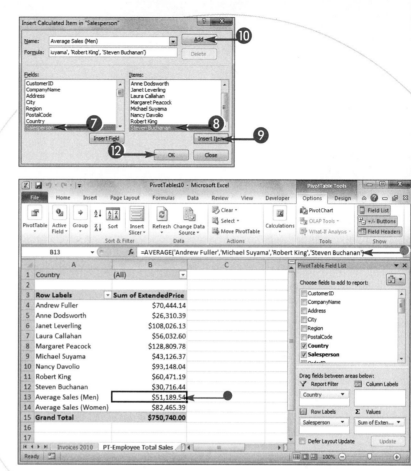

When you insert an item into a field, that item becomes part of the field within the pivot cache. For example, when you select the field in the Insert Calculated Item dialog box, the calculated item appears in the Items list along with the regular field items. This is handy because it enables you to use the calculated item's result in other formulas.

The downside to having the calculated item become part of the field is that Excel includes the calculated item's result in the PivotTable subtotals, row or column totals, and Grand Total. This almost always causes the totals for the affected field to be inaccurate, so double-check field totals when you use a calculated item.

One way to work around this problem is to create a calculated item that uses the SUM() function to add the regular field items. Another workaround is to hide the calculated items; see Chapter 4.

Edit a Custom Calculation

I f you notice an error in a custom calculation, or if your data analysis needs change, you can modify the formula a calculated field or calculated item uses.

When you add a custom calculation to a PivotTable, Excel first checks the formula to make sure that it contains no syntax errors — such as a missing comma or parenthesis; or illegal operands — such as cell addresses, unknown field or item names, or functions not supported by custom calculations. If Excel finds an error, it displays a dialog box to let you know and does not add the custom calculation to the PivotTable.

However, just because a formula contains no syntax errors or illegal operands does not necessarily mean that its results are correct. In a calculated field, you may have

used the wrong function for the result you are seeking. In a calculated item involving several field items, you may have accidentally missed an item.

Alternatively, your formula may be working perfectly, but it may no longer be the result you need if your data analysis needs have changed. For example, you might have a calculated field that determines whether employees get paid a bonus by looking for sales greater than $50,000. If that threshold changes to $75,000, then your calculated field will no longer produce the results you want.

Whether your custom calculation contains an error or your data analysis needs have changed, Excel enables you to edit the formula to produce the result you want.

Edit a Custom Calculation

Edit a Calculated Field

1 Click any cell inside the PivotTable's data area.

2 Click Options→ Calculations→Fields, Items, & Sets→Calculated Field.

The Insert Calculated Field dialog box appears.

3 Click the calculated field you want to edit.

4 Edit the formula.

5 Click Modify.

6 Click OK.

Excel updates the calculated field's results.

Edit a Calculated Item

① Click any cell inside the field that contains the calculated item.

② Click Options→ Calculations→Fields, Items, & Sets→Calculated Item.

The Insert Calculated Item dialog box appears.

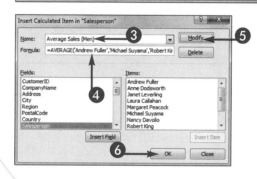

③ Click the calculated item you want to edit.

④ Edit the formula.

⑤ Click Modify.

⑥ Click OK.

You can also edit a calculated item by clicking the item's result. The formula appears in Excel's formula bar, and you can edit it from there.

Excel updates the calculated item's results.

If you use Visual Basic for Applications (VBA) to insert a calculated field or item, then you can modify the custom calculation by editing the macro.

For calculated fields, first note that each PivotTable object has a CalculatedFields collection. To insert a calculated field, use the CalculatedField object's Add method. The following statement inserts a calculated field named Commission (see Chapter 16 for basics on using VBA with PivotTables):

Example:
```
objPT.CalculatedFields.Add _
    Name:="Commission", _
    Formula:="= IF(ExtendedPrice> 50000,ExtendedPrice* 0.1, 0)"
objPT.PivotFields("Commission").Orientation = xlDataField
```

For calculated items, note that each row and column PivotField object has a CalculatedItems collection. To insert a new calculated item, use the CalculatedItems object's Add method. The following statement inserts a calculated item named Average Sales (Men) into the Salesperson field:

Example:
```
objPT.PivotFields("Salesperson").CalculatedItems.Add _
    Name:="Average Sales (Men)", _
    Formula:="=AVERAGE('Andrew Fuller','Michael Suyama'," & _
            "'Robert King','Steven Buchanan')"
```

Change the Solve Order of Calculated Items

Y ou can ensure that your calculated items return the correct results by adjusting the order in which Excel solves the items.

If you have multiple calculated items in a PivotTable, you may end up with cells that have values that rely on two or more formulas. For example, you may have one calculated item in a row field and another in a column field. In the PivotTable cell that lies at the intersection of these two items, the value will be the result of Excel applying one formula and then the other. The default order is the order in which you added the items to the PivotTable. Most of the time, this order does not matter. However, it is often the case that the order that Excel solves calculated items can make a big difference.

For example, suppose you have a PivotTable that shows the number of units that customers ordered based on two different promotional offers — 1 Free with 10 and Extra Discount — broken down by advertisement — Direct

Mail, Magazine, and Newspaper. Suppose further that you have added calculated items in the row field that return the percentage of units ordered for each promotion. For example, with the Magazine advertisement, you might find that 52.5 percent of units were ordered via the 1 Free with 10 promotion, and the other 47.5 percent were ordered via the Extra Discount promotion.

If you also want to know the overall percentages of each promotion, you run into a problem because Excel's default Grand Total calculation will add the percentages. One way to work around this problem is to turn off the Grand Total calculation and create a new calculated item in the column field that adds the various Advertisement items together. However, if this calculated item is solved after the first one, you end up with the same problem: Excel adds the percentages. To fix this, you need to change the solve order so that Excel adds the Advertisement items first and then calculates the percentages.

Change the Solve Order of Calculated Items

① Click any cell in the PivotTable.

● Calculated row items.

● A calculated column item.

● Incorrect results.

② Click Options→ Calculations→Fields, Items, & Sets→Solve Order.

The Calculated Item Solve Order dialog box appears.

③ Click the calculated item you want to move.

④ To move the item up in the list, click Move Up.

Excel moves the item up.

⑤ To move an item down in the list, click Move Down.

⑥ Click Close.

Excel adjusts the solve order and recalculates the results.

The correct results appear.

Calculated Item Solve Order

Solve order:

Total = 'Direct mail' +Magazine +Newspaper
'1 Free with 10 %' = '1 Free with 10'/ ('1 Free with 10'+'Extra Discount')
'Extra Discount %' = 'Extra Discount'/ ('1 Free with 10'+'Extra Discount')

If the value in a PivotTable cell is affected by two or more calculated items, the value is determined by the last formula in the solve order.

Move Up Move Down Delete Close

E7   fx ='1 Free with 10'/ ('1 Free with 10'+'Extra Discount')

	A	B	C	D	E	F	G
1	Product	(All)					
2							
3	Sum of Quantity	Advertisement					
4	Promotion	Direct mail	Magazine	Newspaper	Total		
5	1 Free with 10	935	1,793	1,221	3,949		
6	Extra Discount	879	1,623	1,400	3,902		
7	1 Free with 10 %	51.5%	52.5%	46.6%	50.3%		
8	Extra Discount %	48.5%	47.5%	53.4%	49.7%		

Orders PT-Promotion Percentages

Ready

Apply It

There is another method you can often use to fix solve order problems in a PivotTable. This method relies on the fact that, in a cell that relies on multiple calculated item formulas, Excel applies the last formula in the solve order to the cell. In this section, examine the Excel formula bar in the first screenshot. This is the formula that Excel is applying to cell E7:

```
='Direct mail' + Magazine + Newspaper
```

Now examine the formula bar in the last screenshot. You can see that the formula Excel is now applying to cell E7 is the following:

```
='1 Free with 10' / ('1 Free with 10' + 'Extra Discount')
```

Therefore, in most cases you can fix the solve order problem by copying the correct formula from another cell (such as D7 in the example) and then pasting it into the problem cell.

Note, however, that Excel does not allow you to simply copy the cell and then paste it because Excel does not allow a PivotTable to be changed in this way. Instead, you must open the cell that has the formula you want, copy the cell text, open the destination cell, delete the existing formula, and then paste the copied formula.

List Your Custom Calculations

Y ou can document your PivotTable's custom calculations by displaying the formulas for each calculated field and item on a separate worksheet.

When you add several custom calculations to a PivotTable, the report can become difficult to decipher, particularly with calculated fields because there is nothing in the PivotTable that shows the field's underlying formula to the reader. Calculated items are more transparent because you can see the formula by selecting the cell, but you have no way of knowing if there are multiple calculations that determine the cell's value.

To help the reader decipher a PivotTable's custom calculations, Excel offers a feature that enables you to document all the custom calculations, including the formulas and solve order, in a separate worksheet.

Apply It

You can use a VBA macro to list the custom calculations for a PivotTable. To do this, run the `PivotTable` object's `ListFormulas` method, as shown in the following macro:

```
Sub ListPivotTableFormulas()
    Dim objPT As PivotTable
    '
    ' Work with the first PivotTable on the
active worksheet
    Set objPT = ActiveSheet.PivotTables(1)
    '
    ' List the PivotTable's formulas
    objPT.ListFormulas
End Sub
```

List Your Custom Calculations

① Click any cell in the PivotTable.

② Click Options→ Calculations→Fields, Items, & Sets→List Formulas.

Excel inserts a new worksheet and displays the solve order, name, and formula for each calculated field and item.

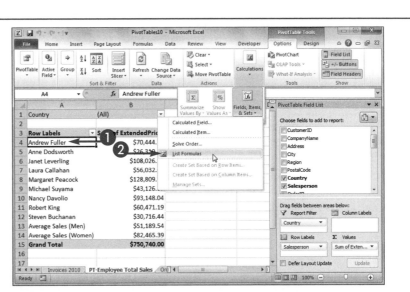

Delete a Custom Calculation

W hen you no longer need a calculated field or calculated item, you can delete the calculation from the PivotTable.

Custom calculations do not always remain a permanent part of a PivotTable report. For example, it is common to add a calculated field or item temporarily to the PivotTable to test the data or get a number to use elsewhere. Similarly, you may find that you create several versions of a custom calculation and you only want to keep the final version. Finally, although custom calculations are a powerful tool, they cannot do everything, so you may find that a calculation does not provide the answer you seek or help you with your data analysis.

For all these situations, Excel enables you to delete those calculated fields or items that you no longer need.

Apply It

The following VBA macro deletes all the custom calculations in a PivotTable:

```
Sub DeleteAllCustomCalculations()
Dim objPF As PivotField
Dim objCF As PivotField, objCI As PivotItem
With ActiveSheet.PivotTables(1)
    For Each objCF In .CalculatedFields
        objCF.Delete
    Next 'objCF
    For Each objPF In .PivotFields
        For Each objCI In objPF.
CalculatedItems
            objCI.Delete
        Next 'objCI
    Next 'objPF
End With
End Sub
```

Delete a Custom Calculation

1. Click any cell in the PivotTable.

2. To delete a calculated field, click Options→ Calculations→Fields, Items, & Sets→Calculated Field.

- To delete a calculated item instead, click Options→ Calculations→Fields, Items, & Sets→Calculated Item.

   The Insert Calculated Field dialog box appears.

3. Click the calculation that you want to delete.

4. Click Delete.

5. Click OK.

   Excel removes the custom calculation.

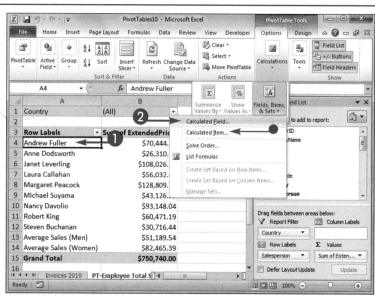

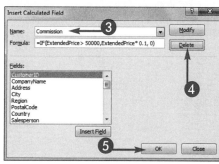

Introducing Formulas

One of the most powerful techniques you can use to enhance PivotTable-based data analysis is custom calculations in your reports, as described in Chapter 10. Whether you create a new calculated field or one or more new calculated items within a field, custom calculations enable you to interrogate your data and return the exact information that you require.

To get the most out of custom calculations, you need to understand formulas: their components, types, and how to build them. In this chapter, you learn how to understand and work with formulas and functions. However, the formulas you use with a PivotTable differ in important ways from regular Excel worksheet formulas. This chapter highlights the differences and focuses on formula ideas and techniques that apply to PivotTable calculations. This section gets you started by showing you the basics of the two major formula components: operands and operators.

For the specifics of implementing custom calculations in your PivotTable reports, see Chapter 10.

Operands

Operands are the values that the formula uses as the raw material for the calculation. In a custom PivotTable calculation, the operands can be constants, worksheet functions, fields from your data source, or items within a data source field. Note that you cannot use cell references or defined names as operands in the PivotTable formula.

Constants

A *constant* is a fixed value that you insert into a formula and use as is. For example, suppose you want a calculated item to return a result that is 10 percent greater than the value of the Beverages item. In that case, you create a formula that multiplies the Beverages item by the constant 110 percent, as shown here:

```
=Beverages * 110%
```

In PivotTable formulas, the constant values are almost always numbers, although when using comparison formulas you may occasionally use a string (text surrounded by double quotation marks, such as "January") as a constant. Note that custom PivotTable formulas do not support constant date values.

Worksheet Functions

You can use many of Excel's built-in worksheet functions as operands in a custom PivotTable formula. For example, you can use the AVERAGE function to compute the average of two or more items in a field, or you can use logic functions such as IF and OR to create complex formulas that make decisions. The major restriction when it comes to worksheet functions is that you cannot use cell addresses or range references in PivotTable formulas, so functions that require such parameters — such as the lookup and reference functions — are off limits. See the section "Introducing Worksheet Functions" later in this chapter for more details.

PivotTable Fields

The third type of operand that you can use in a formula for a calculated field is a PivotTable field. Remember, however, that when you reference a field, Excel uses the sum over all the records in that field, not the individual records in that field. This does not matter for operations such as multiplication and division, because the result is the same either way. However, it can make a big difference with operations such as addition and subtraction. For example, the formula =Condiments + 10 does not add 10 to each Condiments value and return the sum of these results; that is, Excel does not interpret the formula as =Sum of (Condiments + 10). Instead, the formula adds 10 to the sum of the Condiments values; that is, Excel interprets the formula as =(Sum of Condiments) + 10.

PivotTable Items

The fourth and final type of operand that you can use in a formula is a PivotTable field item, which you can only use as part of a calculated item. In the Insert Calculated Item dialog box, click the field, click the item, and then click Insert Item; see Chapter 10. You can also augment the item reference by including the field name along with the item name. With this method, you can either use the item name directly or refer to the item by its absolute or relative position within the field.

Direct Reference

To reference a field and one of its items directly, type the field name followed by square brackets that enclose the item name — surrounded by single quotation marks if the item name includes spaces. For example, in a field named Salesperson, you can reference the Robert King item as follows:

```
Salesperson['Robert King']
```

You can use the field name in this way to make your formulas a bit easier to read and to avoid errors when two fields have items with the same name. For example, a report may have a Country field and a ShipCountry field, both of which might include an item named USA. To differentiate between them, you can use ShipCountry[USA] and Country[USA].

Positional Reference

To reference a field and one of its items by position, type the field name followed by square brackets that enclose the position of the item within the field. For example, to reference the first item in the ProductName field, you can use the following:

```
ProductName[1]
```

This ensures that your formula always references the first item, no matter the sort order you use in the report.

You can also reference a field and one of its items by the position relative to the calculated item that you create. A positive number references items later in the field, and a negative number references items earlier in the field. For example, if the calculated item is the second item in the ProductName field, then ProductName[-1] refers to the first item in the field and ProductName[+1] refers to the third item in the field.

Operators

It is possible to use only an operand in a PivotTable formula. For example, in a calculated field, if you reference just a field name after the opening equals sign (=), then the values in the calculated field are identical to the values in the referenced field.

A calculated field that is equal to an existing field is not particularly useful in data analysis. To create PivotTable formulas that perform more interesting calculations, you need to include one or more operators. The *operators* are the symbols that the formula uses to perform the calculation.

In a custom PivotTable calculation, the available operators are much more limited than they are with a regular worksheet formula. In fact, Excel only allows two types of operators in PivotTable formulas: arithmetic operators such as addition (+), subtraction (−), multiplication (*), and division (/), and comparison operators such as greater than (>) and less than or equal to (<=). See the next section, "Understanding Formula Types," for a complete list of available operators in these two categories.

Understanding Formula Types

Although a worksheet formula can be one of many different types, the formulas you can use in calculated fields and items are more restricted. In fact, there are only two types of formulas that make sense in a PivotTable context: arithmetic formulas for computing numeric results, and comparison formulas for comparing one numeric value with another.

Because you almost always deal with numeric values within a PivotTable report, the type of formula is determined by the operators you use: arithmetic formulas

use arithmetic operators and comparison formulas use comparison operators. This section shows you the operators that define both types. Note, however, that the two types are not mutually exclusive and can be combined to create formulas as complex as your data analysis needs require. For example, the IF worksheet function uses a comparison formula to return a result, and you can then use that result as an operand in a larger arithmetic formula.

Arithmetic Formulas

An arithmetic formula combines numeric operands — numeric constants, functions that return numeric results, and fields or items that contain numeric values — with mathematical operators to perform a calculation. Because PivotTables primarily deal with numeric data, arithmetic formulas are by far the most common formulas used in custom PivotTable calculations.

The following table lists the seven arithmetic operators that you can use to construct arithmetic formulas in your calculated fields or items:

OPERATOR	NAME	EXAMPLE	RESULT
+	Addition	=10 + 5	15
−	Subtraction	=10 – 5	5
−	Negation	=−10	−10
*	Multiplication	=10 * 5	50
/	Division	=10 / 5	2
%	Percentage	=10%	0.1
^	Exponentiation	=10 ^ 5	100000

Comparison Formulas

A comparison formula (also called a relational formula) combines numeric operands — numeric constants, functions that return numeric results, and fields or items that contain numeric values — with special operators to compare one operand with another. A comparison formula always returns a logical result. This means that if the comparison is true, then the formula returns the value 1, which is equivalent to the logical value TRUE; if the comparison is false, then the formula returns the value 0, which is equivalent to the logical value FALSE.

The following table lists the six operators that you can use to construct comparison formulas in your calculated fields or items:

OPERATOR	NAME	EXAMPLE	RESULT
=	Equal to	=10 = 5	0
<	Less than	=10 < 5	0
<=	Less than or equal to	=10 <= 5	0
>	Greater than	=10 > 5	1
>=	Greater than or equal to	=10 >= 5	1
<>	Not equal to	=10 <> 5	1

Operator Precedence

Most of your formulas include multiple operands and operators. In many cases, the order in which Excel performs the calculations is crucial. For example, consider the following formula:

```
=3 + 5 ^ 2
```

If you calculate from left to right, the answer you get is 64 (3 + 5 equals 8, and 8 ^ 2 equals 64). However, if you perform the exponentiation first and then the addition, the result is 28 (5 ^ 2 equals 25, and 3 + 25 equals 28). Therefore, a single formula can produce multiple answers, depending on the order in which you perform the calculations.

To control this problem, Excel evaluates a formula according to a predefined order of precedence. You can also control the order of precedence yourself. See the tip in the section "Build a Formula" later in this chapter. This order of precedence enables Excel to calculate a formula unambiguously by determining which part of the formula it calculates first, which part second, and so on. The order of precedence is determined by the formula operators, as shown in the following table:

OPERATOR	OPERATION	ORDER OF PRECEDENCE
–	Negation	1st
%	Percentage	2nd
^	Exponentiation	3rd
* and /	Multiplication and division	4th
+ and –	Addition and subtraction	5th
= < <= > >= <>	Comparison	6th

Introducing Worksheet Functions

A *function* is a predefined formula that accepts one or more inputs and then calculates a result. In Excel, a function is often called a *worksheet function* because you normally use it as part of a formula that you type in a worksheet cell. However, Excel enables you to use many of its worksheet functions in the PivotTable formulas you create for calculated fields and items.

This section introduces you to worksheet functions by showing you their advantages and structure and by examining a few other worksheet ideas that you should know. The next section, "Understanding Function Types," takes you through the various types of functions that you can use in custom PivotTable calculations, and the section "Build a Function," later in this chapter, shows you a technique for building foolproof functions that you can paste into your custom formulas.

Function Advantages

Functions are designed to take you beyond the basic arithmetic and comparison formulas that you learned about in the previous section. Functions do this in three ways:

- Functions make simple but cumbersome formulas easier to use. For example, suppose that you have a PivotTable report showing average house prices in various neighborhoods and you want to calculate the monthly mortgage payment for each price. Given a fixed monthly interest rate and a term in months, here is the general formula for calculating the monthly payment:

```
House Price * Interest Rate / (1 - (1 + Interest Rate) ^ -Term)
```

Fortunately, Excel offers an alternative to this intimidating formula — the PMT (payment) function:

```
PMT(Interest Rate, Term, House Price)
```

- Functions enable you to include complex mathematical expressions in your worksheets that otherwise are difficult or impossible to construct using simple arithmetic operators. For example, you can calculate a PivotTable's average value using the AVERAGE summary function, but what if you prefer to know the *median* — the value that falls in the middle when all the values are sorted numerically — or the *mode*, which is the value that occurs most frequently? Either value can be time consuming to calculate by hand, but both are easy to calculate using Excel's MEDIAN and MODE worksheet functions.

- Functions enable you to include data in your applications that you could not access otherwise. For example, the powerful IF function enables you to test the value of a field item — for example, to see whether it contains a particular value — and then return another value, depending on the result.

Function Structure

Every worksheet function has the same basic structure:

```
NAME(Argument1, Argument2, ...)
```

Function Name

The NAME part identifies the function. In worksheet formulas and custom PivotTable formulas, the function name always appears in uppercase letters: PMT, SUM, AVERAGE, and so on.

No matter how you type a function name, Excel always converts the name to all-uppercase letters. Therefore, when you type the name of a function that you want to use in a formula, always type the name using lowercase letters. This way, if you find that Excel does not convert the function name to uppercase characters, it likely means you misspelled the name, because Excel does not recognize it.

Arguments

The items that appear within the parentheses are the functions' *arguments*. The arguments are the inputs that functions use to perform calculations. For example, the SUM function adds its arguments and the PMT function calculates the loan payment based on arguments that include the interest rate, term, and present value of the loan. Some functions do not require any arguments at all, but most require at least one argument, and some as many as nine or ten. If a function uses two or more arguments, be sure to separate each argument with a comma, and be sure to enter the arguments in the order specified by the function.

Function arguments fall into two categories: required and optional. A *required argument* is one that you must specify when you use the function, and it must appear within the parentheses in the specified position; if you omit a required argument, Excel generates an error. An *optional argument* is one that you are free to use or omit, depending on your needs. If you omit an optional argument, Excel uses the argument's default value in the function. For example, the PMT function has an optional "future value" argument with which you can specify the value of the loan at the end of the term. The default future value is 0, so you need only specify this argument if your loan's future value is something other than 0.

In the section "Build a Function" later in this chapter, you see that Excel uses two methods for differentiating between required and optional arguments. When you enter a function in a cell, the optional arguments are shown surrounded by square brackets: [and]; when you build a function using the Insert Function dialog box, or if you look up a function in the Excel Help system, required arguments are shown in bold text and optional arguments are shown in regular text.

If a function has multiple optional arguments, you may need to skip one or more of these arguments. If you do this, be sure to include the comma that would normally follow each missing argument. For example, here is the full PMT function syntax — the required arguments are shown in bold text:

```
PMT(rate, nper, pv, fv, type)
```

Here is an example PMT function that uses the type argument but not the fv argument:

```
PMT(0.05, 25, 100000, ,1)
```

Understanding Function Types

Excel comes with hundreds of worksheet functions, and they are divided into various categories or types. These function types include Text, Information, Lookup and Reference, Date and Time, and Database. However, none of these categories is particularly useful in a PivotTable context where you mostly deal with aggregate values: sums, counts, averages, and so on. Therefore, there are only four function types that you will likely use in your custom PivotTable formulas: Math, Statistical, Financial, and Logical. This section introduces you to these four function types and lists the most popular and useful functions in each category. Note that for each function the required arguments appear in bold type.

Mathematical Functions

PivotTables deal with numbers derived by summary operations such as sum, count, average, max, and min. In the formulas for your calculated fields and calculated items, you can often use mathematical worksheet functions to manipulate those numbers.

FUNCTION	DESCRIPTION
CEILING(**number**,**significance**)	Rounds *number* up to the nearest integer
EVEN(**number**)	Rounds *number* up to the nearest even integer
FACT(**number**)	Returns the factorial of *number*
FLOOR(**number**,**significance**)	Rounds *number* down to the nearest multiple of *significance*
INT(**number**)	Rounds *number* down to the nearest integer
MOD(**number**,**divisor**)	Returns the remainder of *number* after dividing by *divisor*
ODD(**number**)	Rounds *number* up to the nearest odd integer
PI()	Returns the value Pi
PRODUCT(**number1**,number2,...)	Multiplies the specified numbers
RAND()	Returns a random number between 0 and 1
ROUND(**number**,**digits**)	Rounds *number* to a specified number of *digits*
ROUNDDOWN(**number**,**digits**)	Rounds *number* down, toward 0
ROUNDUP(**number**,**digits**)	Rounds *number* up, away from 0
SIGN(**number**)	Returns the sign of *number* (1 = positive; 0 = zero; -1 = negative)
SQRT(**number**)	Returns the square root of *number*
SUM(**number1**,number2,...)	Adds the arguments
TRUNC(**number**,digits)	Truncates *number* to an integer

Statistical Functions

Excel's statistical functions calculate a wide variety of highly technical statistical measures. For PivotTable calculations, however, you can only use the basic statistical operations as shown in the following table:

FUNCTION	DESCRIPTION
AVERAGE(**number1**,number2,...)	Returns the average of the arguments
COUNT(**number1**,number2,...)	Counts the numbers in the argument list
MAX(**number1**,number2,...)	Returns the maximum value of the arguments

Statistical Functions *(continued)*

FUNCTION	DESCRIPTION
MEDIAN(**number1**,*number2*,...)	Returns the median value of the arguments
MIN(**number1**,*number2*,...)	Returns the minimum value of the arguments
MODE(**number1**,*number2*,...)	Returns the most common value of the arguments
STDEV(**number1**,*number2*,...)	Returns the standard deviation based on a sample
STDEVP(**number1**,*number2*,...)	Returns the standard deviation based on an entire population
VAR(**number1**,*number2*,...)	Returns the variance based on a sample
VARP(**number1**,*number2*,...)	Returns the variance based on an entire population

Financial Functions

The financial functions that you can use within a PivotTable use the following arguments:

ARGUMENT	DESCRIPTION
rate	The fixed rate of interest over the term of the loan or investment
nper	The number of payments or deposit periods over the term of the loan or investment
pmt	The periodic payment or deposit
pv	The present value of the loan (the principal) or the initial deposit in an investment
fv	The future value of the loan or investment
type	The type of payment or deposit: 0 (the default) for end-of-period payments or deposits; 1 for beginning-of-period payments or deposits

FUNCTION	DESCRIPTION
FV(**rate**,**nper**,**pmt**,*pv*,*type*)	Returns the future value of an investment or loan
IPMT(**rate**,**per**,**nper**,**pv**,*fv*,*type*)	Returns the interest payment for a specified period of a loan
NPER(**rate**,**pmt**,**pv**,*fv*,*type*)	Returns the number of periods for an investment or loan
PMT(**rate**,**nper**,**pv**,*fv*,*type*)	Returns the periodic payment for a loan or investment
PPMT(**rate**,**per**,**nper**,**pv**,*fv*,*type*)	Returns the principal payment for a specified period of a loan
PV(**rate**,**nper**,**pmt**,*fv*,*type*)	Returns the present value of an investment
RATE(**nper**,**pmt**,**pv**,*fv*,*type*,*guess*)	Returns the periodic interest rate for a loan or investment

Logical Functions

The logical functions operate with the logical values TRUE and FALSE, which in your PivotTable calculations are interpreted as 1 and 0, respectively. In most cases, the logical values used as arguments are expressions that make use of comparison operators such as equal to (=) and greater than (>).

FUNCTION	DESCRIPTION
AND(**logical1**,*logical2*,...)	Returns 1 if all the arguments are true; returns 0, otherwise
IF(**logical_test**,**true_expr**,*false_expr*)	Performs a logical test; returns *true_expr* if the result is 1 (true); returns *false_expr* if the result is 0 (false)
NOT(**logical**)	Reverses the logical value of the argument
OR(**logical1**,*logical2*,...)	Returns 1 if any argument is true; returns 0, otherwise

Build a Function

I f you are not sure how to construct a particular function, you can build it within a worksheet cell to ensure that the syntax is correct and that all the required arguments are in place and in the correct order.

When you need to use a function within a custom PivotTable formula, it is common to not know or remember the correct structure of the function. For example, you may not know which arguments are required or what order to enter the arguments. Unfortunately, if you build the function within either the Insert Calculated Field or the Insert Calculated Item dialog box, Excel does not offer any help with the function syntax.

However, when you build a function within a worksheet cell, Excel displays a pop-up banner that shows the correct syntax for the function. This is very useful, so it pays to take advantage of this feature when building your PivotTable formulas. That is, before you display either the Insert Calculated Field or the Insert Calculated Item dialog box, build the function — or even the entire formula — you want in a worksheet cell. You can then copy the function or formula and paste it into the Insert Calculated Field or the Insert Calculated Item dialog box.

Build a Function

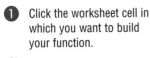 Click the worksheet cell in which you want to build your function.

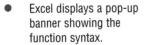 Type = to start a formula.

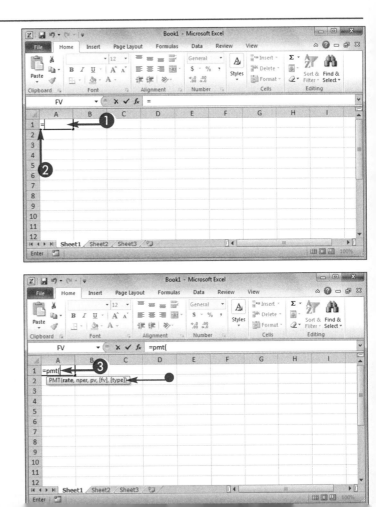

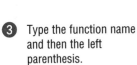 Type the function name and then the left parenthesis.

● Excel displays a pop-up banner showing the function syntax.

- The current argument is bold.

- Optional arguments are surrounded by square brackets ([and]).

④ Type the argument values you want to use.

Note: *If you plan on using the names of PivotTable fields or items as function arguments, type the name of some other placeholder.*

⑤ Type the right parenthesis to complete the function.

⑥ Press Enter to finish editing the cell.

Note: *If you have a PivotTable field or item name in your function, Excel displays a #NAME? error in the cell because it does not recognize the name outside the PivotTable. You can ignore this error.*

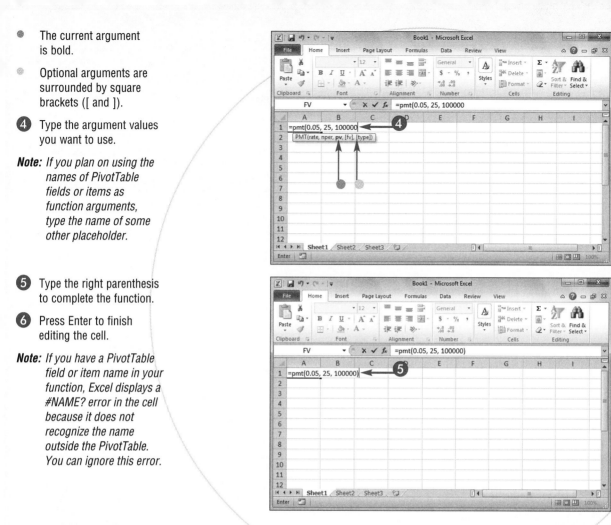

Extra

If you are not sure which function to use, or if you are not sure how to spell the function name, Excel offers an alternative method for building a function: the Insert Function feature. To use this feature, click an empty cell, type an equals sign (=), and then click Formulas➔Insert Function or click the Insert Function button ( ) in the formula bar. Excel displays the Insert Function dialog box.

You can use the Or Select a Category drop-down list to click the function category you want to use, such as Math & Trig, Statistical, Financial, or Logical. Then you can use the Select a Function list to click the function you want to use. Click OK to display the Function Arguments dialog box, which offers text boxes for each argument used by the function. Type the argument values you want to use and then click OK to insert the function into the cell.

If you know the name of the function you want to use, but you want to use the Function Arguments dialog box to type your argument values, type an equals sign (=) and then the function name in an empty cell. Then either press Ctrl+A or click the Insert Function button ( ). Excel displays the Function Arguments dialog box for the function you typed.

Build a Formula

Y ou are now ready to build a custom formula for a calculated field or a calculated item. You learned in the previous section, "Build a Function," that it is helpful to first create a function in a worksheet cell because Excel displays pop-up text that helps you use the correct structure and arguments for the function. Unfortunately, no such help is available when you build a formula in a worksheet cell. Therefore, you will be building your formulas in either the Calculated Field dialog box or the Calculated Item dialog box.

One way to reduce errors when building a custom PivotTable formula is to avoid typing field or item names when you need to use them as operands in your formula. If you are creating a calculated field, for example, it is likely that will use at least one PivotTable field as an operand. Rather than type the field name and introduce the risk of misspelling the name, you can ask Excel to insert the name for you. You learned how to do this in Chapter 10. Similarly, you can also ask Excel to insert field items in a formula for a calculated item, as also described in Chapter 10.

Build a Formula

Note: This chapter uses the PivotTables11.xlsx spreadsheet, available at www.wiley.com/go/pivottablesvb2e, or you can create your own sample spreadsheet.

1 Display the Insert Calculated Field dialog box or the Insert Calculated Item dialog box.

Note: See the sections "Insert a Custom Calculated Field" and "Insert a Custom Calculated Item" in Chapter 10.

2 Type a name for the formula.

3 Type =.

4 Insert an operand.

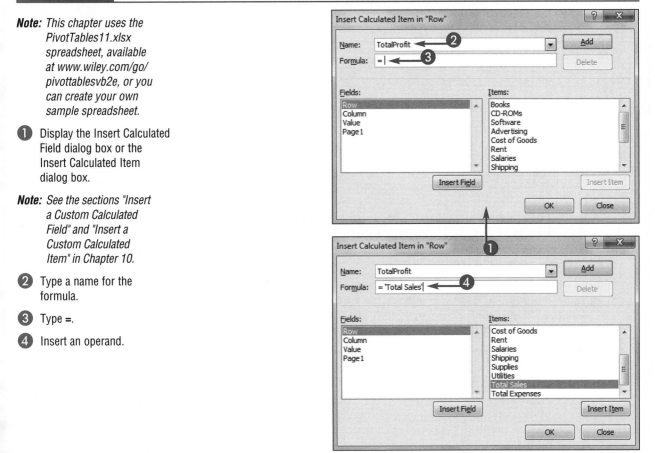

5 Type an operator.

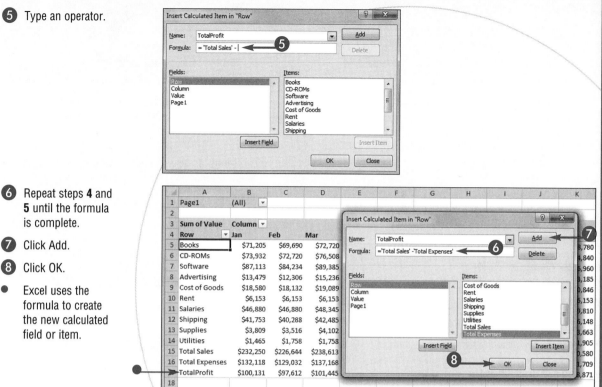

6 Repeat steps **4** and **5** until the formula is complete.

7 Click Add.

8 Click OK.

● Excel uses the formula to create the new calculated field or item.

In the section "Understanding Formula Types" earlier in this chapter, you learn about *operator precedence* — the default order that Excel uses to process the operators in a formula. For example, Excel performs multiplication and division before it performs addition and subtraction. This seems harmless, but it can lead to errors in your formula results. Consider a formula that calculates the gross margin for a business. Gross margin is profit — sales minus expenses — divided by expenses. Therefore, you might start with the following formula:

```
=Profit - Expenses \ Expenses
```

However, when Excel processes this formula, operator precedence tells it to perform the division first, so the formula becomes this:

```
=Profit - 1
```

This is clearly incorrect. To force Excel to perform a particular operation first, surround the expression with parentheses. For example, to force Excel to perform the subtraction first in the gross margin calculation, you can surround the expression Profit - Expenses with parentheses, as shown here:

```
=(Profit - Expenses) \ Expenses
```

Work with Custom Numeric and Date Formats

Y ou can display your PivotTable results exactly the way you want by applying a custom numeric to the values. If your PivotTable includes dates or times, you can also control their display by applying a custom date or time format.

In Chapter 6, you learned how to apply formats to the numbers and dates in your PivotTable. These are predefined Excel formats that enable you to display numbers with thousands of separators, currency symbols, or percentage signs, as well as dates and times using various combinations of days, months, and years or seconds, minutes, and hours.

Excel's list of format categories also includes a Custom category that enables you to create your own formats and display your numbers or dates precisely the way you want. This section shows you the special symbols that you can use to construct these custom numeric and date formats.

Custom Numeric Formats

Every Excel numeric format, whether built in or customized, has the following syntax:

positive format;negative format;zero format;text format

The four parts, separated by semicolons, determine how various numbers are presented. The first part defines how a positive number is displayed, the second part defines how a negative number is displayed, the third part defines how zero is displayed, and the fourth part defines how text is displayed. If you leave out one or more of these parts, numbers are controlled as shown here:

NUMBER OF PARTS USED	FORMAT SYNTAX
Three	positive format;negative format;zero format
Two	positive and zero format; negative format
One	positive, negative, and zero format

The following table lists the special symbols you can use to define each of these parts:

SYMBOL	DESCRIPTION
#	Holds a place for a digit and displays the digit exactly as typed. Displays nothing if no number is entered.
0	Holds a place for a digit and displays the digit exactly as typed. Displays 0 if no number is entered.
?	Holds a place for a digit and displays the digit exactly as typed. Displays a space if no number is entered.
. (period)	Sets the location of the decimal point.
, (comma)	Sets the location of the thousands separator. Marks only the location of the first thousand.
%	Multiplies the number by 100 (for display only) and adds the percent (%) character.
E+ e+ E- e-	Displays the number in scientific format. E- and e- place a minus sign in the exponent; E+ and e+ place a plus sign in the exponent.
/ (slash)	Sets the location of the fraction separator.
$ ( ) : - + <space>	Displays the character.
*	Repeats whatever character immediately follows the asterisk until the cell is full.
_ (underscore)	Inserts a blank space the width of whatever character follows the underscore.
\ (backslash)	Inserts the character that follows the backslash.
"text"	Inserts the text that appears within the quotation marks.

Custom date and time formats generally are simpler to create than custom numeric formats. There are fewer formatting symbols, and you usually do not need to specify different formats for different conditions. The following table lists the date formatting symbols:

SYMBOL	DESCRIPTION
d	Day number without a leading zero (1 to 31)
dd	Day number with a leading zero (01 to 31)
ddd	Three-letter day abbreviation (Mon, for example)
dddd	Full day name (Monday, for example)
m	Month number without a leading zero (1 to 12)
mm	Month number with a leading zero (01 to 12)
mmm	Three-letter month abbreviation (Aug, for example)
mmmm	Full month name (August, for example)
yy	Two-digit year (00 to 99)
yyyy	Full year (1900 to 2078)
/ -	Symbols used to separate parts of dates

The following table lists the time formatting symbols:

SYMBOL	DESCRIPTION
h	Hour without a leading zero (0 to 24)
hh	Hour with a leading zero (00 to 24)
m	Minute without a leading zero (0 to 59)
mm	Minute with a leading zero (00 to 59)
s	Second without a leading zero (0 to 59)
ss	Second with a leading zero (00 to 59)
AM/PM, am/pm, A/P	Displays the time using a 12-hour clock
: .	Symbols used to separate parts of times

Examples

The following table lists a few examples of custom numeric, date, and time formats:

VALUE	CUSTOM FORMAT	DISPLAYED VALUE
.5	#.##	.5
12500	0,.0	12.5
1234	#,##0;-#,##0;0;"Enter a number"	1,234
-1234	#,##0;-#,##0;0;"Enter a number"	–1,234
text	#,##0;-#,##0;0;"Enter a number"	Enter a number
98.6	#,##0.0°F	98.6°F
8/23/2010	dddd, mmmm d, yyyy	Wednesday, August 23, 2010
8/23/2010	mm.dd.yy	08.23.10
3:10 PM	hhmm "hours"	1510 hours
3:10 PM	hh"h" mm"m"	15h 10m

Understanding
Microsoft Query

I f you want to build a PivotTable using a sorted, filtered subset of an external data source, you must use Microsoft Query to specify the sorting and filtering options and the subset of the source data that you want to work with.

Databases such as those used in Microsoft Access and SQL Server are often very large and contain a wide variety of data scattered over many different tables. When your data analysis requires a PivotTable, you rarely use an entire database as the source for the report. Instead, you can extract a subset of the database: a table or

perhaps two or three related tables. You may also require the data to be sorted in a certain way and you may also need to filter the data so that you only work with certain records.

You can accomplish all three operations — extracting a subset, sorting, and filtering — by creating a database query. In Excel, the program that you use to create and run database queries is Microsoft Query. You learn how to use Microsoft Query in this chapter. This section gets you started by introducing you to various query concepts and how they fit into Microsoft Query.

Data Source

All database queries require two things at the very beginning: access to a database and an *Open Database Connectivity*, or *ODBC*, data source for the database installed on your computer. ODBC is a database standard that enables a program to connect to and manipulate a data source. An ODBC data source contains three things: a pointer to the file or server where the database resides; a driver that enables Microsoft Query to connect to, manipulate, and return data from the database; and the logon information that you require to access the database.

You learn how to create a new data source in the next section, "Define a Data Source."

Database Query

Database queries knock a large database down to a more manageable size by enabling you to perform three tasks: selecting the tables and fields you want to work with, filtering the records, and sorting the records.

Select Tables and Fields

The first task you perform when you define a query is to select the table or tables that you want to work with. After you do that, you select the fields from those tables that you want to use in your PivotTable. Because external databases often contain a large amount of data, you can speed up your queries and reduce the amount of memory Excel uses by returning only those fields that you know you need for your PivotTable.

Filter Records

You may not require all of a table's records in your PivotTable report. For example, if a table contains invoice data from

several years, you may only want to work with records from a particular year. Similarly, you may be interested in records for a particular product, country, or employee. In each case, you can configure the database query to *filter* the records so that you only get the records you want.

Sort Records

A database query also enables you to sort the data that you are extracting. This does not matter too much with a PivotTable because Excel sorts the field items in ascending alphabetical order by default. However, the sorting option is important if you import the data into your Excel worksheet, as described in Chapter 13.

You can specify the filtering portion of a database query by specifying one or more *criteria*. These are usually logical expressions that, when applied to each record in the query's underlying table, return either a true or false result. Every record that returns a true result is included in the query, and every record that returns a false result is filtered out of the query. For example, if you only want to work with records where the Country field is USA, then you would set up criteria to handle this, and the query would discard all records where the Country field is not equal to USA. The following table lists the operators you can use to build your criteria expressions:

OPERATOR	VALUE IN THE FIELD
Equals (=)	Is equal to a specified value
Does not equal (<>)	Is not equal to a specified value
Is greater than (>)	Is greater than a specified value
Is greater than or equal to (≥)	Is greater than or equal to a specified value
Is less than (<)	Is less than a specified value
Is less than or equal to (≤)	Is less than or equal to a specified value
Is one of	Is included in a group of values
Is not one of	Is not included in a group of values
Is between	Is between (and including) one value and another
Is not between	Is not between one value and another
Begins with	Begins with the specified characters
Does not begin with	Does not begin with the specified characters
Ends with	Ends with the specified characters
Does not end with	Does not end with the specified characters
Contains	Contains the specified characters
Does not contain	Does not contain the specified characters
Like	Matches a specified pattern
Not like	Does not match a specified pattern
Is Null	Is empty
Is Not Null	Is not empty

Microsoft Query

Microsoft Query is a special program that you can use to perform all the database query tasks mentioned in this section. You can use Microsoft Query to create data sources, add tables to the query, specify fields, filter records using criteria, and sort records. You can also save your queries as query files so that you can reuse them later. If you start Microsoft Query from within Excel, you can return the query records to Excel and use them in a PivotTable.

Define a Data Source

Before you can do any work in Microsoft Query, you must select the data source that you want to use. If you have a particular database that you want to query, you can define a new data source that points to the appropriate file or server.

As you learned in the previous section, "Understanding Microsoft Query," an ODBC data source contains a pointer to the file or server where the database resides; a software driver that enables Microsoft Query to connect to, query, and return data from the database; and the logon information that you require to access the database.

Most data sources point to database files. For example, the relational database management programs Access, Visual FoxPro, Paradox, and dBase all use file-based databases. You can also create data sources based on text

files and Excel workbooks. However, some data sources point to server-based databases. For example, SQL Server and Oracle run their databases on special servers.

As part of the data source definition, you need to include the software driver that Microsoft Query uses to communicate with the database. An Access database requires an Access driver; an SQL Server database requires an SQL Server driver, and so on.

Finally, you must include in the data source any information that you require to access the database. Most file-based databases do not require a logon, but some are protected with a password. For server-based data, you are almost certainly required to provide a username and password.

Define a Data Source

Note: *This chapter uses the Northwind.accdb database, which is based on the sample data that comes with Microsoft Access, or you can create your own sample database.*

1 Click Data→Get External Data→From Other Sources→From Microsoft Query.

The Choose Data Source dialog box appears.

2 Click New Data Source.

3 Deselect Use the Query Wizard to Create/Edit Queries check box.

4 Click OK.

The Create New Data Source dialog box appears.

⑤ Type a name for your data source.

⑥ Click the drop-down arrow (▾) and select the database driver that your data source requires.

⑦ Click Connect.

The dialog box for the database driver appears.

Note: The steps that follow show you how to set up a data source for a Microsoft Access database.

⑧ Click Select.

The Select Database dialog box appears.

Create New Data Source

What name do you want to give your data source?

1. Northwind ← ⑤

Select a driver for the type of database you want to access:

2. Microsoft Access Driver (*.mdb, *.accdb) ▾ ← ⑥

Click Connect and enter any information requested by the driver:

3. Connect... ⑦

Select a default table for your data source (optional):

4.

☐ Save my user ID and password in the data source definition

OK   Cancel

ODBC Microsoft Access Setup

Data Source Name:

Description:

Database

Database:

⑧ — Select...   Create...   Repair...   Compact...

System Database

⊙ None

○ Database:

System Database...

OK   Cancel   Help   Advanced...   Options>>

Apply It

Many medium- and large-sized businesses store their data on Microsoft's SQL Server database system. This is a robust and powerful server-based system than can handle the largest databases and hundreds or thousands of users. If you need to define a data source for an SQL Server installation on your network or some other remote location, first follow steps 1 to 4 to get to the Create New Data Source dialog box.

Type a name for the data source and then, in the list of database drivers, click SQL Server. Click Connect to display the SQL Server Login dialog box. Your SQL Server database administrator should have given you the information you require to complete this dialog box.

Type the name or remote address of the SQL Server in the Server text box. If the SQL Server administrator has associated your Windows login data with the SQL Server login, then you do not need to specify login data, so click OK. Otherwise, deselect the Use Trusted Connection check box, type your SQL Server login ID and password, and then click OK.

Perform steps 13 and 14 later in this task to complete the SQL Server data source.

continued ➡

Your system probably comes with a few data sources already defined, and you can use these predefined data sources instead of creating new ones.

In the Choose Data Source dialog box, the list in the Databases tab often shows one or more predefined data sources. These data sources are created by programs that you install on your system. When you install Microsoft Office and, in particular, the Microsoft Query component, the installation program creates three default data sources: dBase Files, Excel Files, and MS Access

Database. These are incomplete data sources in the sense that they do not point to a specific file. Instead, when you click one of these data sources and then click OK, Microsoft Query prompts you for the name and location of the file. For example, if you use the dBase Files data source, Microsoft Query prompts you to specify a dBase (.dbf) database file. These data sources are useful if you often switch the files that you are using. However, if you want a data source that always points to a specific file, use the steps outlined in this section.

Define a Data Source *(continued)*

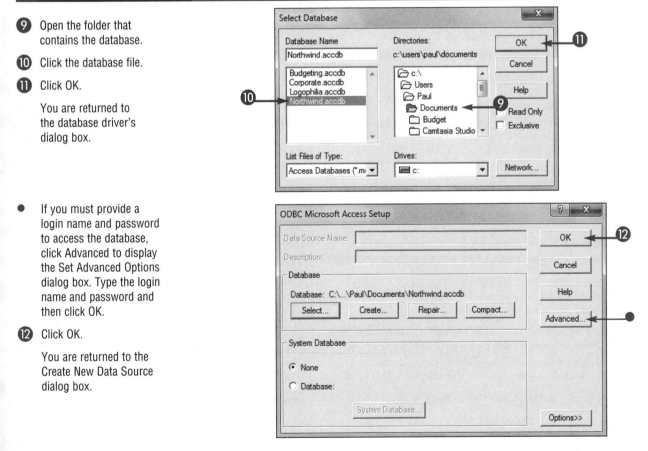

⑨ Open the folder that contains the database.

⑩ Click the database file.

⑪ Click OK.

You are returned to the database driver's dialog box.

● If you must provide a login name and password to access the database, click Advanced to display the Set Advanced Options dialog box. Type the login name and password and then click OK.

⑫ Click OK.

You are returned to the Create New Data Source dialog box.

● If you specified a login name and password as part of the data source, select this check box to save the login data.

⑬ Click OK.

You are returned to the Choose Data Source dialog box.

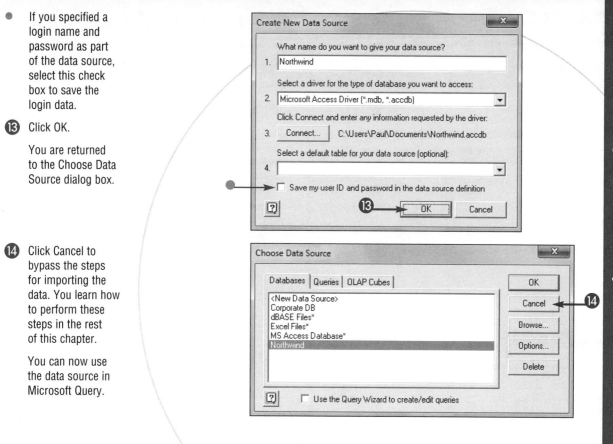

⑭ Click Cancel to bypass the steps for importing the data. You learn how to perform these steps in the rest of this chapter.

You can now use the data source in Microsoft Query.

Apply It

If you have a data source that you no longer use, you should delete it to ensure that only usable data sources appear in the Choose Data Source dialog box. Click Data→Get External Data→From Other Sources→From Microsoft Query to display the Choose Data Source dialog box. Click the data source and then click Delete. When Microsoft Query asks you to confirm the deletion, click Yes.

Unfortunately, the Choose Data Source dialog box does not enable you to reconfigure or rename a data source. To reconfigure a data source, click Start, use the Start menu's Search box to type **odbcad32**, and then click odbcad32 in the search results. In the ODBC Data Source Administrator dialog box that appears, click the File DSN tab. Click the data source you want to work (you may need to open the Queries folder mentioned next) with and then click the Configure button to open the Setup dialog box for the database driver.

To rename a data source, use Windows Explorer to open the following folder:

```
%UserProfile%\AppData\Roaming\Microsoft\Queries
```

Click the data source file, press F2, type the new name, and then press Enter.

Start Microsoft Query

To create a query that defines the fields and records that appear in your PivotTable report, you must begin by starting the Microsoft Query program.

Microsoft Query is part of the Office Tools collection that ships with Microsoft Office. Although you can start the program on its own — click Start→All Programs→ Accessories→Run, type **%programfiles%\microsoft office\office12\msqry32.exe**, and then click OK — you can almost always start it from within Excel. That way, the data you configure with the query is automatically returned to Excel so that you can build your PivotTable report.

Start Microsoft Query

1 Click Data→Get External Data→From Other Sources→From Microsoft Query.

The Choose Data Source dialog box appears.

2 Click the data source you want to work with.

3 Deselect Use the Query Wizard to Create/Edit Queries.

4 Click OK.

The Microsoft Query window and the Add Tables dialog box appear.

Note: To learn how to use the Add Tables dialog box, see the section "Add a Table to the Query" later in this chapter.

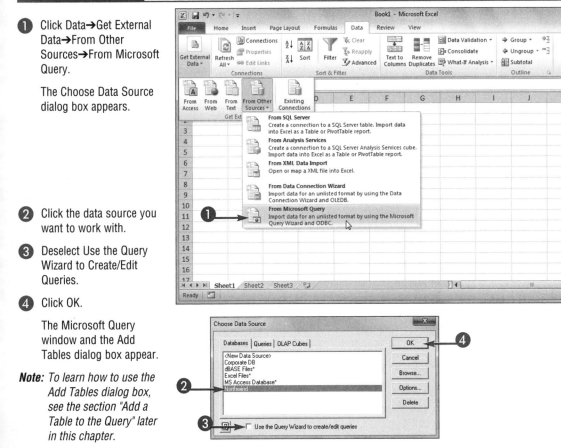

Tour the Microsoft Query Window

You can get the most out of Microsoft Query if you understand the layout of the screen and what each part of the Microsoft Query window represents.

Although you have not yet created a query using the Microsoft Query program, it is worthwhile to pause

now and take a look at the various elements that make up the Microsoft Query window. Do not worry if what you currently see on your screen does not look like the window shown in this section. By the time you finish this chapter, you will see and work with all the elements shown here.

Ⓐ Query Window

This window is where you create and edit, as well as preview, the results. The query window is divided into three panes: the table pane, the Criteria pane, and the results pane.

Ⓑ Toolbar

This toolbar contains buttons that give you one-click access to many of Microsoft Query's most useful features.

Ⓒ Table Pane

This pane displays one list for each table that you add to the query; see the section "Add a Table to the Query" later in this chapter. Each list shows the fields that are part of the table. Click View→Tables to toggle this pane on and off.

Ⓓ Criteria Pane

This pane is where you define the criteria that filter the records you want to return to Excel. See the section "Filter the Records with Query Criteria" later in this chapter. Click View→Criteria to toggle this pane on and off.

Ⓔ Query Results

This pane gives you a preview of the fields and records that your query will return to Excel. As you add fields to the query, change the query criteria, and sort the query; see the task "Sort the Query Records" later in this chapter. Microsoft Query updates the results pane, also called the *data grid*, automatically to show you what effect your changes will have.

Add a Table to the Query

With your data source running and Microsoft Query started, the next step you must take is to add a table to the query.

In a database, a *table* is a two-dimensional arrangement of rows and columns that contains data. The columns are *fields* that represent distinct categories of data, and the rows are *records* that represent individual sets of field data. In some database management systems, the database files themselves are tables. However, in most systems, each database contains a number of tables. Therefore, your first Microsoft Query task in most cases is to select which table you want to work with.

Also note that many database systems enable you to filter and sort data using their own versions of the querying process. Creating a query in Microsoft Access, for example, is similar to creating one in Microsoft Query. By default, when Microsoft Query shows you a list of the tables in the database, it also includes any queries — or *views*, as Microsoft Query calls them — that are defined in the database, so you can add these objects to your query, if required.

However, if the query is based on multiple, related tables, then for best results you may also need to add all the related tables to your query. For example, if you are using the Northwind sample database and you add the Invoices view to your query, it includes the field Customers.CompanyName. This tells you that you should also add the Customers table to your query.

Add a Table to the Query

① Click Table→Add Tables.

   You can also click the Add Tables toolbar button (🖳).

   The Add Tables dialog box appears.

Note: When you start Microsoft Query from Excel, the Add Tables dialog box appears automatically, so you can skip step **1**.

② Click the table you want to add.

③ Click Add.

● Microsoft Query adds the table to the table pane.

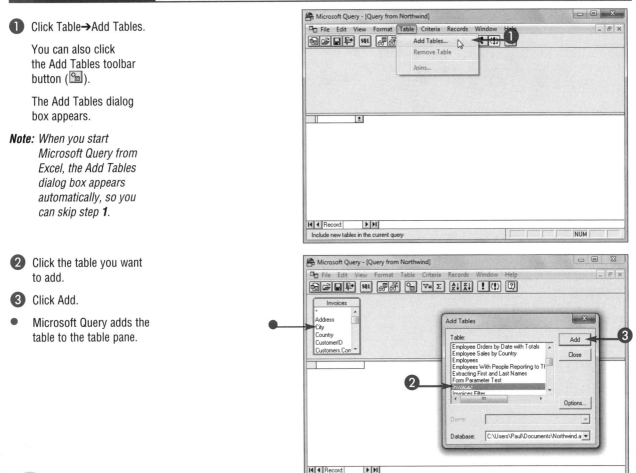

④ Repeat steps **2** and **3** if you want to add multiple, related tables to the query.

● If the tables are related, Microsoft Query displays a join line that connects the common fields.

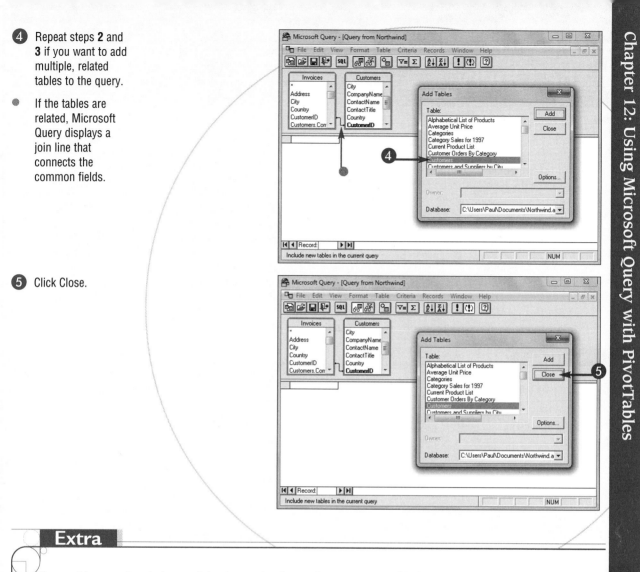

⑤ Click Close.

Extra

If two tables are related, they are joined to each other using a common field. These joins are almost always defined in the original database, so you should not have to worry about creating or editing the joins. However, if you come across two tables that you know are related, but no join line appears when you add them to your query, you can create the join yourself.

After you add the two tables to your query, click Table→Joins to display the Joins dialog box. In the Left list, click the common field from one of your tables. In the Right list, click the common field from the other table. In the Operator list, click = (equals). Click Add to add the join to the query, and then click Close.

To remove a table from the query, first click the table in the table pane. Then click Table→Remove Table. Alternatively, click the table and then press Delete. Microsoft Query deletes the table list. If you added fields from the table to the Criteria pane or the results pane, Microsoft Query removes those fields as well.

Add Fields
to the Query

To display records in the query's results pane, you must first add one or more fields to the query.

After you add one or more tables to the query, your next step is to filter the resulting records so that you return to Excel only the data you need for your PivotTable. Filtering the records involves two tasks: specifying the fields you want to work with and specifying the criteria you want to apply to records. This task shows you how to add fields — or *columns*, as Microsoft Query calls them — to the query. See the next task, "Filter the Records with Query Criteria," to learn how to add criteria to the query.

In the query window's table pane, you see a list for each table in the query. Each list contains an item for each field in the table. At the top of each list, you also see an asterisk (*) item. The asterisk item represents *all* the fields in the table. So if you know that you want to include in your query every field from a particular table, you can do this easily by adding the asterisk "field" to the query.

As you add fields to the query, Microsoft Query automatically shows the corresponding records in the results pane. If you would rather control the display of the results, click the Auto Query toolbar button (▣) to turn off this feature. Then when you are ready to view the results, click the Query Now toolbar button (▯).

Add Fields to the Query

① Click Records→Add Column.

The Add Column dialog box appears.

② In the Field list, click ▾ and then click the field you want to add.

③ If you want to use a different field name, type the new name here.

④ Click Add.

- Microsoft Query adds the field to the results pane.

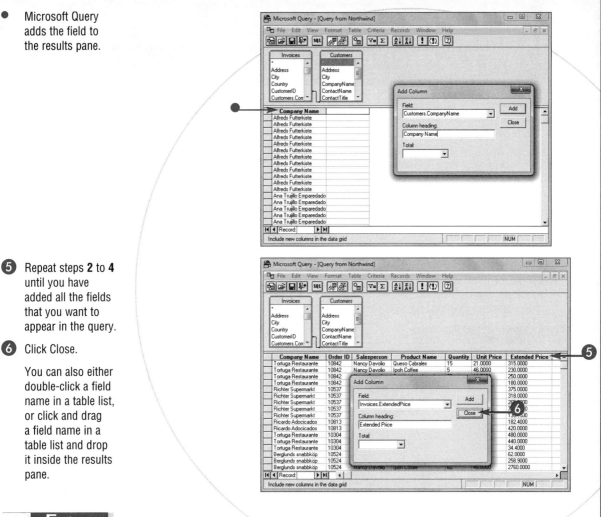

⑤ Repeat steps **2** to **4** until you have added all the fields that you want to appear in the query.

⑥ Click Close.

You can also either double-click a field name in a table list, or click and drag a field name in a table list and drop it inside the results pane.

Extra

The order of the fields in the results pane is not fixed. To change where a field appears in the data grid, first click the field heading to select the entire field. Then click and drag the field heading to the left or right and drop the field into the new position.

If you want to make changes to a field — that is, you want to change to a different field or edit the name displayed in the field header — click the field heading or click any cell in the field, and then click Records→Edit Column. You can also double-click the field heading. You can use the Edit Column dialog box to change the field or edit the field heading, and then click OK.

If you no longer need a field in the query, you should delete it from the data grid. Click the field heading or click any cell in the field; note that Microsoft Query does not ask for confirmation when you delete a field, so be sure you click the correct field. Then either click Records→Remove Column, or press Delete.

Filter the Records with Query Criteria

To display specific records that you want to return to Excel for your PivotTable, you must use criteria to filter the records.

After you add your fields to the data grid, your next step is to specify which records you want to include in the results. You can do this by specifying the conditions that each record must meet to be included in the results. If you are working with invoice data, for example, you may only want to see those orders where the customer name begins with R, the order quantity is greater than 10, the unit price is between $10 and $40, and so on.

In each case, you specify a *criterion*, which is an expression — an operator and one or more values — applied to a specific field. Only those records for which the expression returns a true answer are included in the query results.

You can enter just a single criterion, or you can enter two or more. If you use multiple criteria, you must decide if you want Microsoft Query to include in the results those records that match *all* the criteria, or those records that match *any one* of the criteria.

You learned the various criteria operators in the section "Understanding Microsoft Query" earlier in this chapter. Operators such as "equals" and "is one of" are English language equivalents of the actual operators that Microsoft Query uses. These actual operators include the comparison operators (=, <>, >, >=, <, and <=) as well as keywords such as Between x And y, In, and Like. However, if you use the Add Criteria dialog box, as shown in this section, you do not need to use the actual operators directly.

Filter the Records with Query Criteria

1. Click the Show/Hide Criteria button (⊞).

- Microsoft Query displays the Criteria pane.

2. Click Criteria→Add Criteria.

   The Add Criteria dialog box appears.

3. In the Field list, click ▾ and then click the field to which you want the criterion applied.

4. In the Operator list, click ▾ and then click the operator you want to use.

5. Type the value or values for the criterion.

- To use a value from the selected field, click Values, click the value you want to use, and then click OK.

6. Click Add.

- Microsoft Query adds the criterion to the Criteria pane.

- Microsoft Query filters the results to show only those records that satisfy the criterion.

Note: *If you do not want to specify multiple criteria, skip to step 9.*

⑦ Select And to add another criterion and to display records that meet all the criteria you specify.

● You can also select Or to display records that meet at least one of the criteria you specify.

⑧ Repeat steps **3** to **7** until you have added all the criteria that you want to appear in the query.

⑨ Click Close.

Microsoft Query filters the records to show just those that match your criteria.

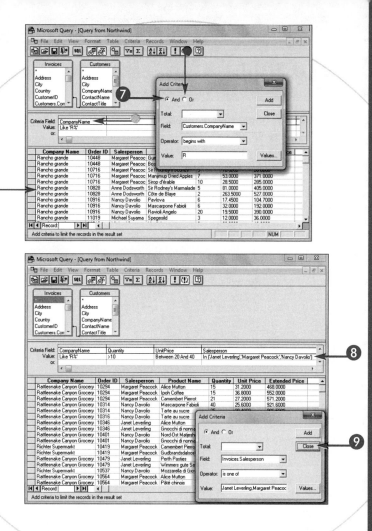

Extra

If you want to change the field to which a criterion expression applies, there are two methods you can use within the Criteria pane:

- Double-click the field name to display the Edit Criteria dialog box. You can use the Field list to click a different field, and then click OK.

- Click the field name. Microsoft Query adds a drop-down arrow to the right of the field cell. Click the arrow to display the Field list, and then click the field you want to use.

If you want to change the criterion expression, again there are two methods you can use with the Criteria pane:

- Double-click the expression to display the Edit Criteria dialog box. You can use the Operator list and Value text box to specify a different expression, and then click OK.

- Edit the expression directly in the Criteria pane.

If you no longer need a criterion in the query, you should delete it from the Criteria pane. Click the bar just above the field name to select the entire criterion; note that Microsoft Query does not ask for confirmation when you delete a criterion, so be sure you click the correct one. Then press Delete. If you want to remove all the criteria and start over, click Criteria→Remove All Criteria.

Sort the Query Records

Y ou can sort the query results on one or more
fields to get a good look at your data.

If you are using the query results within a
PivotTable, it does not matter if the results are sorted,
because Excel uses a default ascending alphabetical sort
when it displays the unique values from a field in the
PivotTable report. However, there are two reasons why
you might want to sort the records that appear in
Microsoft Query's results pane:

- You want to be sure that you are returning the
  correct records, and the records are often easier to
  examine if they are sorted.

- You are importing the query results to Excel instead
  of applying them directly to a PivotTable; see
  Chapter 11. In this case, the sort order you apply in
  Microsoft Query is the order that the records will
  appear in Excel.

You can sort the records either in ascending order (0 to 9,
A to Z) or descending order (Z to A, 9 to 0). You can also
sort the records based on more than one field. In this
case, Microsoft Query sorts the records using the first
field, and then sorts within those results on the second
field. For example, in the invoice data, suppose you are
sorting first on the OrderID field and then on the Quantity
field. Microsoft Query first orders the records by OrderID.
Then, within each OrderID value, Microsoft Query sorts
the Quantity field values.

Sort the Query Records

① Click Records→Sort.

The Sort dialog box
appears.

② In the Column list, click
the field you want to sort.

③ Select a sort order:
Ascending or Descending.

④ Click Add.

- Microsoft Query sorts the records in the results pane.

- Microsoft Query adds the sort to the Sorts in query list.

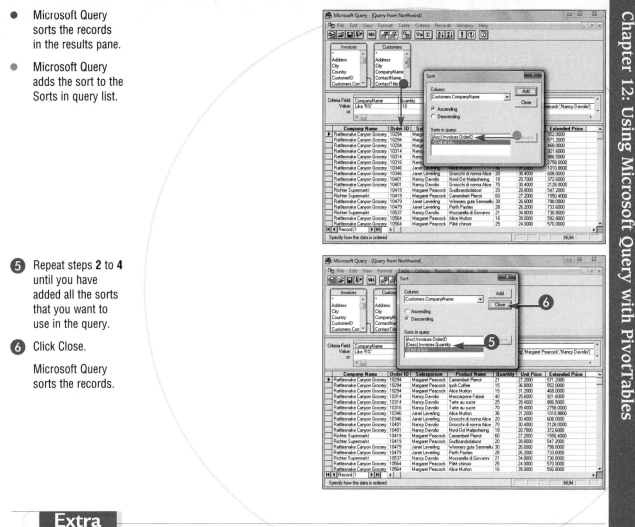

⑤ Repeat steps **2** to **4** until you have added all the sorts that you want to use in the query.

⑥ Click Close.

Microsoft Query sorts the records.

Extra

If you only want to sort the query results on a single field, you can perform the sort much faster by using the toolbar. First, in the results pane, click any cell in the field you want to sort. Then click one of the following buttons:

BUTTON	DESCRIPTION
⬆	Sorts the field in ascending order
⬇	Sorts the field in descending order

If you want to sort on multiple fields, you can still use the toolbar, but it takes a bit more work. First, organize the fields in the results pane so that all the fields you want to use in the sort are side by side in the order you want to apply the sort. Click and drag the mouse pointer from the heading of the first sort field to the heading of the last sort field. You should now have all the sort fields selected. Finally, click either sort button: ⬆ or ⬇.

If you have applied a sort that you no longer want to use, you should remove it from the query. Click Records→Sort to display the Sort dialog box. In the Sort in query list, click the sort that you want to delete, and then click Remove.

Return the Query Results

After you finish adding fields to the query, filtering the data using criteria, and sorting the data, you are ready to return the results to Excel for use in your PivotTable.

Microsoft Query is just a helper application, so the data that resides in the query results does not really "exist" anywhere. To manipulate or analyze that data, you must store it in a different application. In your case, you are interested in using the query results as the source data for a PivotTable report. Therefore, you need to return the query results to Excel, and then start a new PivotTable based on those results.

If you think you will reuse the query at a later date, you should save the query before returning the results. See the tip on the next page to learn how to save and open Microsoft Query files.

Return the Query Results

1. Click File→Return Data to Microsoft Office Excel.

   You can also click the Return Data toolbar button (⊞).

   Microsoft Query closes, and Microsoft Excel displays the Import Data dialog box.

2. Select PivotTable Report.

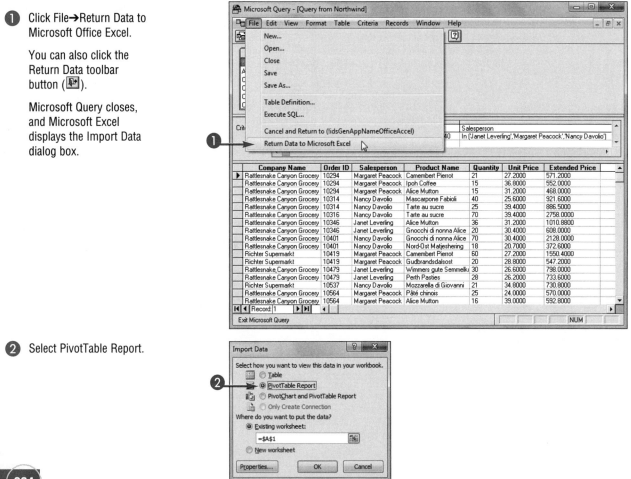

③ Select Existing worksheet.

④ Click the worksheet cell where you want the PivotTable to appear.

● If you prefer to display the PivotTable in a new worksheet, click New worksheet instead.

⑤ Click OK.

Excel builds an empty PivotTable report based on the data returned from Microsoft Query.

⑥ Use the PivotTable Field List to build the report.

Extra

If you want to make changes to your query, you need to edit the results in Microsoft Query. Click any cell in the PivotTable report that you built from the returned data. Then click Options→Change Data Source→Connection Properties (or Options→Refresh→Connection Properties) to open the Connection Properties dialog box. Click the Definition tab and then click Edit Query. This starts Microsoft Query and loads the query results. Make your changes and then return the data to Excel.

If your query includes a complex combination of tables, fields, criteria, and sorting, it can be dismaying to realize that you have to start from scratch if you want to use a similar query for a different PivotTable report. To avoid this extra work, you should save your queries as you work on them, which enables you to reopen the queries any time you need them.

To save a query using Microsoft Query, click File→Save to display the Save As dialog box. Click the folder in which you want to store the query file, type a file name, and then click Save. To use the query file: start Microsoft Query, click File→Open to display the Open Query dialog box, click the query file, and then click Open.

Understanding External Data

xternal data is data that resides outside of Excel in a file, database, server, or Web site. You can import external data into Excel either directly into a PivotTable or into a worksheet for additional types of data analysis.

A vast amount of data exists in the world, and most of it resides in some kind of nonworkbook format. Some data exists in simple text files, perhaps as comma-separated lists of items. Other data resides in tables, either in Word documents or, more likely, in Access databases. There is also an increasing amount of data that resides in Web pages and in XML files.

By definition, all this data is not directly available to you via Excel. However, Excel offers a number of tools that enable you to import external data into the program. Depending on your needs and on the type of data, you can either import the data directly into a PivotTable report, or you can store the data on a worksheet and then build your PivotTable from the resulting worksheet range. In most cases, Excel also enables you to refresh the data so that you are always working with the most up-to-date version of the data.

External Data Types

Excel can access a wide variety of external data types. However, in this chapter you only learn about six of them: data source files, Access tables, Word tables, text files, Web pages, and XML files.

Data Source File

In Chapter 12, you learned about ODBC data sources, which give you access to data residing in databases such as Access and dBase or on servers such as SQL Server and Oracle. However, there are many other data-source types, including data connection files (which connect to specific objects in a data source, such as an Access table), Web queries, OLAP (Online Analytical Processing) cubes, query files (saved via Microsoft Query, as described in Chapter 12), Web-based data retrieval services, and XML files. For more information, see the section "Import Data from a Data Source."

Access Table

Microsoft Access is the Office suite's relational database management system, and so it is often used to store and manage the bulk of the data used by a person, team, department, or company. You can connect to Access tables either via Microsoft Query or by importing table data directly into Excel. For more information, see the section "Import Data from an Access Table."

Word Table

Simple nuggets of nonrelational data are often stored in a table embedded in a Word document. You can only perform so much analysis on that data within Word, and so it is often useful to import the data from the Word table into an Excel worksheet. For more information, see the section "Import Data from a Word Table."

Text File

Text files often contain useful data. If that data is formatted properly — for example, where each line has the same number of items, all separated by spaces, commas, or tabs — then it is possible to import that data into Excel for further analysis. For more information, see the section "Import Data from a Text File."

Web Page

People and companies often store useful data on Web pages that reside either on the Internet or on company intranets. This data is often a combination of text and tables, but you cannot analyze Web-based data in any meaningful way in your Web browser. Fortunately, Excel enables you to create a Web query that lets you import text and/or tables from a Web page. For more information, see the section "Import Data from a Web Page."

XML

XML (Extensible Markup Language) is redefining how data is stored. This is reflected in the large number of tools that Excel now has for dealing with XML data, particularly tools for importing XML data into Excel. For more information, see the section "Import Data from an XML File."

Access to External Data

To use external data, you must have access to it. This usually means knowing at least one of the following: the location of the data or the login information required to authorize your use of the data.

Location

By definition, external data resides somewhere other than in an Excel worksheet on your system. Therefore, to access external data, you must at least know where it is located. Here are some of the possibilities:

- **On your computer.** The data may reside in a file on your hard drive, on a CD or DVD, or on a memory card or other removable storage medium.

- **On your network.** The data may reside in a folder on a computer that is part of your local or wide area network. If that folder has been shared with the network, and if you have the appropriate permissions to view files in that folder, then you can access the data within the files.

- **On a server.** Some data is part of a large, server-based database management system, such as SQL Server or Oracle. In this case, you need to know the name or network address of the server.

- **On a Web page.** If the data resides on a Web page, either as text or as a table, you need to know the address of the Web page.

- **On a Web server.** Some data resides on special Web servers that run data retrieval services such as Windows SharePoint Services. In this case, you need to know the address of the server and the location of the data on that server.

Login

Knowing where the data is located is probably all that you require if you are dealing with a local file or database or, usually, a Web page. However, after you start accessing data remotely — on a network, database server, or Web server — you will also require authorization to secure that access. See the administrator of the resource to obtain a username or login ID as well as a password.

Import Data

After you have access to the data, your next step is to import it into Excel for analysis and manipulation. You have two choices:

Import to PivotTable

If you are building a PivotTable using the external data as the source, then in most cases Excel enables you to import the data directly into a PivotTable. The advantage here is that Excel does not have to store two copies of the data: one on a worksheet and another in the pivot cache. The disadvantage is that you can only analyze the data using the PivotTable report. Other types of data analysis that require direct access to worksheet data are not possible.

Import to Worksheet

In all cases, you can also import the data directly into an Excel worksheet. Depending on the amount of data, this can make your worksheet quite large. However, having direct access to the data gives you maximum flexibility when it comes to analyzing the data. Not only can you create a PivotTable from the worksheet data, but you can also use Excel with other data-analysis tools: lists, database functions, scenarios, and what-if analysis.

Import Data from a Data Source

Y ou can quickly import data into just about any format by importing the data from a defined data source file.

You learn how to create data source files in several places in this book. For data sources and Microsoft Query files, see Chapter 12; for OLAP queries and OLAP cube files, see Chapter 15. You can also create data connection files that point to specific objects in a database, such as an Access table. Excel also considers file types such as Access databases and projects, dBase files, Web pages, text files, and Lotus 1-2-3 spreadsheets to be data sources.

In this section, you learn how to import data from a *data connection file*, which uses the .odc extension. This is a data source that connects you to a wide variety of data, including ODBC, SQL Server, SQL Server OLAP Services, Oracle, and Web-based data retrieval services. See the tip on the following page to learn how to create a data connection file. Note, however, that not all data connection file types support direct import into a PivotTable. For example, if you use a data retrieval service such as MSN MoneyCentral, you cannot import that data directly to a PivotTable.

Import Data from a Data Source

① Click Data→Get External Data→Existing Connections.

The Existing Connections dialog box appears.

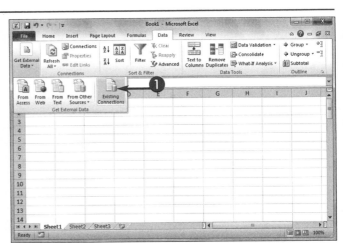

② Click the data source you want to import.

③ Click Open.

The Import Data dialog box appears.

④ Click to select the Table option.

● If you want to import the data directly into a PivotTable, you can select the PivotTable Report option instead.

⑤ Click to select the Existing Worksheet option.

⑥ Click the cell where you want the imported data to appear.

● If you want the data to appear in a new sheet, you can select the New Worksheet option instead.

⑦ Click OK.

Excel imports the data into the worksheet.

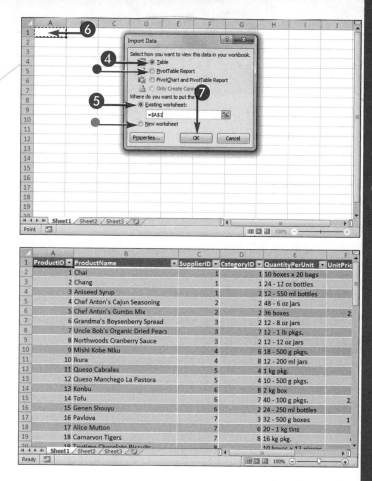

Apply It

If you do not see the data source you want in the My Data Sources folder, you can create one yourself. In most cases, you will want to create a data connection file. To create your own data connection (.odc) file, click Data→ Get External Data→From Other Sources→From Data Connection Wizard to display the Data Connection Wizard. Click the data source you want and then click Next.

The next wizard step depends on the data source you choose:

● For Microsoft SQL Server or Oracle, you specify the server name or address and your server login data.

● For ODBC DSN, you choose the ODBC data source, and then specify the location of the file and the specific table you want to connect to.

● For data retrieval services — including Microsoft Business Solutions — you specify the network name or Web address of the data retrieval server.

Follow the rest of the wizard's steps and then choose your new data source in the Select Data Source dialog box. Note that the Data Connection Wizard stores all new data source files in the My Data Sources folder, which is a subfolder of your user profile's main documents folder (such as My Documents).

Import Data from an Access Table

I f you want to use Excel to analyze data from a table within an Access database, you can import the table to an Excel worksheet.

In Chapter 12, you learned how to use Microsoft Query to create a database query to extract records from a database, filter and sort the records, and return the results to Excel. You also learned that you can create a database query for any ODBC data source, including an Access database.

If you simply want the raw data from an Access table, you can still use Microsoft Query. That is, you add the table to the query, add the asterisk (*) "field" — representing all

the table's fields — to the data grid, and then return the results without adding any criteria to filter the records.

However, Excel gives you an easier way to do this: You can import the table directly from the Access database. To make this technique even easier, Excel automatically creates a data connection file for the database and table that you import. Therefore, you can import the same table in the future simply by opening the data connection file.

Note, too, that you can also use the steps in this section to import data from any query that is already defined in the Access database.

Import Data from an Access Table

Note: This section uses the Northwind.accdb database that comes with Microsoft Access, or you can create your own sample database.

1 Click Data→Get External Data→From Access.

The Select Data Source dialog box appears.

2 Open the folder that contains the Access database.

3 Click the Access database file.

4 Click Open.

Note: If another user has the database open, you may see the Data Link Properties dialog box. If so, make sure the login information is correct and then click Test Connection until you are able to connect successfully. Then click OK.

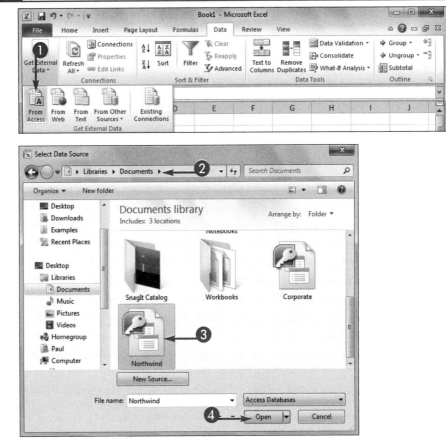

The Select Table dialog box appears.

⑤ Click the table or query you want to import.

⑥ Click OK.

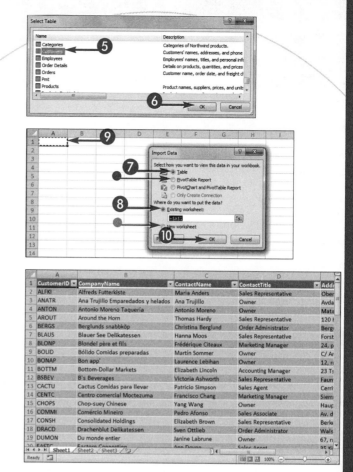

The Import Data dialog box appears.

⑦ Select the Table option.

● If you want to import the data directly into a PivotTable, you can select the PivotTable Report option instead.

⑧ Select the Existing Worksheet option.

⑨ Click the cell where you want the imported data to appear.

● If you want the data to appear in a new sheet, you can select the New Worksheet option instead.

⑩ Click OK.

Excel imports the data to the worksheet.

Extra

Excel automatically creates a new data connection file for the Access table and stores the ODC file in the My Data Sources folder. The name of the data connection file depends on the table name and database name. For example, if you select the Invoices query from the Northwind2007 sample database, the new data connection file is named Northwind2007 Invoices.odc.

If you want to import the same table in the future, you need only click the data connection file in the Existing Connections dialog box, and then click Open.

If the Access database requires a login password, you may need to type the password again when you refresh the imported data. To avoid this extra step, tell Excel to save the database password along with the external data. If you have the Import Data dialog box on-screen, click Properties; if you have already imported the data, click Data→Refresh All→Connection Properties. In the Connection Properties dialog box, click the Definition tab, select the Save Password check box, and then click OK.

Import Data from a Word Table

Y ou can improve your analysis of Word table data by importing the table into an Excel worksheet.

Word tables are collections of rows and columns and cells, which means they look something like Excel ranges. Moreover, you can insert fields into Word table cells to perform calculations. In fact, Word fields support cell references such as B1 — the cell in the second column and first row of the table — and you can use cell references, built-in functions such as SUM and AVERAGE,

and operators such as addition (+), multiplication (*), and greater than (>), to build formulas that calculate results based on the table data.

However, even the most powerful Word field formula cannot perform the functions that are available to you in Excel, which offers far more sophisticated data-analysis tools. Therefore, to analyze your Word table data properly, you should import the table into an Excel worksheet.

Import Data from a Word Table

Note: *This section uses the 2010Budget.docx Word file, available at www. wiley.com/go/2007 pivvotablesvb2e, or you can create your own sample Word table.*

1 Launch Microsoft Word and open the document that contains the table.

2 Click a cell inside the table you want to import.

3 Click Layout→Select→ Select Table.

● You can also select the table by clicking the table selection handle.

4 Click Home→Copy.

You can also press Ctrl+C.

Word copies the table to the Clipboard.

5 Switch to the Excel workbook into which you want to import the table.

6 Click the cell where you want the table to appear.

7 Click Home→Paste.

You can also press Ctrl+V.

Excel pastes the Word table data.

	A	B	C	D	E	F	G	H	I	J	K	L	M
1													
2	Expense Item	Jan	Feb	Mar	Apr	May	Jun	Jul	Aug	Sep	Oct	Nov	Dec
3	Cost of Goods	6,132	5,984	6,300	6,616	6,600	6,572	6,720	6,300	6,300	6,880	6,300	6,300
4	Advertising	4,600	4,200	5,200	5,000	5,500	5,250	5,500	5,200	5,200	4,500	5,200	5,200
5	Rent	2,100	2,100	2,100	2,100	2,100	2,100	2,100	2,100	2,100	2,100	2,100	2,100
6	Supplies	1,300	1,200	1,400	1,300	1,250	1,400	1,300	1,400	1,400	1,250	1,350	1,400
7	Salaries	16,000	16,000	16,500	16,500	16,500	17,000	17,000	17,000	17,000	17,000	17,500	17,500
8	Shipping	14,250	13,750	14,500	15,000	14,500	14,750	15,000	14,500	14,500	15,750	15,250	14,500
9	Utilities	500	600	600	550	600	650	650	600	600	650	600	600

Apply It

The problem with this copy-and-paste method is that there is no connection between the data in Word and the data in Excel. If you make changes to one set of data, those changes are not automatically reflected in the other set of data. You can paste the Word data into Excel as a linked Word object, but you are not able to manipulate the data in Excel.

A better approach is to shift the data's container application from Word to Excel. That is, after you paste the table data into Excel, copy the Excel range, switch to Word, and then click Home→Paste→Paste Special. In the Paste Special dialog box, click HTML Format in the As list, select the Paste link option, and then click OK. The resulting table is linked to the Excel data, which means that any changes you make to the data in Excel automatically appear in the Word table. Note, however, that the link does not work the other way. That is, if you change the data in Word, you cannot update the original data in Excel.

Import Data from a Text File

Y ou can analyze the data contained in certain text files by importing some or all the data into an Excel worksheet.

Nowadays, most data resides in some kind of special format: database object, XML file, Excel workbook, and so on. However, it is still relatively common to find data stored in simple text files because text is a universal format that users can work with on any system and in a wide variety of programs, including Excel.

Note, however, that you cannot import just any text files into Excel. Some or all the files must use one of these two structures:

- **Delimited.** This is a text structure in which each item on a line of text is separated by a character called a *delimiter*. The most common text delimiter is the comma (,), and there is even a special text

format called *Comma Separated Values* (*CSV*) that uses the comma delimiter. A delimited text file is imported into Excel by placing each line of text on a separate row and each item between the delimiter in a separate cell.

- **Fixed-width.** This is a text structure in which all the items on a line of text use up a set amount of space — say, 10 characters or 20 characters — and these fixed widths are the same on every line of text. For example, the first item on every line might use 5 characters, the second item on every line might use 15 characters, and so on. A fixed-width text file is imported into Excel by placing each line of text on a separate row and each fixed-width item in a separate cell.

The Text Import Wizard handles importing text files into Excel, and the steps vary depending on whether you are importing a delimited or fixed-width text file.

Import Data from a Text File

Start the Text Import Wizard

Note: *This section uses the StockPrices.csv and ExchangeRates.txt text files, available at www.wiley.com/go/pivottablesvb2e, or you can create your own sample text file.*

① Click the cell where you want the imported data to appear.

② Click Data→Get External Data→From Text.

The Import Text File dialog box appears.

③ Open the folder that contains the text file.

④ Click the text file.

⑤ Click Import.

The first step of the Text Import Wizard opens.

Note: *For delimited text, continue with Import Delimited Data; for fixed-width text, skip to Import Fixed-Width Data.*

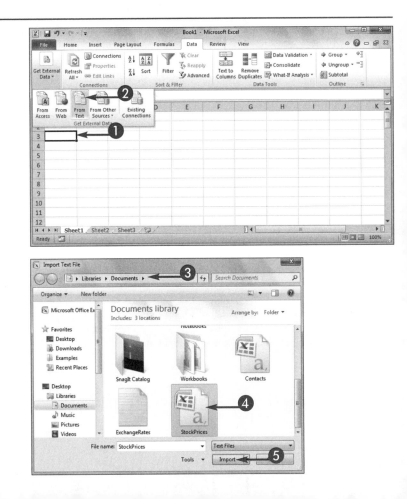

Import Delimited Data

1 Select the Delimited option.

2 Use the Start Import at Row spin box to set the first row you want to import.

3 Click Next.

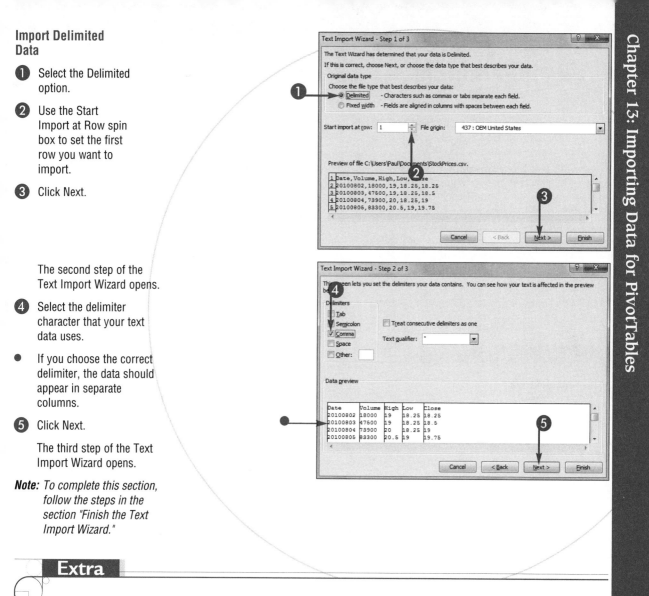

The second step of the Text Import Wizard opens.

4 Select the delimiter character that your text data uses.

● If you choose the correct delimiter, the data should appear in separate columns.

5 Click Next.

The third step of the Text Import Wizard opens.

Note: *To complete this section, follow the steps in the section "Finish the Text Import Wizard."*

It is common for text files to include a title of one or more lines of explanatory text at the top of the document. In this case, you probably do not want to import this introductory text into Excel. The exception to this would be if the text file has a line of column headings. In that case, you should import the headings so that Excel includes them at the top of the range of imported data. To skip text at the beginning of the text file, use the Start import at row spin box in the first step of the Text Import Wizard. Set the value of this control to the row number where the data starts. For example, if you have four lines of introductory text that you want to skip over, set the spin box value to 5.

If your text file originated from a system that is different from the one you are running, then the text may not display properly. To fix this, use the File origin list in the first step of the Text Import Wizard. For example, if the text file originated on a Mac system, click Macintosh in the list. Similarly, if the text file was created in a language that uses different characters or accents, click the appropriate alphabet — such as Cyrillic or Greek — in the list.

continued ➡

Import Data from a Text File (continued)

f you are importing data that uses the fixed-width structure, then you need to tell Excel where the separation between each field occurs.

In a fixed-width text file, each column of data is a constant width. The Text Import Wizard is usually quite good at determining the width of each column of data, and in most cases the wizard automatically sets up *column break lines*, which are vertical lines that separate one field from the next. However, titles or introductory text at the beginning of the file can impair the wizard's calculations, so you should check carefully that the

proposed break lines are accurate. In the second step of the Text Import Wizard, you can scroll through all the data to see if any break line is improperly positioned for the data in a particular field. If you find a break line in the wrong position, you can move it to the correct position before importing the text.

Also note that in some cases the Text Import Wizard adds an extra break line. For example, if the text file has three columns of data, the wizard may suggest three break lines, which divide the data into four columns. In this case, you can delete the extra break line.

Import Data from a Text File *(continued)*

Import Fixed-width Data

Note: *You need to have run through the steps in the section "Start the Text Import Wizard" before continuing with this section.*

① In the first step of the Text Import Wizard, select the Fixed Width option.

② Click here to set the first row you want to import.

③ Click Next.

The second step of the Text Import Wizard appears.

④ Click and drag a break line to set the width of each column.

To create a break line, you can click the ruler at the point where you want the break to appear.

To delete a break line, you can double-click it.

⑤ Click Next.

The third step of the Text Import Wizard appears.

Finish the Text Import Wizard

① Click a column.

② Select the data format you want Excel to apply to the column.

● If you select the Date option, you can use this drop-down list to select the date format your data uses.

③ Repeat steps **1** and **2** to set the data format for all of the columns.

④ Click Finish.

The Import Data dialog box appears.

⑤ Select the Existing Worksheet option.

● If you want the data to appear in a new sheet, you can select the New Worksheet option instead.

⑥ Click OK.

Excel imports the data to the worksheet.

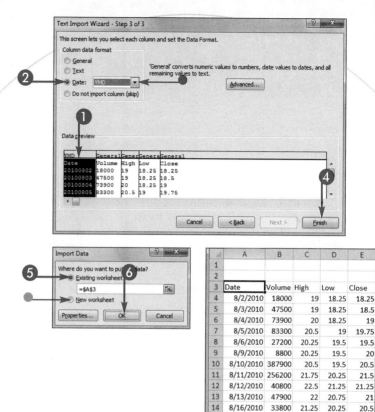

Extra

Some text files may contain numbers that use a comma instead of a dot as the decimal separator, or a dot instead of a comma as the thousands separator. To ensure that Excel imports such numeric data correctly, click Advanced in the third step of the Text Import Wizard to display the Advanced Text Import Settings dialog box. You can use the Decimal Separator drop-down list to click the decimal separator used by the text, and use the Thousands Separator drop-down list to click the thousands separator used by the text. Click OK to put the settings into effect.

If you make a mistake when importing a text file, you do not need to start the import from scratch. Click any cell in the imported data and then click Data→Refresh All→Connection Properties. The Connection Properties dialog box appears. Click the Definition tab and then click Edit Query. The Import Text File dialog box appears. Click the file you want to import and then click Import. Excel launches the Import Text Wizard to enable you to run through the wizard's options again.

Import Data from a Web Page

You can analyze Web page data by importing it into Excel using a Web query.

To make data more readily available to a wide variety of users, many people are placing data on Web pages that are accessible through the Internet or a corporate *intranet* — a local network that uses Web servers and similar technologies to implement Web sites and pages that are accessible only to network users. Although this data is often text, most Web page data comes in one of two formats:

- **Table.** This is a rectangular array of rows and columns, with data values in the cells created by the intersection of the rows and columns.

- **Preformatted text.** This is text that has been structured with predefined spacing. In many cases, this spacing is used to organize data into columns with fixed widths.

Both types of data are suitable for import into Excel, which enables you to perform more extensive data analysis using the Excel tools. To import Web page data into Excel, you must create a *Web query* — a data request that specifies the page address and the table or preformatted text that you want to import.

Import Data from a Web Page

Note: *This section uses the products.html Web page, available at www.wiley. com/go/pivottablesvb2e, or you can create your own sample Web page.*

① Click the cell where you want the imported data to appear.

② Click Data→Get External Data→ From Web.

The New Web Query dialog box appears.

③ Type the address of the Web page that contains the data you want to import.

④ Click Go or press Enter.

● Excel loads the page into the dialog box.

⑤ Click Select Table (☑) beside the table that you want to import.

☑ changes to a check mark.

● Excel selects the table.

⑥ If the page has other tables that you want to import, repeat step **4** for each table.

⑦ Click Import.

The Import Data dialog box appears.

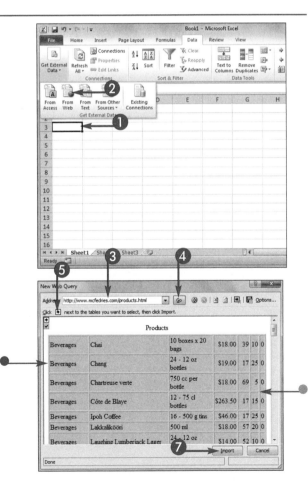

8 Select the Existing Worksheet option.

○ If you want the data to appear in a new sheet, you can select the New Worksheet option instead.

9 Click OK.

Excel imports the data to the worksheet.

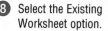

Import Data ? x

Where do you want to put the data?

○ Existing worksheet

=$A$3

○ New worksheet

Properties... OK Cancel

	A	B	C	D	E	F	G
1							
2							
3	Products						
4	Beverages	Chai	10 boxes x 20 bags	$18.00	39	10	0
5	Beverages	Chang	24 - 12 oz bottles	$19.00	17	25	0
6	Beverages	Chartreuse verte	750 cc per bottle	$18.00	69	5	0
7	Beverages	Côte de Blaye	12 - 75 cl bottles	$263.50	17	15	0
8	Beverages	Ipoh Coffee	16 - 500 g tins	$46.00	17	25	0
9	Beverages	Lakkalikööri	500 ml	$18.00	57	20	0
10	Beverages	Laughing Lumberjack Lager	24 - 12 oz bottles	$14.00	52	10	0
11	Beverages	Outback Lager	24 - 355 ml bottles	$15.00	15	30	0
12	Beverages	Rhönbräu Klosterbier	24 - 0.5 l bottles	$7.75	125	25	0
13	Beverages	Sasquatch Ale	24 - 12 oz bottles	$14.00	111	15	0
14	Beverages	Steeleye Stout	24 - 12 oz bottles	$18.00	20	15	0
15	Condiments	Aniseed Syrup	12 - 550 ml bottles	$10.00	13	25	0
16	Condiments	Chef Anton's Cajun Seasoning	48 - 6 oz jars	$22.00	53	0	0

Sheet1 Sheet2 Sheet3

Apply It

Besides the steps you learned in this section, Excel gives you two other methods for creating Web queries. Both of these alternative methods assume that you already have the Web page open in Internet Explorer:

● Right-click the page and then click Export to Microsoft Excel.

● Copy the Web page text, switch to Excel, and then paste the text. When the Paste Options smart tag appears, click the smart tag drop-down arrow and then click Create Refreshable Web Query.

Each of these methods opens the New Web Query dialog box and automatically loads the Web page.

If you want to save the Web query for future use in other workbooks, click the Save Query button (▣) in the New Web Query dialog box and then use the Save Workspace dialog box to save the query file.

Import Data from an XML File

You can analyze data that currently resides in XML format by importing that data into Excel and then manipulating and analyzing the resulting XML list.

XML is a standard that enables the management and sharing of structured data using simple text files. These XML files organize data using tags, among other elements, that specify the equivalent of a table name and field names. Here is a simple XML example that constitutes a single record in a table named "Products:"

```
<Products>
<ProductName>Chai</ProductName>
<CompanyName>Exotic Liquids</CompanyName>
<ContactName>Charlotte Cooper</ContactName>
</Products>
```

These XML files are readable by a wide variety of database programs and other applications, including Excel 2010. Because the XML is just text, if you want to work with the data, you must import the XML file into another application. If you want to perform data analysis on the XML file, for example, then you must import the XML data into Excel.

Excel usually stores imported XML data in an *XML table*, a range that looks and operates much like a regular Excel table, except that it has a few XML-specific features.

Import Data from an XML File

Note: *This section uses the Suppliers.xml file, available at www.wiley. com/go/pivottablesvb2e, or you can create your own sample XML file.*

1. Click the cell where you want the imported data to appear.

2. Click Data→Get External Data→From Other Sources→From XML Data Import.

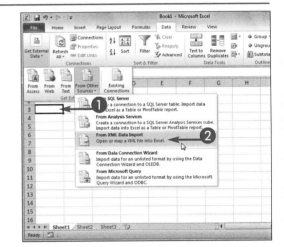

The Select Data Source dialog box appears.

3. Select the folder that contains the XML file.

4. Click the XML file you want to import.

5. Click Open.

The Import Data dialog box appears.

6 Select the XML Table in Existing Worksheet option.

7 Click OK.

Excel imports the data into the worksheet as an XML table.

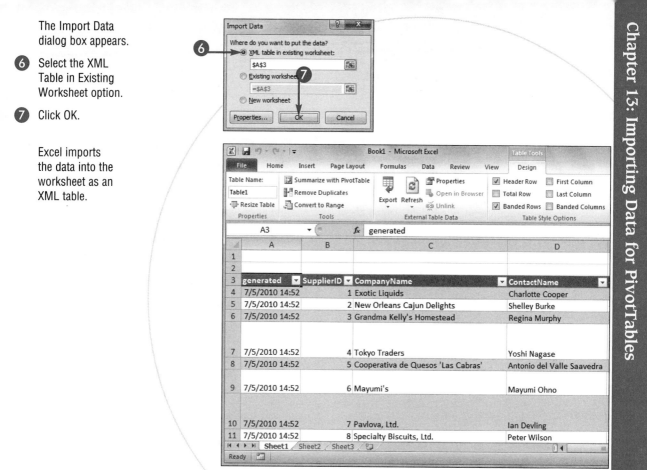

If there are fields in the XML list that you do not want to use, you can remove them. First, display the XML Source pane by right-clicking the XML table and then clicking XML➔XML Source. The XML Source pane displays a list of the fields — called *elements* — including the "generated" field that tells when you imported the data. To remove an element, right-click it and then click Remove element. To add an element back into the XML list, right-click the element and then click Map element.

You can also use the XML Source pane to map the XML elements that you want on your worksheet before importing the data. Press Alt+D, X, X to display the XML Source pane. Click the XML Maps button to display the XML Maps dialog box, and then click Add. In the Select XML Source dialog box, click the XML file you want to import, and then click Open. If the XML data source has multiple roots, Excel prompts you to select one. Click dataroot and then click OK to return to the XML Maps dialog box, and then click OK. You should now see the XML field elements in the XML Source pane. To add an element to the worksheet, either right-click it and then click Map element, or drag the element and drop it on the worksheet. When you are done, import the XML data.

Create a PowerPivot Data Connection

You can quickly connect to and use data from large or complex data sources by using the PowerPivot add-in to connect to those sources.

In Chapter 15, you learn how to create advanced connections to massive server-based data sources that use online analytical processing (OLAP). This is a complex process, but you see in Chapter 15 that it is worthwhile because a PivotTable based on an OLAP data source gives you many more options for analyzing your data.

However, in Excel 2010 these extra options for data analysis are available to just about *any* data source, provided you connect to that data source using a special

add-in called PowerPivot. With the PowerPivot add-in installed, you can create OLAP-like data connections quickly and easily, and you can then use these connections to build a PivotTable based on the source data. The source data can be a database, such as Access or SQL Server; a file, such as a text file or an Excel workbook; or a data feed, such as an Atom feed.

This task shows you how to create a PowerPivot data connection, so be sure you have PowerPivot installed. To download the add-in, go to the Microsoft Download Center at www.microsoft.com/downloads and search for PowerPivot.

Create a PowerPivot Data Connection

1 Click PowerPivot→ PowerPivot Window.

The PowerPivot window appears.

2 Click the Home tab.

3 In the Get External Data group, click the category of data source you want to use.

4 Click the type of data source you want to use for the connection.

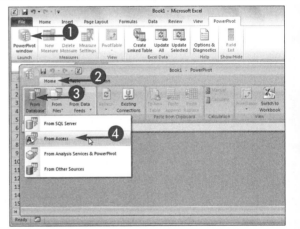

The Table Import Wizard appears.

5 In the Database Name text box, type the location of the data source.

● You can also click Browse and use the Open dialog box to select the data source.

● If your data source requires you to log on, type your credentials in the User Name and Password fields.

6 Click Next.

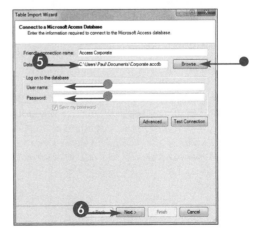

The Choose How to Import the Data page of the Text Import Wizard appears.

7 Leave the Select From a List of Tables and View to Choose the Data to Import option selected.

8 Click Next.

The Select Tables and Views page of the Text Import Wizard appears.

9 Select the check box beside the table or query you want to import.

○ If you always want to connect to all the tables that are related to the table or query you have selected, click Select Related Tables.

10 Click Finish.

PowerPivot connects to the data source and imports the data into a table in the PowerPivot window.

11 Click Close (not shown).

Note: To learn how to create a PivotTable using a PowerPivot data connection, see Chapter 14.

Extra

If you need to make changes to an existing PowerPivot connection, click PowerPivot→PowerPivot Window to open the PowerPivot window. Click Home→Existing Connections to open the Existing Connections dialog box, and then click the connection you want to modify. Click the Edit button to open the Edit Connection dialog box, and then follow steps **5** to **11** in this section to modify the connection properties and options.

You can also use the PowerPivot window to filter the data source before creating your PivotTable report. You filter a PowerPivot table using the same technique that you would use to filter a regular Excel table. That is, the header for each field in a PowerPivot table includes an AutoFilter drop-down arrow, and you click that arrow to see the filter options. For example, you can deselect one or more check boxes to remove those items from the field, or you can select the field's Filters command (such as Text Filters for a text field or Number Filters for a numeric field) and create a custom filter.

Refresh Imported Data

External data often changes; you can ensure that you are working with the most up-to-date version of the information by refreshing the imported data.

Refreshing the imported data means retrieving the most current version of the source data. This is a straightforward operation most of the time. However, it is possible to construct a query that accesses confidential information or destroys some or all of the external data.

Therefore, when you refresh imported data, Excel always lets you know the potential risks and asks if you are sure the query is safe.

Remember, as well, that most external data resides on servers or in remote network locations. Therefore, the refresh may take some time, depending on the amount of data, the load on the server, and the amount of traffic on the network.

Refresh Imported Data

Refresh Nontext Data

1. Click any cell inside the imported data.

2. Click Data→Refresh All→Refresh.

   You can also refresh the current data by pressing Alt+F5.

● To refresh all the imported data in the current workbook, you can click Data→Refresh All→Refresh All, or press Ctrl+Alt+F5.

   Excel refreshes the imported data.

   The refresh may take a long time. To check the status of the refresh, click Data→Refresh All→Refresh Status to display the External Data Refresh Status dialog box. Click Close to continue the refresh.

   If the refresh is taking too long, click Data→Refresh All→Cancel Refresh to cancel it.

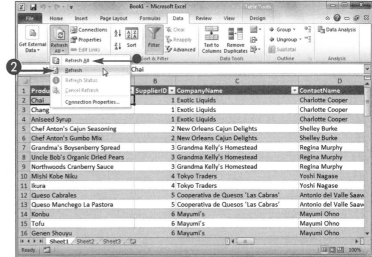

Refresh Text Data

1 Click any cell inside the imported text data.

2 Click Data→Refresh All→Refresh.

You can also refresh the current data by pressing Alt+F5.

The Import Text File dialog box appears.

3 Open the folder that contains the text file.

4 Click the text file.

5 Click Import.

Excel refreshes the imported text data.

Apply It

For certain types of external data, you can set up a schedule that automatically refreshes the data at a specified interval. This is useful when you know that the source data changes frequently and you do not want to be bothered with constant manual refreshes.

Click any cell inside the imported data, and then click Data→Refresh All→Connection Properties. In the Connection Properties dialog box, select the Refresh Every option and then use the spin box to specify the refresh interval in minutes.

Note, however, that you might prefer not to have the source data updated too frequently. Depending on where the data resides and how much data you are working with, the refresh could take some time, which will slow down the rest of your work.

You can also tell Excel to automatically refresh the imported data when you open the workbook. In the Connection Properties dialog box, select the Refresh Data When Opening the File option.

Create a PivotTable from Multiple Consolidation Ranges

I f your source data exists in two or more ranges, Excel can consolidate all the ranges and then produce a PivotTable report based on the consolidated data.

Many businesses create worksheets for a specific task and then distribute them to various departments. The most common example is budgeting. Accounting might create a generic "budget" template that each department or division in the company must fill out and return. Similarly, you often see worksheets distributed for inventory requirements, sales forecasting, survey data, experiment results, and more.

Creating these worksheets, distributing them, and filling them in are all straightforward operations. The tricky part, however, comes when the sheets are returned to the originating department, where all the new data must be combined into a summary report showing companywide totals. This task is called *consolidating* the data, and it is often difficult and time consuming, especially for large worksheets. However, Excel has a powerful PivotTable feature that can make it easy to consolidate the data and summarize it into a simple report.

Create a PivotTable from Multiple Consolidation Ranges

Note: *This chapter uses the workbooks Division1. xlsx, Division2.xlsx, Division3.xlsx, and PivotTables14.xlsm, and the Invoices.accdb database available at www.wiley.com/go/ pivottablesvb2e, or you can create your own sample files.*

1. Open the workbooks that contain the consolidation ranges.

2. Open the workbook in which you want the PivotTable to appear.

3. Press Alt+D, and then press P.

   Step 1 of the PivotTable and PivotChart Wizard appears.

4. Select Multiple Consolidation Ranges.

5. Select PivotTable.

6. Click Next.

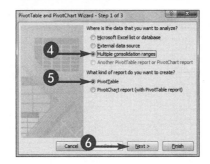

Step 2a of the PivotTable and PivotChart Wizard appears.

⑦ Select I Will Create the Page Fields.

⑧ Click Next.

Step 2b of the PivotTable and PivotChart Wizard appears.

⑨ Click the Collapse Dialog button (⊟).

Excel collapses the dialog box to show just the Range input box.

Extra

Pressing Alt+D, then pressing P is an Office 2003 access key that starts the PivotTable and PivotChart Wizard. Rather than remembering this access key, you can customize either the Ribbon or the Quick Access Toolbar with a command that runs the wizard. Click File→Options and then click either Customize Ribbon or Quick Access Toolbar. If you are customizing the Ribbon, either click New Tab to create a custom tab, or click an existing tab and then click New Group to create a custom group. In the Choose Commands From list, click All Commands, click PivotTable and PivotChart Wizard, and then click Add. Click OK.

Apply It

Another way to summarize data that exists in multiple ranges is to use Excel's Consolidate feature. With this feature, Excel consolidates the data from several worksheets using the same range coordinates on each sheet. You can use this method if the worksheets you are consolidating have an identical layout. To use this feature, click Data→Consolidate to display the Consolidate dialog box. Click the summary Function you want to use, such as Sum or Count; then for each range in the source worksheets, type the range reference and click Add. When you are done, click OK.

continued ➡

I n a PivotTable based on multiple consolidation ranges, Excel only offers a limited layout: a row field, a column field, a value (data) field, and up to four page fields. The items in the row field come from the leftmost columns of the source data ranges; the items in the column field come from the topmost row in the source data ranges; and the items in the value field come from the rest of the source data ranges.

For the page field, Excel sets up the report so that you can display the data from all the ranges or just the data from one of the ranges. In other words, Excel enables you to filter the PivotTable report based on the source ranges, and it uses the page field to do this.

However, if you let Excel set up this page field for you, it uses generic item names such as Item1, Item2, and Item3. To avoid the hassle of renaming these items after you create the PivotTable, you can specify them as you work with the PivotTable and PivotChart Wizard. That is why you selected the "I Will Create The Page Fields" option in step 6. In steps 14 to 17 of this section, you define the page field item names yourself.

Create a PivotTable from Multiple Consolidation Ranges *(continued)*

⑩ Select the range you want to include in the PivotTable report.

⑪ Click the Restore Dialog button.

Excel restores Step 2b of the PivotTable and PivotChart Wizard.

⑫ Click Add.

⑬ Repeat steps **9** to **12** to add the other ranges you want to consolidate.

⑭ Select 1.

⑮ Click the range you want to work with.

⑯ Type a label that identifies the range.

⑰ Repeat steps **15** and **16** for each range.

⑱ Click Next.

Step 3 of the PivotTable and PivotChart Wizard appears.

⑲ Select New Worksheet to place the PivotTable on a new worksheet.

● If you prefer to place the PivotTable on an existing worksheet, select Existing Worksheet, click the Collapse Dialog button, and then click the worksheet and cell where you want the PivotTable to appear.

⑳ Click Finish.

Excel consolidates the ranges and creates the PivotTable.

PivotTable and PivotChart Wizard - Step 3 of 3

Where do you want to put the PivotTable report?

⑲ ● New worksheet
   ○ Existing worksheet
   =$A$3

Click Finish to create your PivotTable report.

Layout... | Options... | Cancel | < Back | ⑳ Finish

	A	B	C	D	E	F	G	H	I
1	Page1	(All)							
2									
3	Sum of Value	Column							
4	Row	Jan	Feb	Mar	Apr	May	Jun	Jul	Aug
5	Advertising	13479	12306	15236	14650	16115	15382.5	16115	1523
6	Cost of Goods	18579.96	18131.52	19089	20046.48	19998	19913.16	20361.6	1908
7	Rent	6153	6153	6153	6153	6153	6153	6153	615
8	Salaries	46880	46880	48345	48345	48345	49810	49810	4981
9	Shipping	41752.5	40287.5	42485	43950	42485	43217.5	43950	4248
10	Supplies	3809	3516	4102	3809	3662.5	4102	3809	410
11	Utilities	1465	1758	1758	1611.5	1758	1904.5	1904.5	175
12	**Grand Total**	**132118.46**	**129032.02**	**137168**	**138564.98**	**138516.5**	**140482.66**	**142103.1**	**13863**
13									
14									
15									
16									

Sheet4 / Sheet1 / Sheet2 / Sheet3

Extra

When you complete the wizard, the PivotTable Field List shows only four items: Row, Column, Value, and Page1. You can add up to three more page fields, but other than that you cannot add any other fields to the Field List. However, you are free to rename the fields to provide more meaningful names; for more on this, see Chapter 6. You can also perform most other PivotTable tasks, including pivoting the fields and changing the summary calculation.

To create more page fields, press Alt+D, press P, and then click Back to display Step 2b of the PivotTable and PivotChart Wizard. Select the number of page fields you want: 2, 3, or 4. Then perform steps **15** and **16** to define the item names for each page field. For step **16**, be sure to use the appropriate text box: Field Two for the second page field; Field Three for the third page field; or Field Four for the fourth page field.

If you allowed Excel to create the page field automatically, you need to rename the page field items to give them more meaningful names. Pivot the page field into the row area so that the items are visible. Rename each item, and then pivot the field back into the page area.

Create a PivotTable from an Existing PivotTable

Y ou can save time and effort by creating a new PivotTable based on the data in an existing PivotTable.

You learned in several places throughout this book that Excel maintains a pivot cache for each PivotTable. This pivot cache is a memory location that holds the source data and other information relating to the PivotTable. Keeping this data in memory means that your PivotTable recalculates quickly when you change the layout, grouping, filtering, or summary calculation. The price you pay for having the pivot cache is extra workbook size and less memory available for other tasks, but the trade-off is usually worth it.

You can minimize the downside of the pivot cache by building new PivotTables based on existing PivotTables wherever possible. You can't do this directly from a PivotTable using the Excel Ribbon. However, if you use the old PivotTable and PivotChart Wizard, you can create a new PivotTable from any existing PivotTable in a workbook. Doing this not only means that the two PivotTables share the same pivot cache, but it also takes less time and effort to build the new PivotTable because the PivotTable and PivotChart Wizard lets you build the new report with just a few mouse clicks.

Create a PivotTable from an Existing PivotTable

1 Press Alt+D, and then press P.

Step 1 of the PivotTable and PivotChart Wizard appears.

2 Select Another PivotTable Report or PivotChart Report.

3 Select PivotTable.

4 Click Next.

PivotTable and PivotChart Wizard - Step 1 of 3

Where is the data that you want to analyze?
- Microsoft Excel list or database
- External data source
- Multiple consolidation ranges
- 2 → Another PivotTable report or PivotChart report

What kind of report do you want to create?
- 3 → PivotTable
- PivotChart report (with PivotTable report)

Cancel   < Back   4 → Next >   Finish

Step 2 of the PivotTable and PivotChart Wizard appears.

5 Click the PivotTable upon which you want to base the new PivotTable.

6 Click Next.

PivotTable and PivotChart Wizard - Step 2 of 3

Which PivotTable report contains the data you want to use?

5 → [PivotTables14.xlsm]PT-Employee Total Sales!PivotTable2
[PivotTables14.xlsm]PT-Product Sales By Month!PivotTable3

Cancel   < Back 6 → Next >   Finish

Step 3 of the PivotTable and PivotChart Wizard appears.

7 Select Existing Worksheet.

8 Click the worksheet and cell where you want the PivotTable to appear.

● If you prefer to place the PivotTable on a new worksheet, select New Worksheet instead.

9 Click Finish.

Excel creates an empty PivotTable.

● The fields available in the PivotTable that you choose in step **5** appear in the PivotTable Field List.

10 Click and drag fields from the PivotTable Field List and drop them in the PivotTable areas.

Apply It

If you know the name of the PivotTable report from which you want to create your new PivotTable, you can use the Worksheet object's `PivotTableWizard` method to create the new PivotTable. Set the `SourceType` parameter to `xlPivotTable` and set the `SourceData` parameter to the name of the existing PivotTable, including the workbook name — enclosed in square brackets ([]) — worksheet name, and PivotTable name, as shown in the following example:

Example:
```
ActiveSheet.PivotTableWizard _
    SourceType:=xlPivotTable, _
    SourceData:="[PivotTables14.xlsm]PT-Employee Total Sales!PivotTable2"
```

Create a PivotTable from External Data

You can create a PivotTable using an external data source, which enables you to build reports from extremely large datasets and from relational database systems.

So far in this book, you have learned about data sources that reside on Excel worksheets as ranges or lists. This is a convenient way to work with PivotTables because you have access to the source data, enabling you to easily change field names, add and delete fields, insert records, and so on. However, working with data in Excel has two major drawbacks:

- Excel offers only simple row-and-column database management. You cannot use Excel to perform relational database management where, when two or

more datasets are related on a common field, you can combine those datasets in powerful ways.

- Excel worksheets are limited to 1,048,576 rows, so that is the maximum number of records you can have in a range or list data source.

To overcome these limitations, you need to use a relational database management system (RDBMS) such as Microsoft Access or SQL Server. With these programs, you can set up a table, query, or other object that defines the data you want to work with. In most cases, the data object can be as complex and as large as you need. You can then build your PivotTable based on this *external data source*.

Create a PivotTable from External Data

1. Press Alt+D, and then press P.

   Step 1 of the PivotTable and PivotChart Wizard appears.

2. Select External Data Source.

3. Select PivotTable.

4. Click Next.

   Step 2 of the PivotTable and PivotChart Wizard appears.

5. Click Get Data.

Note: *If your external data source requires a login, you see the Login dialog box, which you then use to type your login credentials.*

The Choose Data Source dialog box appears.

6 Click the data source you want to use.

Note: *To learn how to create data sources, see the Chapter 12.*

7 Select Use the Query Wizard to Create/Edit Queries.

8 Click OK.

The Choose Columns page of the Query Wizard appears.

9 Click the table or column you want to use as the source data for your PivotTable.

10 Click >.

● The table's fields appear in the Columns In Your Query list.

11 Click Next.

The Filter Data page of the Query Wizard appears.

12 Click Next.

Extra

You can reduce the size of the new PivotTable's pivot cache by including only those fields that you need for your PivotTable. In the Choose Columns page of the Query Wizard, each table has a plus sign (+). Click a table's plus sign to display a list of that object's fields, or columns, as the Query Wizard calls them. You can then click a field and click > to add it to the list of fields to be used with your PivotTable. You can also double-click the field.

If you are not sure what items a field contains, click the field in either list and then click Preview Now. The Query Wizard displays the field's items in the Preview Of Data In Selected Column list.

If you add a table, query, or field by mistake, click the item in the Columns In Your Query list, and then click < to remove it. If you want to start over, click << to remove everything from the Columns In Your Query list.

continued ➜

Create a PivotTable from External Data (continued)

The Choose Data Source dialog box and the various Query Wizard pages are not part of Excel. Instead, they are components of a program called Microsoft Query. You can use this program to work with external data. For more details on how this program works, see Chapter 12. For the purposes of this section, I assume that you have already defined the appropriate data source, as shown in Chapter 12, and that you do not want to work with Microsoft Query directly; see Chapter 12. Also note that steps **12** and **13** essentially skip over the Query Wizard pages that enable you to filter and sort the external data because this is not usually pertinent for a PivotTable report. For the details of these steps, see the section "Define a Data Source" in Chapter 12.

The other assumption I made in this section is that you do not want the external data imported to Excel. Rather, in this section, the external data resides only in the new PivotTable's pivot cache; you do not see the data itself in your workbook. This is particularly useful if the external data contains more than 1,048,576 records, because otherwise Excel would not allow you to import so much data. (1,048,576 is the maximum number of rows in an Excel 2007 and Excel 2010 worksheet.) However, you can still easily refresh and rebuild your PivotTable, just like you can with a report based on a local range or list. If you want to learn how to import external data into Excel, see Chapter 13.

Create a PivotTable from External Data *(continued)*

The Sort Order page of the Query Wizard appears.

13 Click Next.

The Finish page of the Query Wizard appears.

14 Select Return Data to Microsoft Excel.

15 Click Finish.

Step 2 of the PivotTable and PivotChart Wizard appears.

⑯ Click Finish.

Excel creates an empty PivotTable.

● The fields available in the table or query that you chose in step **11** appear in the PivotTable Field List.

⑰ Click and drag fields from the PivotTable Field List and drop them in the PivotTable areas.

Extra

The most common drawback to using an external data source is that you often have no control over the external file itself. This may mean that the database login data changes or that the file might get moved to a new location, renamed, or even deleted. If this happens and you attempt to refresh the PivotTable, Excel displays an error message. For example, if the external data source is an Access database, Excel might display an error dialog box telling you that it cannot find the external database file. In this case, click OK to close the dialog box and display the Login dialog box.

If you suspect the problem is a change to the login data, find out the correct login name and password from the database administrator, type the new data in the Login dialog box, and then click OK.

If you suspect the problem is that the database file has been moved or renamed, click Database in the Login dialog box. You can use the Select Database dialog box to find and click the database file, and then click OK to return to the Login dialog box. Click OK to return to Excel.

Create a PivotTable Using PowerPivot

Y ou can create a PivotTable that unlocks some of Excel 2010's powerful new features by basing that PivotTable on a PowerPivot data connection. In Chapter 13, you learned about the PowerPivot add-in for Excel. This add-in enables you to import data from a variety of data sources, particularly large data sets in SQL Server that would be otherwise difficult to manage without specialized knowledge. The PowerPivot add-in enables you to set up a connection with the data source using a few relatively straightforward steps.

Although you can manipulate the imported data within the PowerPivot window — for example, you can filter the data and customize the resulting table — you will most likely want to display the data in an Excel PivotTable. This not only lets you see a summary of the data, but it also enables you to analyze that data using Excel's PivotTable tools. However, PivotTable reports based on PowerPivot data connections also enable some new features in Excel, such as performing what-if analysis on the data. You learn about some of these new features in Chapter 15.

Create a PivotTable Using PowerPivot

① Use PowerPivot to create a connection to a data source.

Note: See Chapter 13 to learn how to set up a PowerPivot data connection.

② Click Home→PivotTable→ Single PivotTable.

- If you want to create a PivotChart instead, you can click Single PivotChart.

- If you want to create a PivotTable and a PivotChart at the same time, you can click one of these Chart and Table commands.

The Insert Pivot dialog box appears.

③ Click New Worksheet.

◉ If you prefer to place the PivotTable on an existing worksheet, click Existing Worksheet, click ⊟, and then click the cell where you want the PivotTable to appear.

④ Click OK.

Excel creates an empty PivotTable.

◉ The fields available in the PivotTable that you choose in step **5** appear in the PivotTable Field List.

⑤ Click and drag fields from the PivotTable Field List and drop them in the PivotTable areas.

Extra

One of the main differences between a regular PivotTable and a PivotTable generated from a PowerPivot data connection is that the Field List task pane for a PowerPivot-based report includes two new drop areas: Slicers Vertical and Slicers Horizontal. You learned about slicers in Chapter 5, but with PowerPivot-based reports you can create slicers right from the Field List. If you drop a field in the Slicers Vertical area, Excel creates a vertical slicer to the left of the PivotTable; if you drop a field in the Slicers Horizontal area, Excel creates a horizontal slicer above the PivotTable

Automatically Refresh a PivotTable that Uses External Data

If you built a PivotTable directly from an external data source, as described in the previous section, you can configure the connection between the PivotTable and the data source to refresh automatically. This ensures that you are always working with the most up-to-date version of the information.

External data often changes, but because the data is located elsewhere — either in another file or on a remote server — you can never be sure when the data underlying your PivotTable report has changed. The easiest way to make sure you are working with the latest is to refresh the PivotTable, as described in Chapter 3.

However, for certain types of external data, you can set up a schedule that automatically refreshes the PivotTable at a specified interval. This is useful when you know that the source data changes frequently and you do not want to be bothered with constant manual refreshes. For example,

you can set up the connection to refresh every 60 minutes. Note that you might prefer not to have the source data updated too frequently. Depending on where the data resides and how much data you are working with, the refresh could take some time, which will slow down the rest of your work. You can also tell Excel to automatically refresh the imported data when you open the workbook.

In both cases, when you refresh the PivotTable, Excel queries the external data source to retrieve the latest data. While the query is in progress, you cannot do anything else in Excel. This is fine if the query takes only a few seconds, but it can be a problem for queries that take a very long time. Therefore, you can also configure the connection to run the refresh in the background, which enables you to perform other work in Excel while the PivotTable refreshes.

Automatically Refresh a PivotTable that Uses External Data

① Click any cell in the PivotTable that you created from external data.

② Click Options→Refresh→Connection Properties.

The Connection Properties dialog box appears.

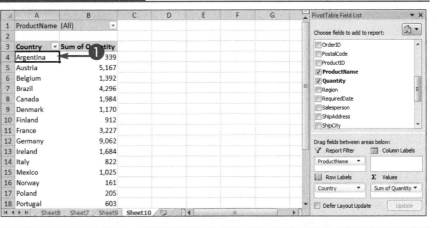

3 Select Refresh Every.

4 Type the refresh interval in minutes that you want to use for the schedule.

● If you want Excel to automatically refresh the PivotTable each time you open the workbook, you can select Refresh Data When Opening the File.

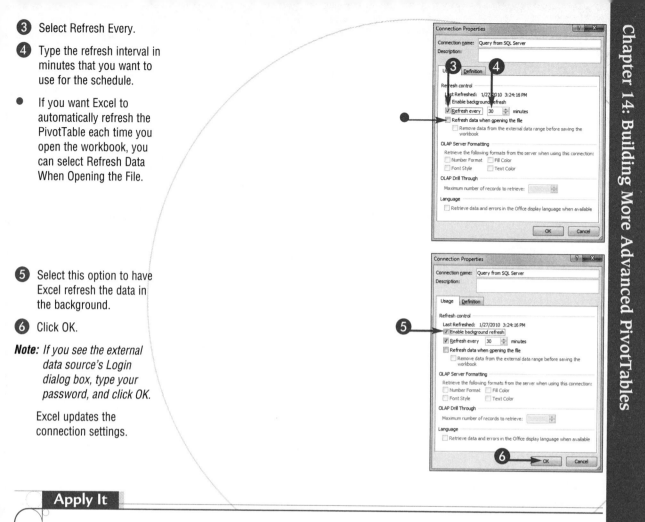

5 Select this option to have Excel refresh the data in the background.

6 Click OK.

Note: *If you see the external data source's Login dialog box, type your password, and click OK.*

Excel updates the connection settings.

Apply It

You can control the external data refresh settings using Visual Basic for Applications (VBA). You can use the `PivotTable` object's `PivotCache` property, which is itself an object with three properties that correspond to the three check boxes: `RefreshPeriod`, `RefreshOnFileOpen`, and `BackgroundQuery`. The following macro toggles these three properties on and off (see Chapter 16 for VBA basics):

Example:
```
Sub ToggleExternalDataRefreshSettings()
    ' Work with the active PivotTable
    With ActiveCell.PivotTable.PivotCache
        ' Toggle the "Refresh every X minutes" setting
        If .RefreshPeriod > 0 Then
            .RefreshPeriod = 0
        Else
            .RefreshPeriod = 60
        End If
        ' Toggle the "Refresh data when opening the file" setting
        .RefreshOnFileOpen = Not .RefreshOnFileOpen
        ' Toggle the "Enable background refresh" setting
        .BackgroundQuery = Not .BackgroundQuery
    End With
End Sub
```

Save Your Password with an External Data Connection

You can save time and typing by configuring an external data connection to save your password.

Some external data sources require a login name and password to access the data. By default, Excel does not save the login password in the pivot cache. If you close the workbook, reopen it, and then refresh the PivotTable, you must log in again to the external data source. As you saw in the previous section, you also have to log in again each time you make manual changes to the connection properties.

To prevent Excel from prompting you for a password each time you refresh a PivotTable after opening a workbook

or after you make changes to the connection, you can configure the connection to save your password. Excel stores the password with the other connection properties, so you do not need to type it again.

You should know that Excel does not encrypt or hide the password in any way. After saving the password, when you examine the connection properties, the password is visible in plain text. This is not a problem if you are the only person who uses your computer. However, if other people use or have access to your computer, then you might not want your password so easily visible.

Save Your Password with an External Data Connection

① Click any cell in the PivotTable that you created from external data.

② Click Options→Refresh→ Connection Properties.

The Connection Properties dialog box appears.

③ Click the Definition tab.

④ Select the Save Password check box.

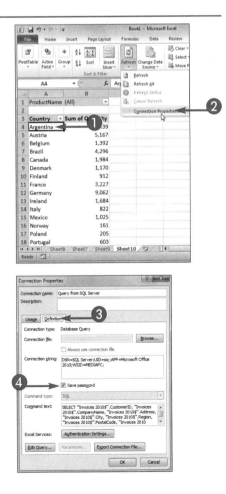

Excel asks you to confirm that you want to save the password.

⑤ Click **Yes**.

● The password appears in plain text in the Connection String box.

⑥ Click **OK**.

Note: *If you see the external data source's Login dialog box, type your password and click OK.*

Excel updates the connection settings.

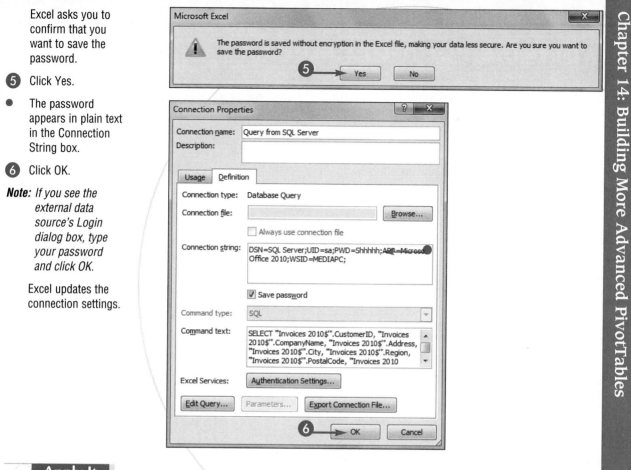

Apply It

You can control whether Excel stores the password with the connection using VBA. Use the `PivotTable` object's `PivotCache` property, which returns an object that has a `SavePassword` property. The following macro toggles this property on and off (see Chapter 16 for VBA basics):

```
Example:
Sub ToggleSaveExternalDataPassword()
    ' Work with the active PivotTable
    With ActiveCell.PivotTable.PivotCache
        ' Toggle the "Save password" setting
        .SavePassword = Not .SavePassword
    End With
End Sub
```

Extra

If you are concerned that other people might see your password when you are not at your computer, you should lock your computer each time you leave your desk. To lock your computer, press Windows Logo+L. Alternatively, press Ctrl+Alt+Delete and then click Lock Computer. In Windows 7, you can also click Start, click the Shut Down arrow, and then click Lock; in Windows Vista, click Start, and then click Lock.

Export an Access PivotTable Form to Excel

I f you are working with a PivotTable form in an Access 2007 database, you can export the PivotTable form's data from the Access database to a PivotTable in Excel.

In Access 2007 and Access 2010, you can create a PivotTable form that looks and operates much like an Excel PivotTable. Using an Access table or query as the data source, you can create a new PivotTable form and then populate the row, column, and filter areas with items from fields in the table or query fields. You can also summarize the data in a numeric field by adding that field to the data area.

Once the PivotTable form is complete, you can then perform actions such as pivoting the fields, filtering the field items, hiding and showing details, and even creating calculated items and detail fields. However, these actions are only a small subset of what you can do with an Excel PivotTable. Therefore, if you want to perform more advanced data analysis on the PivotTable, you should export the PivotTable form to an Excel PivotTable. This gives you a regular Excel PivotTable in a read-only file, which you can then save to your computer.

Note that for this operation to proceed smoothly, you should shut down Excel if it is currently running.

Export an Access PivotTable Form to Excel

① Open the database containing the PivotTable form you want to export.

② Open the PivotTable form.

③ Click Design→Export to Excel.

If Access encounters problems exporting the data, the Problems During Load dialog box appears.

Note: *This dialog box is common when you export an Access PivotTable form and appears to be a bug in Access. No data is lost or corrupted during the transfer, so you can safely ignore the problem.*

④ Click OK.

The PivotTable appears in a temporary Excel workbook.

Problems During Load

Problems came up in the following areas during load:

PivotTable

A log file has been created listing the load errors. This file has been saved to the following location: C:\Users\Paul\AppData\Local\Microsoft\Windows\Temporary Internet Files\Content.MSO\8748D4C8.log.

④ → OK   Cancel

	A	B	C	D	E	F
1	Country	(All)				
2						
3	Sum of ExtendedPrice	CategoryName				
4	Salesperson	Beverages	Condiments	Confections	Dairy Products	Grains/Cerea
5	Andrew Fuller	$9,009.10	$6,036.77	$11,706.13	$12,440.05	$6,838
6	Anne Dodsworth	$5,469.33	$2,918.05	$226.80	$8,012.45	$1,021
7	Janet Leverling	$23,069.66	$7,589.14	$18,967.59	$20,257.05	$17,723
8	Laura Callahan	$6,414.95	$8,197.25	$10,643.19	$9,722.59	$5,087
9	Margaret Peacock	$27,560.90	$15,966.45	$11,375.84	$16,890.10	$10,552
10	Michael Suyama	$4,492.20	$2,416.74	$4,090.28	$9,511.70	$6,581
11	Nancy Davolio	$13,112.07	$6,797.84	$14,297.46	$18,538.19	$6,183
12	Robert King	$12,633.71	$3,821.48	$9,738.30	$16,006.90	$1,495
13	Steven Buchanan	$2,162.37	$1,624.84	$1,612.11	$4,008.59	$1,388
14	Grand Total	$103,924.29	$55,368.56	$82,657.70	$115,387.62	$56,871
15						
16						
17						
18						

Sheet1 / Sheet2

Apply It

After Access exports the PivotTable form, you end up with a new Excel PivotTable in a read-only workbook. You can work with this PivotTable using the normal Excel techniques. However, if you want to preserve your changes, you need to save the workbook to a file. Click File→Save As, select a location, type a file name, and then click Save. Also note that the resulting PivotTable uses the classic layout. If you prefer the Excel 2007 and later layout, click Options→PivotTable→Options, click the Display tab, and then deselect the Classic PivotTable Layout check box.

Extra

To create a PivotTable form in Access 2010 and 2007, first select the table or query you want to use as the data source. Then click Create→More Forms→PivotTable. Access displays a blank PivotTable form. Click Design→Field List to display the PivotTable Field List (you may need to click this button twice to see the list). Then, for each field you want to add, click and drag the field and drop it inside the PivotTable area you want to use. For a data field, click the field you want to use, select Data Area in the Add To list, and then click Add To.

Reduce the Size of PivotTable Workbooks

You can reduce the size of your Excel workbooks by not saving the PivotTable source data in the pivot cache.

If you build a PivotTable from data that resides in a different workbook or in an external data source, Excel stores the source data in the pivot cache. This greatly reduces the time it takes to refresh and recalculate the PivotTable. The downside is that it can increase both the size of the workbook and the amount of time it takes Excel to save the workbook. If your workbook has become too large or it takes too long to save, you can tell Excel not to save the source data in the pivot cache.

Apply It

You can control whether Excel uses the pivot cache via VBA. To do this, set the `PivotTable` object's `SaveData` property to `True` with the pivot cache on, or to `False` with the pivot cache off, as shown in the following macro (see Chapter 16 for VBA basics):

Example:
```
Sub TogglePivotCache()
    With ActiveSheet.PivotTables(1)
        ' Toggle the SaveData property
        .SaveData = Not .SaveData
        ' Display the current state
        MsgBox "pivot cache is now " & _
                IIf(.SaveData, "on.", "off.")
    End With
End Sub
```

Reduce the Size of PivotTable Workbooks

1. Click any cell in the PivotTable.

2. Click Options→ PivotTable→Options.

   The PivotTable Options dialog box appears.

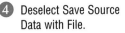

3. Click the Data tab.

4. Deselect Save Source Data with File.

5. Click OK.

   Excel no longer saves the external source data in the pivot cache.

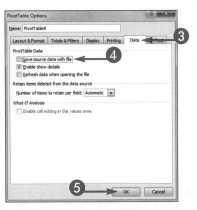

Use a PivotTable Value in a Formula

Y ou may need to use a PivotTable value in a worksheet formula. You normally reference a cell in a formula by using the cell's address. However, this does not work with PivotTables because the addresses of the report values change as you pivot, filter, group, and refresh the PivotTable.

To ensure accurate PivotTable references, use Excel's GETPIVOTDATA function. This function uses the data field, PivotTable location, and one or more (row or column) field/item pairs that specify the exact value you want to use. This way, no matter what the PivotTable layout is, as long as the value remains visible in the report, your formula reference remains accurate.

Extra

If you want to reference a PivotTable value only temporarily, click Options→Options→Generate GetPivotData to turn off that command. You can also do this using VBA:

Example:
```
Sub ToggleGenerateGetPivotData()
    With Application
        .GenerateGetPivotData = Not
 .GenerateGetPivotData
        MsgBox "Excel will " & _
            IIf(.GenerateGetPivotData,
 "generate", "not generate") & _
                " the GETPIVOTDATA function."
    End With
End Sub
```

Use a PivotTable Value in a Formula

❶ Click the cell in which you want to build your formula.

❷ Type =.

❸ Click the PivotTable cell containing the value you want to include in your formula.

● Excel generates a GETPIVOTDATA function for the PivotTable value.

❹ Complete the formula and press Enter.

● Excel includes the PivotTable value in the formula result.

Note: The GETPIVOTDATA function looks complicated, but it really only contains a few parameters. The first parameter is the name of the data field ("Quantity" in the example); the second parameter is the location of the PivotTable ($A$3); subsequent parameters come in pairs: a field name ("ShipRegion") and an item in that field ("Oregon").

Understanding OLAP

So far in this book you have worked with relatively small data sources such as the Northwind sample database that comes with Microsoft Access. In the business world, however, it is common to work with data sources that are much larger — from hundreds of thousands of records to millions, even billions, of records. You cannot place such a huge data source on a worksheet, and even trying to manipulate all that data via a regular external data source is extremely time consuming and resource intensive. Fortunately, such huge data sources often reside on special servers that use a technology called *Online Analytical Processing*, or *OLAP*. OLAP enables you to retrieve and summarize immense and complex data sources. When combined with Excel, OLAP enables you to view the data in a PivotTable or PivotChart report and manipulate the data quickly and easily.

Data Warehouse

In a traditional relational database management system, or RDBMS, such as Access, multiple tables are related using common fields. In the Northwind sample database, for example, the Customers table is related to the Orders table based on the common Customer ID field, and the Orders table is related to the Order Details table on the common Order ID field. You can use a query to pick and choose fields from each table and return them in a dataset. However, this can be a very slow process with a massive data source, so OLAP uses a different concept called the *data warehouse*. This is a data structure — called a *star schema* — with a central fact table that contains the numeric data you want to summarize and pointers to surrounding related tables.

Fact Table

A *fact table* is the primary table in a data warehouse and it contains data on events or processes — the facts — within a business, such as sales transactions or company expenses. Each record in the fact table contains two types of data: measures and dimensions.

Measure

A *measure* is column of numeric values within the fact table and it represents the data that you want to summarize. In a data warehouse of sales transactions, for example, there might be one measure for units sold and another for dollars sold. An OLAP measure is analogous to a data field in a regular data source.

Dimension

A *dimension* is a category of data, so it is analogous to a row, column, or report filter in an ordinary data source. However, dimensions often contain hierarchical groupings called *levels*. For example, a Store dimension may have a hierarchy of location levels, such as Country, State, and City. Similarly, a Time dimension may have Year, Quarter, and Month levels. Each level has its own set of items, called *members*. For example, the Month level has the items January, February, and so on. Because most fact tables contain keys to multiple dimension tables, OLAP data is often called *multidimensional data*.

OLAP Cube

An *OLAP cube* is a data structure that takes the information in a data warehouse and summarizes each measure by every dimension, level, and member. For example, a three-dimensional cube might summarize sales based on the dimensions of Time, Product, and Store. The cube could then tell you, for example, the units sold of rye bread at store #6 in January, or the dollars worth of scissors sold in California in the second quarter. All the measures come precalculated in the cube, so Excel does not have to perform any calculations when you use an OLAP cube as a source for a PivotTable.

Non-OLAP and OLAP PivotTables look and operate much the same. However, OLAP PivotTables have a number of limitations and differences of which to be aware:

Calculations

- You cannot change the summary function in the OLAP PivotTable data area. The summary function used by a measure is defined in advance and the calculations are performed on the OLAP server.

- You cannot change the summary function for PivotTable subtotals.

- You cannot create calculated fields or calculated items. However, there may be calculated members that are defined on the OLAP server.

Layout

- In the PivotTable Field List, measures appear at the top of the list in the Values section. The rest of the PivotTable Field List contains separate sections for each dimension.

- Dimensions can only be used in the PivotTable's row, column, and page areas.

- Measures can only be used in the PivotTable's data area.

- You cannot display the underlying detail for an OLAP summary value.

- Items initially appear in the sort order defined by the OLAP server. However, you can sort the PivotTable results yourself; see Chapter 4.

- You cannot use the Show Pages command to display each PivotTable page on a separate worksheet.

- If you rename a dimension or member, hide it, and then add it back into the PivotTable, Excel displays the dimension or member using its original name.

Other Differences

- You cannot disable the Enable background refresh option; see Chapter 14.

- Excel does not save the external data with the PivotTable layout. Only the data used in the PivotTable report is returned from the OLAP server or cube file.

- Excel can only work with OLAP data in a PivotTable or PivotChart report. You cannot save OLAP data to a worksheet.

- You cannot change the summary function used by a measure.

- You cannot create custom calculated fields or items in an OLAP PivotTable.

Create an OLAP Cube Data Source

Before you can use an OLAP cube as the underlying data for a PivotTable, you must first create a data source that points to either a database on an OLAP server or to an offline cube file.

If you are on a network that runs an OLAP server — such as Microsoft SQL Server with Analysis Services, SAS OLAP Server, or Oracle OLAP Server — then you can get

the most flexibility by connecting to the server and working with a database that has one or more OLAP cubes defined. This ensures that you are always working with the most recent data. Check with your database administrator to learn how to find the OLAP server and whether you need a separate login user name and password to access the server.

Create an OLAP Cube Data Source

Start the Data Source

Note: *Portions of this chapter use the SalesCube.cub offline cube file, available at www.wiley.com/go/pivottablesvb2e, or you can create your own sample cube file.*

① Click Data→Get External Data→From Other Sources→From Microsoft Query.

The Choose Data Source dialog box appears.

② Click the OLAP Cubes tab.

③ Click New Data Source.

④ Click OK.

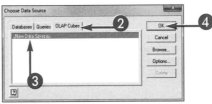

The Create New Data Source dialog box appears.

⑤ Type a name for the OLAP cube.

⑥ Click ▼ and select the OLAP provider that you use to connect to the OLAP server or cube file.

⑦ Click Connect.

The Multidimensional Connection dialog box appears.

Note: *If you want to use an OLAP server, follow the steps in the section "Connect to an OLAP Server." If you want to use a cube file, follow the steps in the section "Connect to a Cube File."*

Connect to an OLAP Server

1. Select Analysis Server.

2. Type the server name or address.

3. If you are connecting to the server via the Internet, type the User ID and password, if required.

4. Click Next.

   A list of databases on the OLAP server appears.

5. Click the database that contains the OLAP cube you want to use.

6. Click Finish.

   The Create New Data Source dialog box appears.

Note: *To finish the data source, follow the steps in the section "Complete the Data Source."*

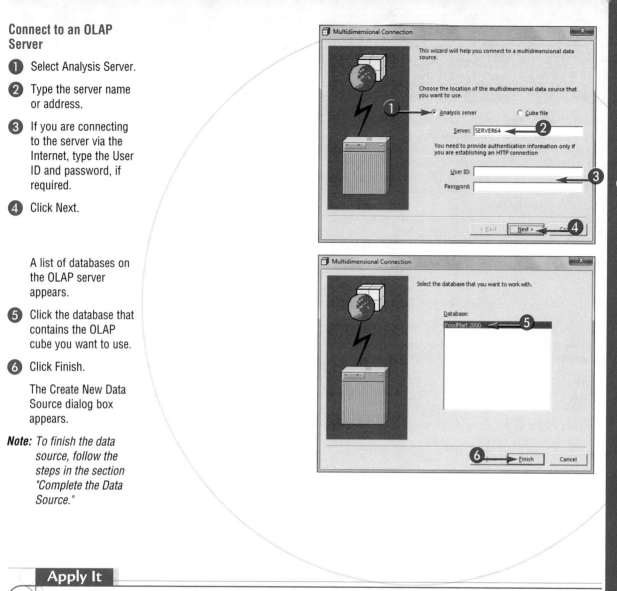

Apply It

You can also create OLAP cubes from relational data by creating a query for, say, an Access object, and then saving it as an OLAP cube. First, set up a data source that points to the Access database; see the section "Define a Data Source" in Chapter 12. Then select the data source using the Query Wizard; see Chapter 12. In the final Query Wizard page, select Create an OLAP Cube From The Query and then click Finish to launch the OLAP Cube Wizard.

The OLAP Cube Wizard has three steps. In the first step, you can select the measures you want to include in the cube. In the second step, you can specify the dimensions and levels you want to include in the cube — drag a dimension field and then drag its levels onto it. In the third step, you can either create a cube file or you can create an online cube.

continued ➡

Instead of connecting to an OLAP server, you may have access to a *cube file*, which is a version of an OLAP cube that has been saved to a local or network folder. A cube file is offline in the sense that the data is not connected to an OLAP server, so it is a static snapshot of the data. This is useful if you are working out of the office and do not have access to the OLAP server. However, you may also want to work with a cube file while you are connected to the network. If you know

the data is not going to change soon, working with a cube file tends to be faster than working online with a server because network traffic may slow down the server connection.

Your database administrator may be able to create a cube file for you. Alternatively, you can use the OLAP Cube Wizard to create a cube file, as described in the tip on the previous page. See also the section "Create an Offline OLAP Cube" later in this chapter.

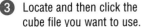

Create an OLAP Cube Data Source *(continued)*

Connect to a Cube File

1 Select Cube File.

2 Click here to specify the cube file you want to use.

The Open dialog box appears.

3 Locate and then click the cube file you want to use.

4 Click Open.

5 Click Finish.

The Create New Data Source dialog box appears.

Note: *To finish the data source, follow the steps in the section "Complete the Data Source."*

Complete the Data Source

1 Click ▾ and select the cube you want to work with.

2 Click OK.

The Choose Data Source dialog box appears.

3 Click the OLAP Cubes tab.

● The cube data source appears in the OLAP Cubes tab.

4 Click Cancel.

You can now use the cube data source to create a PivotTable.

Note: *If you want to create the PivotTable right away, click OK instead of Cancel in the Choose Data Source dialog box.*

Apply It

If your network uses SQL Server with Analysis Services as its OLAP server, then you should also have access to a sample database. Older versions of SQL Server use the Foodmart database, which is a relatively large database of transactions based on a fictional grocery store chain. The database includes a number of fact tables, such as sales_fact_1998, which contains more than 160,000 records. On the OLAP server, there are several built-in cubes, including Sales, HR, and Budget. For SQL Server 2005 and 2008, you may have access to the AdventureWorks database, which simulates a bicycle retailer. It includes several fact tables, most of which contain tens of thousands of records.

If you do not see one of these databases when you access your OLAP server, ask your database administrator whether the sample database can be made available.

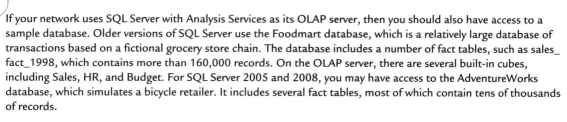

Create a PivotTable from an OLAP Cube

After you define a data source for the OLAP cube you want to work with, you can then use that data source as the basis of a PivotTable.

By definition, an OLAP cube is already a summary of the underlying data in the OLAP database. When creating an OLAP cube, the database administrator specifies one or more measures, and then the OLAP server applies those measures to every dimension, level, and member. So every possible combination of measure and dimension is already part of the cube. This is what makes cubes so powerful: Because all the summarizing work has already been done and the results are part of the cube, Excel requires very little processing power to pivot, filter, and summarize the data.

Because the OLAP cube is already a summary of data, it can only appear in Excel as part of a PivotTable or a PivotChart. So if you want to work with an OLAP cube within Excel, you must do it as part of a PivotTable.

Create a PivotTable from an OLAP Cube

① Click Data→Get External Data→From Other Sources→From Microsoft Query.

The Choose Data Source dialog box appears.

② Click the OLAP Cubes tab.

③ Click the OLAP cube you want to work with.

④ Click OK.

The Import Data dialog box appears.

5 Select the PivotTable Report option.

6 Select the New Worksheet option.

● If you want to place the PivotTable on an existing worksheet, select the Existing Worksheet option and then click the cell where you want the report to appear.

7 Click OK.

Excel creates an empty PivotTable and displays the PivotTable toolbar and the PivotTable Field List.

● Cube measures appear in the Values section of the PivotTable Field List.

● The rest of the PivotTable Field List displays the cube dimensions.

● To display a dimension's levels, click the plus sign (**+**).

8 Click and drag one or more dimensions to the Row Labels, Column Labels, or Report Filter area.

9 Click and drag a measure to the Values area.

Excel displays the completed PivotTable.

Extra

If your network uses SQL Server Analysis Services and you are working with OLAP cubes extensively, consider downloading and installing the Excel 2002/2003 Add-in for SQL Server Analysis Services from www.microsoft.com/downloads/. This add-in works with Excel 2010 and 2007 as well.

After you install this add-in, restart Excel and you will see an Add-Ins tab that includes a Cube Analysis menu. You can use the options on this menu to connect to a cube and to build special reports that enable you to analyze the data in more detail than you can with a PivotTable report. For example, you can use the Drillthrough command to drill down into the measure values to see the underlying data.

Show and Hide Details for Dimensions and Levels

You can enhance your data analysis by displaying the details for one or more of the dimensions and levels in an OLAP PivotTable.

When you add a dimension to an OLAP PivotTable, Excel shows the members that comprise the top level of the dimension's hierarchy. For example, if you add the Product dimension in the Foodmart Sales cube, Excel displays the members of the Product Family level: Drink, Food, and Non-Consumable. However, the dimension hierarchy may have more levels. For example, in the Foodmart Sales cube, the Product Family's Drink member has another level that includes the items Alcoholic Beverages, Beverages, and Dairy. Similarly, the Beverages

member has another level that includes Carbonated Beverages, Drinks, and Hot Beverages.

Some dimensions have only a single level, but others can have four or five. For these multilevel dimension hierarchies, you can drill down into the dimension's details to see more specific slices of the cube data.

In this section, you learn how to move up and down through a dimension's hierarchy one level at a time. An OLAP PivotTable also enables you to display only selected levels and members, and you learn how to do that in the section "Display Selected Levels and Members" later in this chapter.

Show and Hide Details for Dimensions and Levels

Show Details

Note: For the VBA macro code in this chapter, see the PivotTables15.xlsm workbook available at www.wiley.com/go/pivottablesvb2e.

① Click **+** for the level item you want to work with.

You can also double-click the level item.

- To expand all the details for a dimension, click any cell in the dimension and then click Options→ Expand Entire Field ().

- Excel shows the detail.

Hide Details

1 Click the Minus button
(—) for the level item
you want to work with.

You can also double-click
the level item.

● To hide all the details for
a dimension, click any
cell in the dimension and
then click Options→
Collapse Entire Field (▦).

Excel hides the detail.

Apply It

You can use VBA to control whether a cube field displays details by setting the `PivotField` object's
`DrilledDown` property to `True`. You can access all the members in a cube field by using the `PivotField` object's
`CubeField.PivotFields` collection, as shown in the following macro, which shows details for up to five levels of
the cube field in the active cell (see Chapter 16 for VBA basics):

Example:

```
Sub ShowAllDetails()
    Dim objPF1 As PivotField, objPF2 As PivotField
    Dim objPF3 As PivotField, objPF4 As PivotField, objPF5 As PivotField
    On Error Resume Next
    Set objPF1 = ActiveCell.PivotField
    For Each objPF2 In objPF1.CubeField.PivotFields
        objPF2.DrilledDown = True
        For Each objPF3 In objPF2.CubeField.PivotFields
            objPF3.DrilledDown = True
            For Each objPF4 In objPF3.CubeField.PivotFields
                objPF4.DrilledDown = True
                For Each objPF5 In objPF4.CubeField.PivotFields
                    objPF5.DrilledDown = True
                Next 'objPF5
            Next 'objPF4
        Next 'objPF3
    Next 'objPF2
End Sub
```

Hide Levels

After you show the details for one or more levels in a hierarchical cube field, you can reconfigure the PivotTable to hide all the levels above a specified level in the hierarchy.

Displaying details is useful because it enables you to see more specific slices of the OLAP cube data. However, the extra levels can sometimes make the PivotTable more difficult to read. You can work around that problem by hiding the levels you do not want to see. For example, in the Foodmart Sales cube, the Product dimension has six levels: Product Family, Product Department, Product Category, Product Subcategory, Brand Name, and Product Name. If you want to view some measure with respect to the Product Name level, you must display details for all the upper levels. The resulting PivotTable is difficult to read and cumbersome to navigate, but you can make it easier by hiding the upper levels — the ones from Product Family to Brand Name.

Hide Levels

① Right-click any cell in the PivotTable.

② Click Show/Hide Fields.

③ Click the field you want to hide.

④ Repeat steps 2 and 3 to hide the other fields.

Excel hides the levels that you selected.

To show the levels again, repeat steps 2 and 3 to turn on each field.

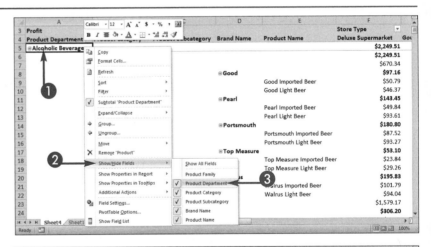

Display Selected Levels and Members

You can control exactly which levels and members Excel displays for a dimension that you have added to a PivotTable.

By default, Excel displays all the members of the top level when you add a dimension to the PivotTable. If you click a cell inside the level and then run the Expand Entire Field command, Excel displays all the members of the next level. If, on the other hand, you only want to display the members associated with a particular item in a level, then you can click the item's **+** button.

However, your data analysis might require even more control over the display of levels and members. Excel enables you to hide members of any level, and this section shows you how to do that.

Extra

When you are working in the dimension drop-down list, you see the following check box states:

☑ — The level or member is displayed; for a level, all of its lower levels or members are displayed.

☐ — The level or member is not displayed; for a level, none of its lower levels or members is displayed.

▣ — The level or member is displayed; for a level, only some of its lower levels or members are displayed.

Display Selected Levels and Members

① Click ▾ in the dimension you want to work with.

Excel displays a hierarchical list of the levels and members in the dimension.

② Click **+** to open a level and see its members (**+** changes to **—**).

③ Deselect the check box of any level or member that you do not want to display.

④ Repeat steps **2** and **3** to set the levels and members you want to display.

⑤ Click OK.

Excel displays just the levels and members that you selected.

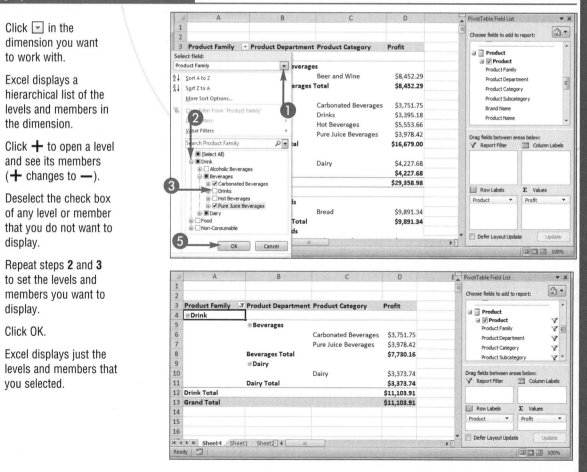

257

Display Multiple Report Filter Items

W ith an OLAP PivotTable, you can filter the report using two or more items in the report filter.

A major component of good PivotTable-based data analysis is the ability to filter the report so that you see only the data you want to work with. In a regular PivotTable, you can filter the report by selecting an item from the report filter. However, filtering on a single item is often not exactly what you want. For example, suppose your report shows the store sales of beverages to

consumers in various income groups and you want to filter that report based on the education level of the consumers. Filtering the report to show just those consumers with a bachelor's degree or a graduate degree is useful, but your analysis may require that you examine both types of consumers together. In a regular PivotTable, it is possible to filter on multiple report filter items, but it requires hiding all the items you do not want to include in the report. In an OLAP PivotTable, you can do this more directly by selecting just the items you want to include in the report filter.

Display Multiple Report Filter Items

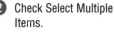 ① Click ⏷ in the report filter.

② Check Select Multiple Items.

③ Click ✛ to open the dimension and see the top-level members.

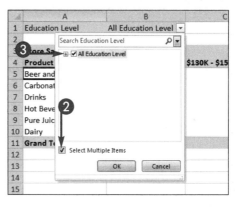

Excel displays a hierarchical list of the levels and members in the dimension.

④ Click **+** to open a level and see its members.

⑤ Deselect the check box of any level or member that you do not want to display.

⑥ Repeat steps **4** and **5** to set the levels and members you want to display.

⑦ Click OK.

Excel displays the results for just the report filter items that you selected.

	A	B	C
1	Education Level	All Education Level	
2		Search Education Level	
3	Store Sa	☐☐ All Education Level	
4	Product	☑ Bachelors Degree	$130K - $15
5	Beer and	☑ Graduate Degree	
6	Carbonat	☐ High School Degree	
7	Drinks	☐ Partial College	
8	Hot Beve	☐ Partial High School	
9	Pure Juic		
10	Dairy		
11	Grand T	☑ Select Multiple Items	
12			
13	⑦ OK Cancel		
14			

	A	B	C	D	E
1	Education Level	(Multiple Items)			
2					
3	Store Sales	Yearly Income			
4	Product Category	$110K - $130K	$130K - $150K	$150K +	Grand T
5	Beer and Wine	$279.80	$322.07	$127.98	$72!
6	Carbonated Beverages	$154.71	$130.32	$51.14	$33!
7	Drinks	$122.12	$73.33	$46.70	$24!
8	Hot Beverages	$180.36	$212.92	$80.06	$47!
9	Pure Juice Beverages	$57.37	$114.54	$49.09	$22!
10	Dairy	$175.56	$120.74	$47.62	$34!
11	Grand Total	$969.92	$973.92	$402.59	$2,34!
12					
13					
14					
15					
16					
17					
18					
19					
20					

Sheet3 Sheet4

Apply It

A quick way to reset the report to display the data for all the report filter items is to use the drop-down report filter list and deselect the Select Multiple Items check box. When you deactivate this check box, Excel automatically selects the All item in the list. Click OK to reset the report.

You can also do this via VBA by setting the `CubeField` object's `EnableMultiplePageItems` property to `False`. The following macro toggles this property on and off (see Chapter 16 for VBA basics):

Example:
```
Sub ToggleMultiplePageFieldItems()
    Dim objPF As PivotField
    ' Work with the first report filter in the active PivotTable
    Set objPF = ActiveCell.PivotTable.PageFields(1)
    ' Work with the CubeField object
    With objPF.CubeField
        ' Toggle the EnableMultiplePageItems property
        .EnableMultiplePageItems = Not .EnableMultiplePageItems
    End With
End Sub
```

Include Hidden Items in PivotTable Totals

I f you have configured your PivotTable to hide one or more items within a dimension or level, you can set a PivotTable option to include the results from those hidden items in your report totals.

When working with a dimension of level field, you can hide one or more of the pages; for the details, see Chapter 5. When you do this, Excel normally reconfigures the PivotTable report in two ways. First, it removes the hidden items from the report. Second, it does not include the values associated with the hidden items in the PivotTable totals. This is reasonable because in most cases you probably want those items completely hidden from the reader.

However, what if you only want to prevent the reader from seeing one or more field items, while still including the data from all the items in the PivotTable totals? You can set this up in two steps. First, exclude those items you do not want the reader to see — again, see Chapter 5. Second, activate a PivotTable option that forces Excel to include all the report filter items in the PivotTable results. This section shows you how to perform this second step. Also note that you can also configure the PivotTable to show an asterisk with the PivotTable total fields to indicate that the totals include values not shown in the report.

Include Hidden Items in PivotTable Totals

① Click any cell within the PivotTable.

② Click Options→ PivotTable→Options.

You can also right-click any PivotTable cell and then click PivotTable Options.

The PivotTable Options dialog box appears.

③ Click the Totals & Filters tab.

④ Select the Include Filtered Items In Totals check box.

● If you do not want to display the asterisk beside the report totals, deselect the Mark Totals With * check box.

⑤ Click OK.

Excel recalculates the PivotTable totals to include the hidden items.

● The labels of the total fields appear with an asterisk (*).

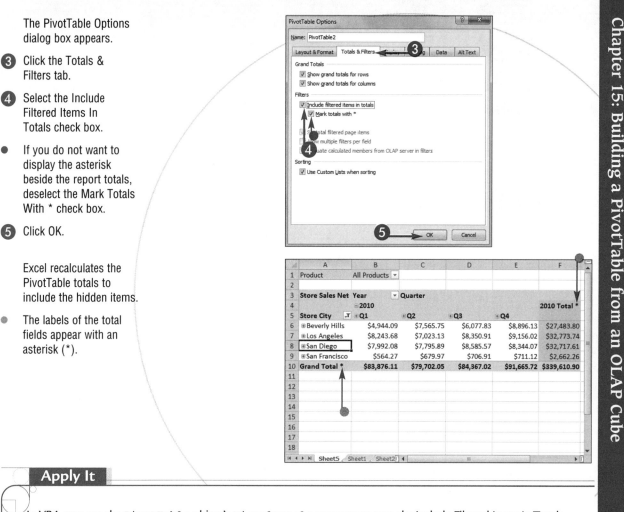

Apply It

In VBA, you use the `PivotTable` object's `VisualTotals` property to turn the Include Filtered Items In Totals option on (`False`) or off (`True`). Here is a VBA procedure that toggles the value of this property between `True` and `False` (see Chapter 16 for VBA basics):

Example:

```
Sub ToggleSubtotalHiddenPageItems()
    Dim objPT As PivotTable
    '
    ' Work with the first PivotTable on the active worksheet
    Set objPT = ActiveSheet.PivotTables(1)
    With objPT
        '
        ' Toggle the VisualTotals property
        .VisualTotals = Not .VisualTotals
        '
        ' Display the current setting
        MsgBox "The Include Filtered Items in Totals option is now " & _
        IIf(.VisualTotals, "off", "on") & "."
    End With
End Sub
```

Performing What-if Analysis on the PivotTable

You can configure your OLAP-based PivotTable to allow changes to the data field values, which enables you to perform what-if analysis on the PivotTable data by trying out different data values.

One of the most common data analysis techniques is *what-if analysis*, where you set up worksheet models to analyze hypothetical situations. The what-if part comes from the fact that these situations usually come in the form of a question: "What happens to the monthly payment if the interest rate goes up by 2 percent?" "What will the sales be if you increase the advertising budget by 10 percent?" Excel offers four what-if analysis tools: data tables, Goal Seek, Solver, and scenarios.

What-if analysis is often difficult with PivotTables created from OLAP server-based data because it requires you to modify the source data and then rebuild the report. This is time consuming at best, and impossible at worst because you may not have direct access to the data. Excel 2010 overcomes these limitations by enabling you to perform what-if analysis directly on the OLAP PivotTable data. You can then recalculate the PivotTable to see what effect your changes made to the report. If you want to keep your changes, you can publish them to the source data.

Performing What-if Analysis on the PivotTable

Enable What-if Analysis

1 Click any cell within the PivotTable.

2 Click Options→What-if Analysis→Enable What-if Analysis.

Excel enables what-if analysis on the PivotTable.

You can now edit the PivotTable values to perform your analysis.

Recalculate the PivotTable

① Click a changed data cell.

● Excel displays a red triangle in the bottom-right corner of each changed cell.

● When you select a changed cell, the What-if Analysis Options smart tag appears.

② Click the What-if Analysis Options smart tag.

③ Click Calculate PivotTable with Change.

Excel recalculates the PivotTable with your changed data values.

Publish Your Changes

① Click any cell within the PivotTable.

② Click Options→What-if Analysis→Publish Changes.

Excel writes the changes back to the source data.

Extra

It is almost always most efficient to manually recalculate the PivotTable after you have made changes to the data. However, you may occasionally prefer to have Excel automatically update the PivotTable after you make each change. To set this up, click any cell in the PivotTable and then click Options→What-if Analysis→Automatically Calculate Changes.

When you write data back to the server, Excel takes the new value and divides it by the number of items that comprise the source data for that value. This is usually the most straightforward method to use, but Excel can also write the data by incrementing the source items based on the difference between the original value and the new value you entered. To switch to this method, click any cell in the PivotTable and then click Options→What-if Analysis→Settings to open the What-if Analysis Settings dialog box. Select the Increment Based On The Old Value option, and then click OK.

Create an Offline OLAP Cube

You can work with an OLAP PivotTable while your computer is not connected to the network by creating and using an offline version of the cube that includes some or all of the data stored on the OLAP server.

We live in a world of mobile computing where the "desktop" is any reasonably flat surface upon which you can balance your notebook or handheld computer. Unfortunately, although your computer may be quite portable, your data is not always so prepared to travel. This is particularly true when that data resides on a network server. After you disconnect from the network, you lose access to the server and to your data.

Many solutions exist that enable a roaming computer to make a remote connection to the network. But technologies such as Virtual Private Networking and dial-up connections are often expensive, difficult to set up, and too slow for heavy-duty data work.

A better solution is to take some or all the data on the road with you. By storing a version of the data on your traveling computer, you can work with the data at any time, without needing a remote connection. For most OLAP data, Excel offers the Create Cube File Wizard, which takes you step by step through the process of creating an offline cube file. (Note, however, that this wizard does not work with all data warehouse software.) You can then take that cube file with you when you travel and work with the cube's associated OLAP PivotTable, just as though it resided on an OLAP server.

Create an Offline OLAP Cube

① Click any cell in the OLAP PivotTable you want to work with.

② Click Options→OLAP Tools→Offline OLAP.

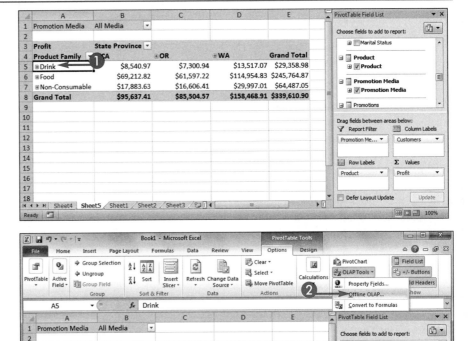

The Offline OLAP
Settings dialog box
appears.

③ Click Create Offline
Data File.

Step 1 of the the
Create Cube File
Wizard appears.

④ Click Next.

Apply It

If you simply want to create a cube file that uses the same dimensions, levels, members, and measures that are in the current PivotTable, VBA gives you an easy way to do it. You can use the `PivotTable` object's `CreateCubeFile` method and specify only the `File` parameter, which is a string that specifies the location and name of the cube file. The following macro prompts the user for a file path and name and then uses the active PivotTable to create just such a cube file (see Chapter 16 for VBA basics):

Example:
```
Sub CreateDefaultCubeFile()
    Dim strFilePath As String
    ' Build the default path from the USERPROFILE environment variable
    strFilePath = Environ("USERPROFILE") & "\Documents\"
    ' Get the user's file path and name
    strFilePath = InputBox("Type the location of the cube (.cub) file:", _
                        "Create Default Cube File", _
                        strFilePath)
    ' Did the user click Cancel?
    If strFilePath <> "" Then
        ' If not, create the cube file with the specified pathname
        ActiveCell.PivotTable.CreateCubeFile _
            File:=strFilePath
    End If
End Sub
```

continued ➡

Y ou can use the Create Cube File Wizard to specify exactly the data that you require while you work with the OLAP PivotTable offline.

Depending on how much data is stored in the online OLAP cube, the offline version can be massive. In fact, most OLAP cubes contain enough multidimensional data to create offline cube files that are dozens, or even hundreds, of megabytes in size. If you are not transferring the cube file to a different computer (such as your notebook PC), if you are not e-mailing the cube file, and if your computer contains lots of free hard drive space, then the size of the OLAP cube is probably not a concern.

However, it is common to require a cube file transfer — either to a portable machine or via e-mail. Alternatively, you may be running low on hard drive space and cannot store a huge file. For these situations, you need to restrict the size of the offline cube file. You can do this in the Create Cube File Wizard by specifying the data that you are certain you need while disconnected from the network. The wizard gives you two ways to do this. First, you can select for inclusion in the cube file just those dimensions that you want to work with. Second, you can select just those top-level items that you want to work with. These top-level items include all the measures in the OLAP cube and all the items in the dimensions that you selected for inclusion in the cube file.

Create an Offline OLAP Cube *(continued)*

Step 2 of the Create Cube File Wizard appears.

5 Select the check box beside each dimension you want to include in the cube file.

6 To exclude lower levels of a dimension from the cube file, first click **+** to display the levels (**+** changes to **—**).

7 Deselect the check box beside each level you want to exclude from the cube file.

8 Repeat steps **5** to **7**, as needed.

9 Click Next.

Step 3 of the Create Cube File Wizard appears.

10 To include items from a top level in the cube file, first click **+** to display the items (**+** changes to **—**).

11 Select the check box beside each item you want to include in the cube file.

12 Repeat steps **10** and **11** to specify all the top-level items you want in the cube file.

13 Click Next.

Step 4 of the Create Cube File Wizard appears.

⑭ Type the location and name of the cube file.

● Alternatively, click Browse and use the Save As dialog box to specify a folder and file name for the cube file.

⑮ Click Finish.

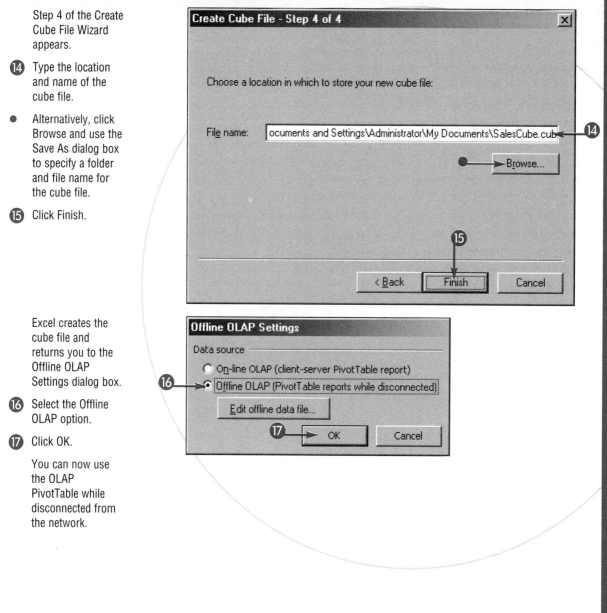

Excel creates the cube file and returns you to the Offline OLAP Settings dialog box.

⑯ Select the Offline OLAP option.

⑰ Click OK.

You can now use the OLAP PivotTable while disconnected from the network.

Extra

When you are offline and using the cube file for your PivotTable, you are free to create other PivotTables using the same cube file. First, you need to create a data source that connects to the cube file. In the section "Create an OLAP Cube Data Source," see the subsection "Connect to a Cube File." When that is done, you can then create the new PivotTable using the cube file data source; see the section "Create a PivotTable from an OLAP Cube."

When you reconnect to the network, you should switch to using the online OLAP data so that you can refresh the PivotTable report to get the latest data. To switch from the offline OLAP cube, click any cell in the PivotTable report and then click Options→OLAP Tools→Offline OLAP. In the Offline OLAP Settings dialog box, select the On-line OLAP option and then click OK.

Open the VBA Editor

I f you want to add a macro to a workbook, or if you want to create macros from scratch, you need to open the VBA Editor.

VBA is a powerful language that can perform a wide variety of tasks, but its main purpose is to operate on the application in which it is running. With Excel VBA, for example, you can create macros that add text and formulas to cells, format ranges, insert or delete worksheets, create and manipulate PivotTables, and much more.

You can store macros in any workbook, but Excel provides a special workbook for this purpose: the Personal Macro Workbook. Whichever workbook you use, Excel stores the

macro code in a *module*, a special window in which you can view, edit, and run macros. If you want to add macro code to a workbook, or if you want to edit existing macro code, then you need to view the module to work with the macro. Similarly, you also require access to the module if you want to create new macros from scratch.

In both cases, you can access the module using the VBA Editor, a program that enables you to view, create, edit, and run VBA macros. This section shows you how to start the VBA Editor and how to open a module.

Open the VBA Editor

1. Click Developer→Visual Basic.

Note: To display the Developer tab, right-click the Ribbon, click Customize the Ribbon, select the Developer check box, and then click OK.

You can also press Alt+F11.

The Microsoft Visual Basic for Applications window appears.

2. Click the plus sign to open the branch of the workbook that contains the recorded macro.

Note: If you do not see the Project pane, click View→Project Explorer, or press Ctrl+R.

- Personal.xlsb is the Personal Macro Workbook.

③ Click the plus sign to open the Modules branch.

● Excel displays the workbook's modules.

Note: *If your workbook does not contain any modules, click Insert→Module to create one.*

④ Double-click the module you want to open.

◉ The VBA Editor opens the module window in a new window.

◉ The macro code appears in the module window.

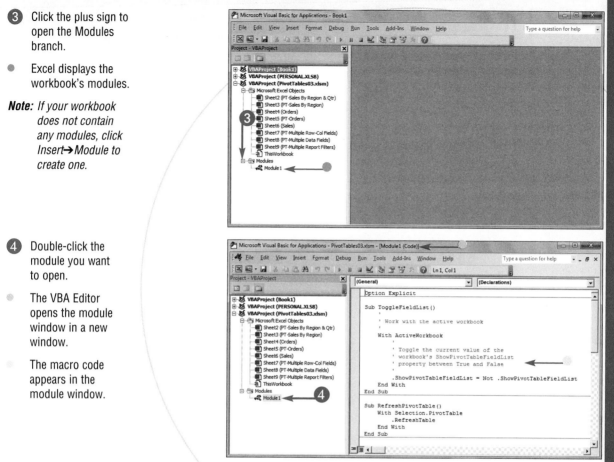

Apply It

It is a good idea to store all your macros in the Personal Macro Workbook. Excel keeps this workbook open all the time, so the macros you store in it are always available to you. Note, however, that Excel keeps the Personal Macro Workbook hidden, which is why you do not see it when you are working in Excel.

If you want to see the Personal Macro Workbook, you need to unhide it. Switch to Excel and click View→Unhide to display the Unhide dialog box. Click Personal and then click OK.

If the Unhide command is disabled, or if you do not see the Personal Macro Workbook in the Unhide dialog box, then it is likely that the Personal Macro Workbook does not exist. In most cases, Excel only creates this workbook after you use it to store a recorded macro for the first time. In Excel, click Developer→Record Macro to open the Record Macro dialog box, use the Store Macro In list to select Personal Macro Workbook, click OK, and then click Developer→Stop Recording.

Add a Macro
to a Module

I f you have a macro that you want to create or copy, you need to add the VBA code for the macro to a module in the VBA Editor.

As you become familiar with manipulating PivotTables using VBA, you will likely come up with many ways to simplify complex tasks and automate routine and repetitive chores using macros. To implement these macros, you need to type your code into an existing module in the VBA Editor.

Similarly, you may run across a macro that you want to use for your own work, either as is or by modifying the code to suit your needs. For example, you have seen many PivotTable macro examples throughout this book, and these examples are available on the Web; see www.wiley.com/go/pivottablesvb2e. You can either transcribe these macros into a module on your system or better yet, copy the macros and then paste them into a module.

Add a Macro to a Module

① Start the VBA Editor.

Note: *For more information, see the section "Open the VBA Editor."*

② Double-click the module into which you want to add the macro.

If you prefer to add your code to a new module, you can click Insert→ Module instead.

Excel opens the module window.

③ Position the cursor where you want to start the new macro.

Note: *You must add the new macro either before or after an existing macro.*

④ Type **sub**, a space, and then type the name of the new macro.

Note: *Make sure the name you use is not the same as any existing macro name in the module.*

⑤ Press Enter.

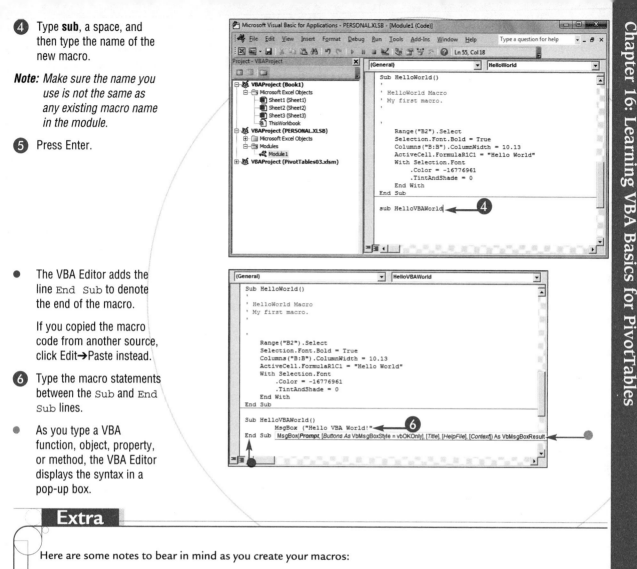

● The VBA Editor adds the line End Sub to denote the end of the macro.

If you copied the macro code from another source, click Edit➔Paste instead.

⑥ Type the macro statements between the Sub and End Sub lines.

● As you type a VBA function, object, property, or method, the VBA Editor displays the syntax in a pop-up box.

Extra

Here are some notes to bear in mind as you create your macros:

● If you want to begin your macro with a few comments — notes that describe what the macro does — type an apostrophe (') at the beginning of each comment line.

● To make your code easier to read, indent each statement by pressing the Tab key at the beginning of the line — you do not need to do this for the Sub and End Sub lines. VBA preserves the indentation on subsequent lines, so you only have to indent the first line.

● After you type a statement, VBA formats the color of each word in the line. By default, VBA keywords are blue, comments are green, errors are red, and all other text is black.

● After you type a statement, VBA converts keywords to their proper case. For example, if you type **msgbox**, VBA converts it to MsgBox when you press Enter.

● By always typing VBA keywords in lowercase letters, you can catch typing errors by looking for those keywords that VBA does not recognize; in other words, the ones that remain in lowercase.

● Click Tools➔Options and then the Editor tab. Select the Require Variable Declaration check box and click OK. This adds Option Explicit to the top of all new modules, which requires you to declare all variables to avoid errors. Add Option Explicit to any existing modules as well.

● After you type a statement, VBA checks for syntax errors, which are errors when a word is misspelled, a function is entered incorrectly, and so on. VBA signifies a syntax error either by displaying a dialog box to let you know what the problem is, or by not converting a word to its proper case or color.

Run a
Macro

Y ou can run a macro from any open workbook. You have the option of running the macro from the VBA Editor or from Excel.

Excel maintains a list of the macros that are stored in each open workbook. When you want to run a macro, you can either open the module that contains the macro or display the list of available Excel macros. Either way, to run a macro, you must first open the workbook in which the macro is stored.

Note, however, that Excel's default macro security settings may prevent you from running any macros stored outside the Personal Macro Workbook. If you cannot perform the steps in this section — particularly after you create one or more macros and then close and

restart Excel — then you either need to lower Excel's macro security settings or "self-sign" your own macros. See the next section, "Set Macro Security," for the details.

After you open a workbook, you then have two ways to run one of its macros:

- From the VBA Editor
- From Excel

It is best to use the VBA Editor if you are testing the macro, because although VBA switches to Excel to execute the code, it returns to the VBA Editor when it is done. Therefore, you can run the code, see whether it works properly, and then adjust the code as necessary. When your code is working properly, you can run it from Excel without having to load the VBA Editor.

Run a Macro

Run a Macro from the VBA Editor

1. Open the module that contains the macro.

2. Click any statement within the macro you want to run.

- The macro name appears in the list of macros.

3. Click Run→Run Sub/UserForm.

   You can also press F5 or click the Run button (▶).

   The VBA Editor runs the macro.

Run a Macro from Excel

1. Open the workbook that contains the macro.

   You can skip step **1** if the macro is stored in the Personal Macro Workbook.

2. Click View→Macros.

   If you have the Developer tab displayed, you can also click Developer→Macros.

   You can also press Alt+F8.

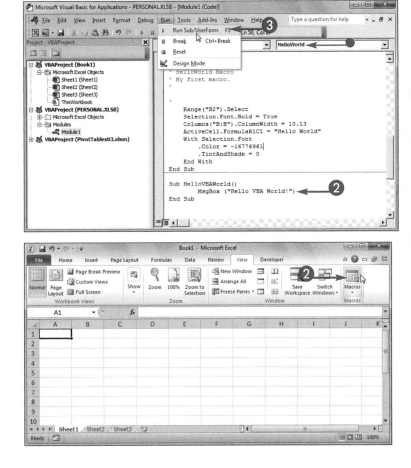

The Macro dialog box appears.

3 Click the Macros In ⊡ and select the workbook that contains the macro you want to run.

If you are not sure which workbook contains the macro, select All Open Workbooks instead.

● Excel displays a list of macros in the workbook.

4 Click the macro you want to run.

5 Click Run.

If you assigned a shortcut key to the macro, you can avoid steps **1** to **4** by pressing the shortcut key.

Excel runs the macro.

Extra

Some macros expect a particular workbook, worksheet, or cell to be active. You can tell this if you see the following in your code:

● `ActiveWorkbook` — This keyword references the active workbook.

● `ActiveSheet` — This keyword references the active worksheet.

● `ActiveCell` — This keyword references the active cell.

In each case, "active" means that the object — the workbook, worksheet, or cell — has the focus. That is, the active workbook or active worksheet is the one that is displayed in Excel, while the active cell is the one that is currently selected.

If your code uses any of these keywords, make sure that the appropriate workbook, worksheet, or cell is active. For example, it is common to generalize a PivotTable macro to work with any PivotTable by using the `PivotTable` object referenced by the following code:

```
ActiveCell.PivotTable
```

This is convenient, but it means that before you run the macro, you must select a cell in the PivotTable report that you want the macro to work with.

Set Macro Security

You can gain more control over how Excel treats macros by setting the macro security level.

Unfortunately, VBA's power is all too often used for nefarious ends — such as viruses that can destroy entire systems — so Microsoft Office comes with VBA macros disabled as a security precaution. The exception is macros stored in Excel's Personal Macro Workbook, which you can always run.

You can adjust Excel's macro security setting to one of the following values:

- **Disable all macros without notification.** Excel disables all macros and does not give a way to enable them. This gives you total macro safety, but it is more than what most people require.

- **Disable all macros with notification.** Excel warns you when a document you are about to open contains macros. It disables the macros but gives

you the option of enabling them. This is useful if you often open third-party documents.

- **Disable all macros except digitally signed macros.** Excel only enables macros if they come from a trusted source — that is, a source that has digitally signed the VBA project using a trusted code-signing certificate. Macros from any other source are automatically disabled. This is Excel's default security level, and it gives you almost total macro safety. However, you need to self-sign your own macros, as described later in this section.

- **Enable all macros.** Excel runs all macros without prompting. If you do not have a virus scanner installed, use this level if you only run your own macros and you never open documents created by a third party. If you do have a virus scanner, this level is probably safe if you only open third-party documents from people or sources you know.

Set Macro Security

Set the Macro Security Level

① Click File→Options.

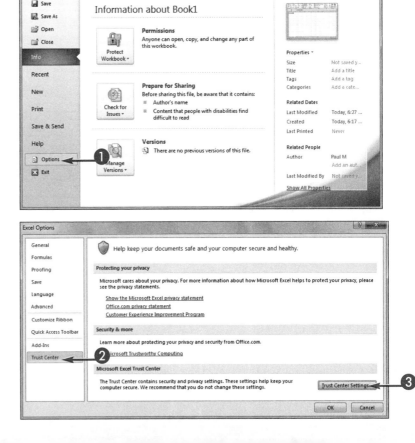

The Excel Options dialog box appears.

② Click Trust Center.

③ Click Trust Center Settings.

The Trust Center dialog box appears.

If you have the Developer tab displayed, a quicker way to open the Trust Center is to click Developer→Macro Security.

④ Click Macro Settings.

⑤ Select the security level you want to use.

⑥ Click OK.

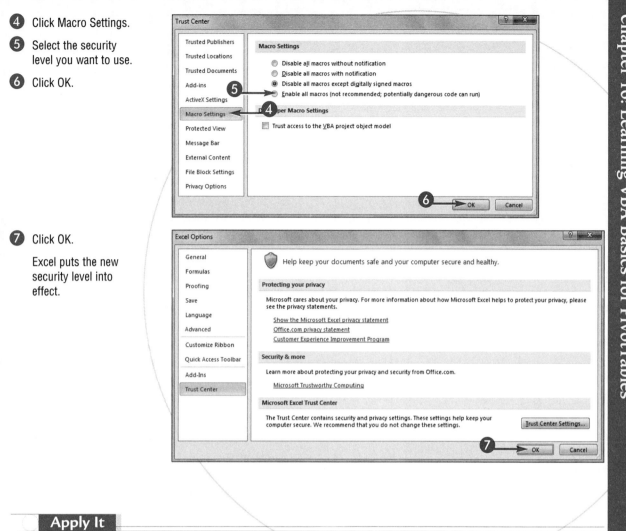

⑦ Click OK.

Excel puts the new security level into effect.

continued ➡

275

Apply It

To create a digital certificate for signing your own macros, click Start➔All Programs➔Accessories➔Run (or, in Windows XP, click Start➔Run). In the Run dialog box, type the following address and then click OK:

%ProgramFiles%\Microsoft Office\Office14\SelfCert.exe

In the Create Digital Certificate dialog box, use the Your Certificate's Name text box to type your name and then click OK. Excel creates a digital certificate in your name and displays a dialog box when it is done. Click OK. You can now use the digital certificate to sign your VBA code. See the next page to learn how to apply the digital certificate to your VBA projects.

I f you are a VBA programmer and you set Excel's macro security at the Disable All Macros Without Notification level, you immediately run into a problem: Excel does not allow you to run any of your own macros that reside outside the Personal Macro Workbook. This seems like overkill at first, but this stringent security policy is not without its fair share of common sense. That is, Excel has no way to tell whether you are the author of such macros. By definition, macros in the Personal Macro Workbook are yours, but code in any other file could have come from a third party, which makes that code a potential security risk.

Does this mean that you have to store *all* your macros in the Personal Macro Workbook? That would make it difficult to distribute your macros to other people, so

fortunately the answer is "no." That is, because it is possible to "prove" that you are the author of your own macros. You can do that by *self-certifying*, which creates a trust certificate that applies only to your own work and to using that work on your own computer. The certificate is not valid on any other computer, so it is not a substitute for getting a proper code-signing digital certificate. However, if all you want to do is run your own macros, then self-certifying enables you to do that while still using the High macro security level.

After you run the SelfCert.exe program to create your personal digital certificate, as described on the previous page, the next step is to assign that certificate to a VBA project. Note that you need to assign the certificate to each project that contains macros you want to run.

Set Macro Security *(continued)*

Assign a Digital Certificate

① In the VBA Editor, click the project to which you want to assign the certificate.

② Click Tools→Digital Signature.

The Digital Signature dialog box appears.

③ Click Choose.

The Windows Security - Confirm Certificate dialog box appears.

● Windows displays your digital certificate.

Note: *Remember that you only see this digital certificate after you run the SelfCert.exe program, as described on the previous page.*

④ Click OK.

● The certificate appears in the Digital Signature dialog box.

⑤ Click OK.

⑥ Switch to Excel, save the workbook that you just signed, and then close the workbook.

⑦ Reopen the signed workbook.

If you have macros disabled, the Security Notice dialog box appears.

⑧ Click Trust All from Publisher.

Excel opens the workbook with macros enabled.

Excel no longer displays the Security Notice dialog box for workbooks signed with your digital signature.

Apply It

If you distribute your VBA projects to people running High macro security, the only way they can run your macros is if you get a proper code-signing digital certificate from a trusted certification authority. If you work for a large corporation or a software company, your network administrator may be able to generate a certificate for you. Otherwise, you need to purchase a certificate from a third-party certification authority. To see a list of trusted authorities, see the following page on the Microsoft Developer Network (MSDN) site:

http://msdn2.microsoft.com/en-us/library/ms995347.aspx

By clicking the Trust all from publisher button in the Security Notice dialog box, you add yourself to Excel's list of trusted publishers. If you add another person's or company's certificate to your list of trusted publishers, you may need to revoke that trust later on. To do this, open the Trust Center as described earlier in this section. Click the Trusted Publishers tab, click the publisher you want to delete, and then click Remove.

Assign a Shortcut Key to a Macro

If you have a VBA macro that you use fairly often, you can quickly access the code by setting up a shortcut key that runs the macro.

You saw earlier in this chapter — see the section "Run a Macro" — that it takes quite a few mouse clicks to run a macro from Excel. That is not so bad if it is a macro that you use only once in a while. However, macros are meant to be timesavers, so it is not unusual to have a macro that you run several times each day, or even several times in a row. In such situations, those mouse clicks can start to add up and you may begin to wonder whether the macro is really saving you time.

To work around this problem, you can assign a shortcut key to a macro. You can assign a shortcut key when you record an Excel macro. Fortunately, it is also possible to assign a shortcut key to a macro later on, either after you have recorded the macro or after you have added a macro to a module using the VBA Editor. In either case, as long as the workbook containing the macro is currently open, you can press the shortcut key within Excel to run the macro.

To ensure your macro shortcut keys do not interfere with Excel's built-in shortcut keys (see the Tips on the next page), access Excel's Help system and locate the Help article titled "Keyboard shortcuts in Excel 2010."

Assign a Shortcut Key to a Macro

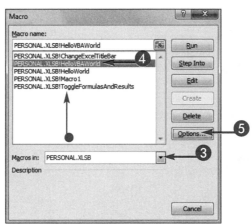

1 Open the workbook that contains the macro.

You can skip step 1 if the macro is stored in the Personal Macro Workbook.

2 Click View→Macros.

If you have the Developer tab displayed, you can also click Developer→ Macros.

You can also press Alt+F8.

The Macro dialog box appears.

3 Click the Macros In ☑ and select the workbook that contains the macro you want to run.

If you are not sure which workbook contains the macro, select All Open Workbooks instead.

● Excel displays a list of macros in the workbook.

4 Click the macro you want to work with.

5 Click Options.

The Macro Options dialog box appears.

⑥ Type the character you want to use as part of the shortcut key.

⑦ Click OK.

Excel assigns the shortcut key to the macro.

⑧ Click Cancel.

You can now run the macro by pressing the shortcut key.

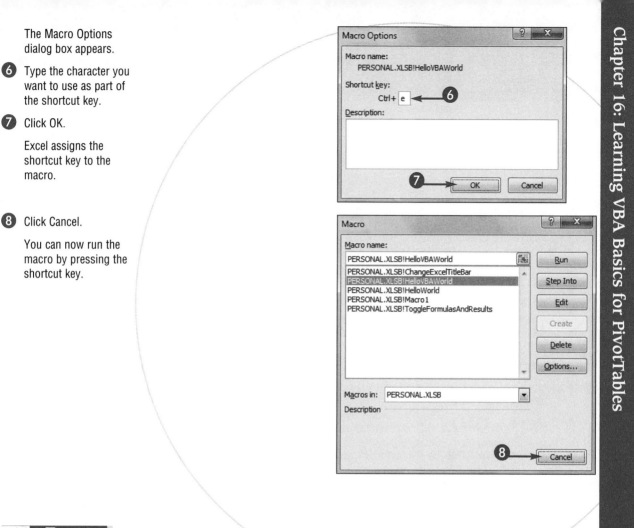

Extra

Make sure you do not specify a shortcut key that conflicts with Excel's built-in shortcuts — such as Ctrl+B for Bold or Ctrl+C for Copy. If you use a key that clashes with an Excel shortcut, Excel overrides its own shortcut and runs your macro instead, provided that the workbook containing the macro is open. Also remember that your macro shortcut keys apply only to your copy of Excel. If you share the workbook with another user, that person does not have access to your shortcut keys.

The shortcut key you specify in step **6** is case sensitive, meaning you can create separate shortcuts with uppercase and lowercase letters. For example, if you type **e** into the Ctrl+ text box, you have to press Ctrl+E to run the macro. However, if you type **E** into the Ctrl+ text box, you have to press Ctrl+Shift+E to run the macro.

There are only five letters not assigned to Excel commands that you can use with your macros: e, j, m, q, and t. You can get extra shortcut keys by using uppercase letters. For example, Excel differentiates between Ctrl+b and Ctrl+B, or more explicitly, Ctrl+Shift+b. Note, however, that Excel uses four built-in Ctrl+Shift shortcuts: A, F, O, and P.

Glossary of PivotTable Terms

Argument

A value that is used as an input for a function and which the function uses to calculate a result. The arguments of a function must correspond to the function's parameters.

Arithmetic Formula

A formula that combines numeric operands — numeric constants, functions that return numeric results, and fields or items that contain numeric values — with mathematical operators to perform a calculation.

AutoFormat

A collection of formatting options — alignments, fonts, borders, and patterns — that Excel defines for different areas of a PivotTable.

Background Query

A query that Excel executes behind the scenes so that you can continue to perform other work in Excel.

Base Field

In a running-total summary calculation, the field on which to base the accumulation.

Break-Even Analysis

The number of units of a product that you must sell for the profit to be 0.

Calculated Field

A new data field in which the values are the result of a custom calculation formula.

Calculated Item

A new item in a row or column field in which the values are the result of a custom calculation.

Category Area

The PivotChart drop area in which the category field appears.

Category Field

A source data field added to the PivotChart's category area; the field's items form the chart's X-axis values.

Column Area

The PivotTable drop area in which the column field appears.

Column Field

A source data field added to a PivotTable's column area; the field's items form the report's columns.

Comma-separated Values

A type of text file in which the items on each line are separated by commas.

Comparison Formula

A formula that combines numeric operands — numeric constants, functions that return numeric results, and fields or items that contain numeric values — with operators such as less than (<) or greater than (>) to compare one operand with another.

Conditional Formatting

Formatting — a custom font, border, and pattern — applied to any cells that match criteria that you specify.

Consolidation

Data that is combined from two or more ranges but have a similar structure.

Constant

A fixed value that you insert into a formula and use as is.

Criteria

One or more expressions that filter a query by specifying the conditions that each record must meet to be included in the results.

Custom Calculation

A formula that you define to produce PivotTable values that otherwise do not appear in the report if you use only the source data fields and Excel's built-in summary calculations.

Data

The calculated values that appear within the data area.

Data Analysis

The application of tools and techniques to organize, study, reach conclusions about, and sometimes also make predictions about, a specific collection of information.

Data Area

The PivotTable drop area in which the data field appears.

Data Connection File

A data source that connects to a wide variety of data, including ODBC, SQL Server, SQL Server OLAP Services, Oracle, and Web-based data retrieval services.

Data Field

A source data field added to a PivotTable's data area; Excel uses the field's numeric data to perform the report's summary calculations.

Data Model

A collection of cells designed as a worksheet version of some real-world concept or scenario. The model includes not only the raw data, but also one or more cells that represent some analysis of the data.

Data Source

A file, database, or server that contains data.

Data Table

A range of cells where one column consists of a series of input cells. You can then apply each of those inputs to a single formula, and Excel displays the results for each case.

Data Warehouse

A data structure with a central fact table that contains the numeric data you want to summarize and pointers to surrounding related tables.

Delimited Text File

A text file that contains data and each line item is separated by a delimiter.

Delimiter

The character used to separate items on each line in a text file.

Dimension

A category of data in a data warehouse. A dimension is analogous to a row field, column field, or report filter in an ordinary data source.

Drill Down View

The details that underlie a specific data value in a PivotTable.

Drop Area

A region of the PivotTable onto which you can drop a field from the source data or from another area of the PivotTable.

External Data

Source data that comes from a non-Excel file or database, or from a remote source such as a server or Web page.

Fact Table

The primary table in a data warehouse. The fact table contains data on events or processes — the *facts* — within a business, such as sales transactions or company expenses.

Field

A distinct category of data in a PivotTable or a database table.

Fixed-width Text File

A text file containing data where the items on each line use up a set amount of space.

Formula

A set of symbols and values that perform some kind of calculation and produce a result. All Excel formulas have the same general structure: an equals sign (=) followed by one or more operands separated by one or more operators.

Function

A predefined formula that is built in to Excel.

Grand Totals

The totals that appear in a PivotTable for each row and column item.

Inner Field

The field that is closest to the data area in the row or column area.

Input Cells

The cells used as input values by a data table.

Item

A unique value from a row field, column field, or report filter.

continued

Labels

The non-data-area elements of a PivotTable. The labels include the field buttons, field items, and page area drop-down lists.

Levels

A collection of hierarchical groupings in a data warehouse dimension.

List

A worksheet collection of related information with an organizational structure that makes it easy to add, edit, and sort data. A list is a type of database where the data is organized into rows and columns, with each column representing a database field and with each row representing a database record.

Measure

A column of numeric values within a data warehouse fact table. A measure represents the data that you want to summarize.

Member

The items that appear within each level in a data warehouse dimension.

Method

In VBA, a function or procedure that manipulates an object.

Module

A special window in which you can view, edit, and run VBA macros.

Multidimensional Data

OLAP data in which the fact table contains keys to multiple dimension tables.

Object

A distinct item that you can manipulate with VBA code.

Object Model

A complete summary of the objects associated with a particular program or feature, the hierarchy used by those objects, and the properties and methods supported by each object.

ODBC

Open Database Connectivity. A database standard that enables a program to connect to and manipulate a data source.

OLAP

Online Analytical Processing. A database technology that enables you to quickly retrieve and summarize immense and complex data sources.

OLAP Cube

A data structure that takes the information in a data warehouse and summarizes each measure by every dimension, level, and member.

OLAP Cube File

A version of an OLAP cube that has been saved to a local or network folder. A cube file is "offline" in the sense that the data is not connected to an OLAP server, so it is a static snapshot of the data.

Operand

In a worksheet formula, a literal value, cell reference, range, range name, or worksheet function. In a custom calculation formula, a literal value, worksheet function, PivotTable field, or PivotTable item.

Operator

In a formula, a symbol that combines operands in some way, such as the plus sign (+) and the multiplication sign (*).

Operator Precedence

The order in which Excel processes operands in a formula.

Optional Argument

A function argument that you are free to use or omit, depending on your needs.

Outer Field and Inner Field

In the row or column area, the field that is farthest from the data area.

Parameter

A placeholder in a function that specifies the type of argument value.

Phantom Field Item

A PivotTable field item that no longer exists in the source data.

Pivot

To move a field from one drop area of a PivotTable to another.

Pivot Cache

Source data that Excel keeps in memory to improve PivotTable performance.

Property

A programmable characteristic of an object.

Query

An operation that retrieves data from an external data source, particularly by specifying the tables and fields you want to work with, filtering the records using criteria, and sorting the results.

Record

An individual set of field data in a database table.

Refresh

To rebuild a PivotTable report using the most current version of the source data.

Report Filter

A source data field added to a PivotTable's report filter area; you use the field's items to filter the report.

Report Filter Area

The PivotTable drop area in which the report filter appears.

Required Argument

A function argument that must appear between the function's parentheses in the specified position.

Row Area

The PivotTable drop area in which the row field appears.

Row Field

A source data field added to a PivotTable's row area; the field's items form the report's rows.

Running Total

A type of summary calculation that returns the cumulative sum of the values that appear in a given set of data. Most running totals accumulate over a period of time.

Scenario

A collection of input values that you plug into formulas within a model to produce a result.

Self-Certify

To create a trust certificate that applies only to your own VBA projects and only to those projects on your own computer.

Series Area

The PivotChart drop area in which the series field appears.

Series Field

A source data field added to the PivotChart's series area; the field's items form the chart's data series.

Solve Order

The order in which Excel solves the calculated items in a PivotTable.

Source Data

The original data from which you built your PivotTable. The source data can be an Excel range or list, an Access table, a Word table, a text file, a Web page, an XML file, SQL Server data, or OLAP server data, among others.

Star Schema

A type of data warehouse.

Summary Calculation

The mathematical operation that Excel applies to the values in a numeric field to yield the summary that appears in the data area. Excel offers 11 built-in summary calculations: Sum, Count, Average, Maximum, Minimum, Product, Count Numbers, Standard Deviation (sample), Standard Deviation (population), Variance (sample), and Variance (population).

Table

A two-dimensional arrangement of rows and columns that contains data in a database.

What-if Analysis

The creation of worksheet models designed to analyze hypothetical situations.

XML

Extensible Markup Language. A standard that enables the management and sharing of structured data using simple text files.

INDEX

SYMBOLS

' (apostrophe), 271
* (asterisk), 85, 210

A

Access (Microsoft)
  database password, 211
  exporting PivotTables forms to Excel, 242–243
  tables, 206, 210–211
accessing external data, 207
Accounting format, 100
Add Columns dialog box, 198
Add Criteria dialog box, 200–201
Add Tables dialog box, 194, 196
add-ins (OLAP), 253
Advanced Text Import Settings dialog box, 217
analysis
  break-even, 3, 280
  data, 2–3, 281
  relationship with PivotTables, 9
  trend, 9
  what-if, 3, 262–263, 283
apostrophe ('), 271
arguments
  defined, 3, 280
  optional, 179, 282
  overview, 179
  required, 179, 180, 182, 283
arithmetic formulas, 176, 280
asterisk (*), 85, 210
AutoFilter feature, 15
AutoFormat feature, 280
Automatic Subtotals feature, 15
AutoSort feature, 60–61, 65
Average calculation, 148

B

background query, 280
base field, 150, 280
base item, 150
break-even analysis, 3, 280

C

calculated fields, 162–165, 280
Calculated Item Solve Order dialog box, 170–171

calculated items
  changing solve order of, 170–171
  as custom calculation type, 162, 166–167
  defined, 280
  limitations of, 163
calculations. *See* custom calculations; summary
  calculations; *specific types*
category area, 112, 280
category axis, 13
category field, 12, 55, 117, 121, 280
category item, 13
cells, 3, 98–99, 144–145, 281
Change Chart Type dialog box, 122–123
Change PivotTable Data Source dialog box, 22–23
chart categories (X-axis), 12
chart data series, 12
chart values (Y-axis), 12
charts. *See* PivotCharts
Choose Data Source dialog box
  creating
    OLAP cube data sources, 248, 251
    PivotTables from external data, 233–234
    PivotTables from OLAP cubes, 252
  defining data sources, 190, 192–193
  starting Microsoft Query, 194
Classic layout, 38–39, 57
column areas
  adding fields to, 40–41
  compared with series area, 112
  overview, 10, 280
column break lines, 216
column chart, clustered, 117
column fields
  defined, 10, 280
  hiding items in, 82–83
  selecting, 26
  showing hidden items in, 86–87
  sorting, 60
column items, 62–63, 78–79
Comma Separated Values (CSV), 214, 280
Compact layout, 59
comparison formulas, 177, 280
computer, locking, 241
conditional formatting, 104–105, 280
Connection Properties dialog box
  editing queries, 205, 217
  importing data from Access tables, 211
  refreshing
    imported data, 225
    PivotTables, 238–239
  saving passwords, 240–241

INDEX

INDEX

For more professional instruction in a visual format, try these.

All designed for visual learners—just like you!

Read Less–Learn More®

Excel PivotTables and PivotCharts
2nd Edition

Your visual blueprint for creating dynamic spreadsheets

978-0-470-59161-1

Ric Shreves

Ubuntu Linux Desktop

Your visual blueprint to using the Linux operating system

978-0-470-34520-7

iPhone OS Development

Your visual blueprint for developing apps for Apple's mobile devices

978-0-470-55651-1

For a complete listing of *Visual Blueprint*™ titles and other Visual books, go to wiley.com/go/visual

Visual
An Imprint of **WILEY**
Now you know.

Portland Community College